# Memory Power

# 101

## A Comprehensive Guide to Better Learning for Students, Businesspeople, and Seniors

**W. R. Klemm, DVM, PhD**

**a.k.a. "Memory Medic"**

Skyhorse Publishing

Skyhorse Publishing books may be purchased in bulk at special discounts for sales promotion, corporate gifts, fund-raising, or educational purposes. Special editions can also be created to specifications. For details, contact the Special Sales Department, Skyhorse Publishing, 307 West 36th Street, 11th Floor, New York, NY 10018 or info@skyhorsepublishing.com.

Skyhorse® and Skyhorse Publishing® are registered trademarks of Skyhorse Publishing, Inc.®, a Delaware corporation.

Visit our website at www.skyhorsepublishing.com.

10 9 8 7 6 5 4 3 2 1

Library of Congress Cataloging-in-Publication Data

Klemm, William. Memory power 101 : a comprehensive guide to a better memory for students, businesspeople, and seniors / William Klemm.        p. cm. ISBN 978-1-61608-612-1 (alk. paper)1. Memory. 2. Mnemonics.        I. Title. BF371.K534 2012 153.1'4--dc23 2012019719

ISBN: 978-1-61608-612-1

Printed in the United States of America

Learning has always been important to me, from soaking up the knowledge of the wild on the edge of the Everglades as a child, to attaining my DVM and a PhD in physiology, to over 50 years of research on how the brain works.

Learning is not only empowering but fulfilling. It gives our lives meaning and can benefit us professionally. Learning is also perhaps the best antidote to boredom and depression.

I know that few people are as compulsive about learning as I am. That is their loss. Even so, everyone has times in their life when effective learning becomes important, whether it's in school, on the job, or entering the mental decline of old age. When you learn, whether it's because you really want to or because you have to, it is of great benefit to do so powerfully. Once learned, the greatest advantage of the new learning comes from making the memory last.

For all those who want power memory, this is the book for you. There is no comparable book. I say that with confidence, because I think I have read them all.

# TABLE OF CONTENTS

# INTRODUCTION—*HOW THIS BOOK IS DIFFERENT*

Why are you reading this book? I put myself in your shoes when I undertook this writing project. But I could only speculate on what you expected to get from the book I was about to write.

I knew from my own experience as a student decades ago that you might have a need to get better grades, maybe to get nagging parents off your back or maybe to get admitted to a highly selective university. I knew as a young person that for sure I wanted to spend less time studying.

I knew from my experience as a veterinarian, and later a scientist, that you probably wanted to have more mastery of the knowledge in your field, again, preferably, without having to work too hard to acquire it.

Though I am not much of a businessman (I owned a long-gone software company), I know from observing successful businesspeople trying to function in this increasingly competitive and complex global economy that they too want to have more mastery over the deluge of information they have to process every day.

And then I knew as I became a senior citizen, those of you who have reached that point in life might be concerned about your slipping memory, maybe looming Alzheimer's disease. Many people worry about their memory. Billions of dollars are spent each year on herbs, vitamins, and assorted supplements to improve memory. This interest is growing as more and more baby boomers come to the age when forgetting is becoming a problem.

Memory is such an important issue for so many people that the pharmaceutical industry is frantically searching for a "memory pill," not only to treat the growing incidence of Alzheimer's disease, but also to help students and working people in their everyday lives. Someday, such a pill may arrive (don't hold your breath). In the meanwhile, you need to be doing the things I explain in this book.

So, why did I write this book? Foremost was my desire to meet those expectations that I speculated you would have. But it was more than that. My life experience has taught me that competence is a precious commodity, one that cannot be gained without knowing and remembering a lot of stuff.

Competence seems increasingly needed in our modern age, yet our culture seems to attack excellence and professionalism. It could seem like there is a conspiracy against effective memory and reasoning. Yet, memory and reasoning, according to physician Julian Whitaker, are what make us human—"they are the essence of our beings."

We are becoming an attention-deficit riddled culture wherein people do not read well and do their thinking in sound bites, phone text messages, bullet points, and tweets. They think less and talk more. This cultural shift in communication will probably worsen, given that our information load seems to be expanding exponentially.

Yet it is fundamental human nature to seek superiority. One of the nation's founding fathers, John Adams, has been quoted as having said in 1777, "I believe there is no one principle which predominates in human nature so much… as this passion for superiority." A good memory is needed to get superior performance, whether it is in school, business, or a profession.

One thing that makes this book different from other memory books is that it is timely. Most memory books were written before the advent of computers, Internet communication, and on-line information repositories. As a consequence, those books focused on the old issues of memory, that is how to move from the inefficiency and tedium of rote memorization to the use of assorted memory tactics, such as those of employing mental images. I explain all that in this book too, but this book addresses many of the challenges of today, like knowledge superficiality, information overload, multitasking, attention deficit, the stress of modern competitive life, and the increasing problems of mental decline that come from living longer.

Today's information explosion is overloading our Stone Age brains. We are forced to distractibility and attention deficit, to multitasking, to relying on Google. We not only skim read, we skim think. That is not how you become an expert in anything. My book shows the approaches and tactics to learning that are more necessary now than ever to succeed in this complicated world.

*We not only skim read, we skim think.*

Yet, despite all this need for more and better learning, people increasingly disparage memorization skills. Many school children don't have to learn multiplication tables, because now we have calculators. In science education, the emphasis is on inquiry, where it used to be on knowledge and understanding. We don't learn much history, because we can always "look it up" (trouble is, we usually don't, and thus have to keep re-learning the lessons of history). We don't memorize Bible verses, poems, songs, the Bill of Rights, or other things like people used to do.

People today seem to think Google is the source of competence. My book challenges that naive idea. I have to wonder if reliance on external knowledge, as opposed to having it in our heads, is part of the reason more and more kids are dropping out of school—school work is too frustrating for them because they never acquired the necessary learning and memory skills.

Yet all this is happening at a time in our culture where there is a premium on education and skilled workers. As a result, we may be evolving a permanent underclass of workers trapped in unemployment or menial, low-pay jobs.

Learning and memory are not exactly the same, but rather should be thought of as two sides of the same coin. Doing the things advocated in a good book on learning and memory would make people more competent and increase the likelihood of a more successful life. In this book, I tried to give the reader the best of what is known about how to become more competent.

*You can learn without remembering. But you can't remember what you haven't learned.*

I bring to this book a unique background of experience and expertise you won't find elsewhere. I was an exceptional student. I went on to become my high-school valedictorian—with the highest average in the Memphis metropolitan area—and an Honors student at three universities (including graduating with a DVM degree and later securing a PhD in two-and-a-half years). It's not that I was so smart—it's that I studied smart. I've since discovered much about learning from observing students in my years as a professor.

My job as a professor for almost 50 years has been about helping students become more competent (trust me, if there is a way to study poorly, students will find it). A major part of those efforts incorporated what I had learned that helped me become competent as a student and professional.

My work as a neuroscientist gave me a background in how the brain works and an appreciation for how brain function determines the degree of memory capability. For example, I share with you in this book some of what we know about memory influences on IQ and thinking ability, and vice versa. You won't find that in other books.

Now as a greying senior citizen, I saw the need to make the book useful to those readers who are at that stage of life. You might say, I have touched all the bases needed to talk about learning and memory.

Books on improving memory are almost as ubiquitous as cookbooks. I have 35 memory books in my own personal library. Cookbooks are popular because everybody likes to eat. Memory books are popular because everybody, at one time or another in their life, has a real need to remember better.

So, who needs another memory book? Everybody, if it is a book unlike the rest. Most memory books tell you the tricks that memory "athletes" use in memory contests. My book does that too (see Chapter III). But my book is more practical, because the memory athlete tricks are hard work. Memory athletes train for hours every day all year long to make these tricks work for them. This is not what the average person wants to do. Even so, normal people can more casually use some of these tricks in everyday life, such as in school, playing cards, and practical things like remembering names and faces.

No other memory book (at least the 35 I have read) gives you a comprehensive understanding of the things that influence learning and memory. This understanding can vastly improve memory performance in everyday life, even if you don't feel up to working at it like a memory athlete. This book, for example, has a whole chapter on learning (Chapter II), the point of which is to help the reader down the path of learning how to learn. This book shows that learning and memory are separate yet interdependent processes.

This book explains working memory and how central it is to our ability to think clearly and with power. I report experiments that show how to improve working memory capacity and even raise your IQ.

This book has practical things you can do to improve your attentiveness (lack of which is the major cause of memory problems in seniors and, of course, children with ADHD).The book explains the role of stress in memory and hopefully will encourage you to improve your stress-coping skills. This is the only memory book I know of that explains important new discoveries on the role of sleep in memory formation. This book has research-based information on how to improve motor-memory, like improving your golf game or playing a musical instrument.

This book is built around published memory research with practical applications. I will try not to make any glib promises, but I can tell you that this research will give you fresh insights into making your memory better. Hopefully when you've finished reading you will have learned some interesting things in addition to improving your memory skills. Each small step in raising your memory capacity makes it easier to advance to the next level of memory competency.

Unlike other memory-book authors, I continuously read this literature   (I write some of it too) and have the educational background to understand it. That brings me to this point: I have actually performed memory research on subjects such as laboratory rats and college sophomores.

Memory research, once out of fashion, is published more often these days. This creates a lot of sometimes bewildering ideas. We confront a lot of hype about new memory-enhancing supplements and diet, teaching methods, neural plasticity, "mind healing," and the like. You need an expert like me to help sort through all the chaff.

Unlike most scientists, my experience as an author and blog writer helps me translate research reports into everyday language. While I am on the topic of my blogging, you may want to know that this book will be updated as new research comes out in my Learning and Memory blog site (http://thankyoubrain.blogspot.com) and my postings at *Psychology Today* (http://www.psychologytoday.com/blog/memory-medic). At this writing I only have a few posts at *Psychology Today*, but they already have had over 150,000 reader views.

How should you read this book? You could just jump to the memory task currently most pressing in your life. You could be looking for a better way to remember playing cards, or computer passwords, or jokes, or whatever. This kind of specific information occurs in the last chapter. I urge you to read this chapter last. It you skip to the end, as in a novel or a movie—you will miss the plot and, more importantly, the total experience needed to get the most benefit.

Chapter II explains the basic principles of memory: the kinds, the processes, and core principles about optimizing memory in general.

Chapter IV explains what I am calling "Lifestyle Effects." This material is typically omitted in memory books, because most authors don't realize how such things as attitude, emotions, lifestyle, etc., affect memory profoundly. Memory is a brain function and therefore affected by whatever affects the brain. Even if the effect on memory is indirect, it can nonetheless be crucial.

The last chapter gives specific advice for the most common learning and memory tasks that so many people face in school, on the job, or in social situations. This is perhaps the most important section of the book—it might even improve your golf game.

*Whatever affects the brain affects the memory.*

*Whatever affects the memory affects the brain.*

The upshot is this: you are now launching into a book jam-packed with the author's lifetime of learning and memory experiences, the essence of 35 other memory books, and the practical applications of modern neuroscience research on learning and memory. Read on. It may change your future.

# I. HOW YOU SHOULD THINK ABOUT LEARNING AND MEMORY

Picture this: a donkey is pulling a two-wheeled cart. Hundreds of people run around the cart dumping stuff into it until the cart gets so heavy it lifts the donkey into the air. That's what I feel it is like to work and live in a world that overflows with information. Do you feel that way sometimes too?

In terms of Information Theory, we get bombarded with up to 100 million bits of information per second, but we can only consciously process at most about 45 bits per second. In terms of working memory, which is what we think with, our capacity is at most about 16 bits. And we're supposed to be effective learners and have good memories?

This chapter explains why learning and memory are more important today than ever before—Google notwithstanding. Schools are failing, jobs get more technical and complex, the workplace is more competitive, and we seem to have less time. Is it any wonder that people like you are looking for more effective ways to learn and remember?

Fortunately, in the face of increased demand on our brains, we are not limited to the learning and memory strategies and tactics of the past. Today, as this chapter points out, we are being helped by the discoveries of brain research, "neuroscience" as it is called. This chapter explains the role of neuroscience in improving our learning and memory abilities and the new trend of "neuro-education," which is a movement to apply the findings of neuroscience to schools.

This chapter also explains something we don't think enough about. What we learn and remember largely determines our attitudes, our character, our abilities—and even our brain!

Finally, the chapter sets the stage for the rest of the book by explaining what we know about learning and memory, such as how they relate to each other, where memory is located in the brain and the kinds of memory and how they differ.

## Learning and Memory in Everyday Life

"Mommy, Grandma can't find her glasses. Have you seen them?"

"I know we've met somewhere—I'm sorry, but I can't remember your name."

"I know I came to the kitchen for a reason. What was I looking for?"

"Professor, I studied like a demon for this test and I still barely passed. What am I doing wrong?"

These common problems in today's culture were less prevalent in ancient times. Before the advent of written language and means of large-scale printing, whole cultures were transmitted from generation to generation by prodigious feats of memory. Greek orators, for example, memorized speeches and stories lasting seven hours or more. I will tell you how they did that later.

But who needs memory skills today? Not only do we have books where we can look something up, but now we can always just "Google it." But Google can't learn a foreign language for you. What about students trying to pass high-stakes exams? Google isn't enough. And can Google make businesspeople more knowledgeable and competent?

Being able to find information is not the same as knowing it. Access to the Internet is not always available or practical. Looking stuff up instead of memorizing it breeds mental laziness, which I think is a major problem with today's schoolchildren. Memory needs exercise or it atrophies like a muscle. Memory-contest competitors train for months to become mental athletes, but when they stop training, their memory capability shrivels back to a more ordinary level.

*Being able to find information is not the same as knowing it.*

More importantly, memory is crucial for powerful thinking. I will explain that in Chapter III when discussing "working memory" and how to train it. Here I would like to discuss some of the negative attitudes about the value of memory, often held by those in education who think emphasis on memory is old-fashioned and we should focus on teaching children to be creative and critical thinkers.[1] I agree that the ultimate goal should be to teach people how to think, solve problems, and create. Central to these capabilities, however, is the ability to remember things.

---

### Memory Myth Buster

*The focus of learning should be on developing critical thinking skills.* Not if that's all you do! A person can't think in a vacuum. Critical thinking requires knowledge and acquired thinking and problem-solving skills. These things require a powerful memory.

---

Think about all the time and money we spend trying to learn, whether it's in school, on the job, or anywhere else. What good is it trying to learn something if you don't remember it?[2] The only benefit I can think of is that such temporary learning makes it easier to learn something a second time.

The more one knows (remembers), the more intellectual competencies one has to draw upon for thinking, problem solving, and even creativity. Society does not need a workforce of trained seals, but it needs people with knowledge and skills that they can apply appropriately to different situations. US manufacturing company executives are complaining that, since manufacturing technology is so complicated, they have to rely on foreign workers who have better educational backgrounds than most US students do. The same problem exists for recruiters to graduate education programs at US colleges of engineering.

Think back to your school days. How many teachers explicitly taught you how to remember effectively and efficiently? Your teachers may have used a couple of acrostics and limericks, or warned you not to cram, but chances are that was the extent of your formal education in how to learn. The emphasis in school is always on what to learn. Who teaches how to learn?

The problem is that learning is hard for so many people. They have not learned much about how to learn from parents or teachers, or on their own. When learning is hard it's not fun, so they avoid learning until it is absolutely necessary. These people miss out on all the fun and rewards of lifelong learning.

Maybe you are a student trying to make better grades, especially with less effort. Maybe your work requires you to have a good memory, and you are not advancing in your career because of memory limitations. Maybe you have reached the stage of life when you begin to worry about your memory and that is why you have sought this book.

Let's be honest. The vast majority of us have problems with our memory. Politicians know this; they must remember many people, especially their benefactors. Businesspeople who must remember key details about their business and their clients know this. Shoppers who forget to pick up certain groceries know this. Professional football players know how hard it is to memorize the playbook. Students who have to prepare for exams know this. When I was younger, competing for good grades in school, and later competing to get into and excel in veterinary college, I quickly learned I had to work on improving my memory. Now, as I age, I have lost some of the memory capability of my youth.

Whatever memory failings we have are due to failure to use our innate memory capabilities to their full potential. The reason is mostly a matter of faulty education. In some cases we have been told erroneous things about memory, but, for the most part, we haven't been taught much about memory at all.

---

### Memory Myth Buster

*The cause of poor memory is typically a biological limitation or disease.* WRONG. Most people with memory problems are not doing the right things to have a good memory. That is what this book is all about, to show them what works and what interferes with memory.

---

Learning and remembering open doors to new experiences, new career possibilities, new achievements, and new rewards and benefits. Knowledge and the insights that go with it move us from a narrow, shallow life into a big, expansive one. Our world becomes larger and more fulfilling.

Learning is the reason that humans dominate the planet. Our extraordinary ability to learn enables us to live in hostile environments, cope with difficult situations, solve new problems, and create new tools and procedures.

Humans have a special gift for learning how to learn. The more we learn, the more learning skills we acquire. And learning is self-reinforcing: the more we learn and remember, the stronger and faster our capacity for learning becomes.

Learning effectiveness depends on several things:

*Degree of interest and enjoyment*. Too often, people have limited interests, which limit what they learn. It pays to develop interest in many things. The drive to learn is killed by telling yourself that something is uninteresting or boring. Schoolchildren and young adults do this routinely.

*Paying attention and thinking about what you are trying to learn*. Thinking involves relating new information to existing knowledge by asking and attempting to answer questions. This is a part of the next item in this list.

*Actively engage.* This relates to the idea of learning by doing, either mentally or physically. Strive to identify meaning and gain insight. Getting involved with and applying what you are trying to learn is much more effective than passively watching a video or listening to a lecture without taking notes or otherwise engaging with the material. This point applies to lazy reading, too.

*Striving for continuous improvement of learning skills and knowledge expansion.* Learning-to-learn skills are cumulative and, I think, super-additive. Without continual striving to become a better learner, you will reach an "OK" plateau that keeps you from expanding your learning and memory capabilities. You will never know the satisfaction and joy you have missed.

*Knowing memorization principles and tricks.* There are lots of techniques to help you absorb new information, many of which will be discussed later in this book.

*Confronting challenging learning material.* When you make a conscious decision to learn hard material, you can move out of your OK plateau and begin expanding your learning and memory capabilities. Deliberate practice must be difficult in order to gain maximum benefit. It's like the physical-exercise mantra: "no pain, no gain."

---

### Memory Myth Buster

*It's not what you know. It's who you know that counts.* This quip is a half-truth at best.

---

I concede that networking and knowing important people can open many doors of opportunity, but at some point you have to produce in order to get ahead. And that requires certain skills, and all skills require knowledge. This truth was enshrined in the famous quote from the classic 1982 best-seller, *In Search of Excellence*:[3] career people typically "rise to their level of incompetence." In other words, at some point in a career, your level of knowledge and skill limits how far you progress.

Competence matters and competence comes from your ability to learn and remember. Capacity to learn is itself a learned skill, one that this book aims to teach. Employers have always understood this principle, which is why they typically prefer to hire college graduates, even for menial jobs. The assumption is that if you can graduate from college, you have at least demonstrated some minimal capacity for learning how to learn. However, my nearly fifty years of experience as a college professor has taught me not to be too sanguine about this assumption. Graduating from college in many curricula doesn't demand much these days. Post-graduate studies are a different matter. The Ph.D. degree obtained from a rigorous graduate program signifies that the holder has substantial learning and discovery skills.

In high school and lower college levels, students tend to focus on learning for short term retention, just long enough to pass the next exam. In the real world, what matters is not what you once knew, but what you know now.

I began to learn these lessons in the seventh grade, but not for the most noble of reasons. My seventh grade teacher, Ms. Torti, was a real babe. My hormones were surging at that stage, and I developed a crush on her. But the student she paid the most attention to was the "teacher's pet," a girl who always knew the right answers and made the top grades. If that is how the game was played, I decided I must find a way to get Ms. Torti's attention by making good grades. So I tried. The more my hormones churned, the harder I worked, and the more I thought about how to create and optimize an approach to learning. And it worked. Of course, I never got anywhere with Ms. Torti, but I did discover that I could make good grades if I thought hard enough about how to do it. From the seventh grade until I graduated from high school, I never made a grade in any subject less than an A (with only a couple of exceptions, that also applied to seven years of college course work). And this was before today's era of grade inflation.

One high-school teacher (who never had me in class) said my good grades were a fluke, not truly representative, because I had a modest IQ score. He and other teachers called me an "overachiever" as if that were a dirty word. At least one teacher openly predicted I would have trouble in college. Oh really? These teachers didn't know how well I knew how to learn. I performed exceptionally well academically. This book shares a lot of what I learned about learning.

*Knowledge is power, and is accessible to everyone who knows how to get it.*

## The Role for Neuroscience

Where do we get our ideas about improving learning and memory? In the old days, the advice in memory books originated from anecdotes and informal trial-and-error experiences. Today, we can add to such advice rigorously tested ideas in scientific experiments. Most of these new ideas come from the field of neuroscience—the study of the brain and psychology. And these ideas are beginning to find their way into educational practice. As I was finishing the final drafts of this book, I attended a great "neuro-education" conference in Aspen, Colorado. Neuro-education is a hot new movement based on applying discoveries about brain function to teaching practices. Actually, this is what I have been doing since 2004 with my efforts to find the practical applications of memory research and explain them to the public.

You would never guess who the conference's keynote speaker was. It was Goldie Hawn. Yes, I mean the famous actress many of us think of as the ditsy blonde in TV shows like *Rowan & Martin's Laugh-In* and movies like *Private Benjamin*. She is a grandmother now, but still vivacious and attractive. Goldie has created a neuroscience-based educational foundation and teaching program called "MindUP" which is designed to improve learning in elementary school children (see http://www.thehawnfoundation.org/mindup).

Her program espouses some of the things that are central to neuroscience-based education. Elementary school teachers are using her approach not only to teach neuroscience (see, brain research is not arcane), they also teach kids to be more introspective about how their thoughts, feelings, and actions affect their brain and how it learns.

Showing kids how to recognize and control their feelings and behavior is a key part of neuro-education. The experts refer to this capability as "executive function," which they ascribe to the prefrontal cortex (PFC). The PFC is the part of the brain that is most developed in higher primates such as chimps, apes and humans. As such, the PFC is certainly crucial to executive brain functions. However, I and many other researchers have shown that higher cognitive functions arise from widespread concerted action across many parts of the cerebral cortex (the outer surface of the brain).

Anyway, from a teaching perspective, what is important about executive function training is that kids need to learn how to be more self-aware and self-controlled. Goldie's program emphasizes teaching kids to recognize when they are wired, distracted, upset, angry, or have other emotions that interfere with their learning. By being more self-aware, they have a better chance to control themselves. Research in neuro-education also includes such things as reasoning training, improving working memory and long-term memory consolidation and retrieval, and treatments for reading disabilities and ADHD.

At the same conference I met Nobel Prize physicist, Carl Wieman, now Associate Director for Science at the White House Office of Science and Technology Policy. His talk stressed the need for educators to emphasize concepts and principles to their students. This is an emphasis throughout this book: optimal learning and memory requires more than memorizing bullet points, gimmicks, and short-cuts (though you'll find plenty of those here, too). Another point Dr. Wieman made was that everybody who has gone to school tends to think they are an expert in learning. But he emphasized, "Novices seldom recognize what they do not know, especially in education." This is a problem not only with politicians and educational policy makers, but also the typical person's attitude about learning and memory. Too many people think that, when it comes to learning and memory, they are what they are and it's too late to change. This book should prove that it is possible to improve learning and memory capabilities regardless of where you are right now.

We all know that US education is in crisis. Many think the solution is to spend more money. But there is plenty of non-partisan research showing no correlation between funding and educational achievement. The solution is to stop doing things that don't work and do more of what does. Neuro-education principles are crucial to effective reform.

In developing countries, education problems run even deeper, as ignorance and illiteracy are common in burgeoning populations. Surveys by the UN's Development Program indicate that under-education is prevalent in nations that are widely considered seedbeds of economic dependency, dysfunctional governments, and extreme political unrest. When I spoke with Helen Abadzi, education specialist and senior evaluation officer at the UN World Bank (and fellow Auburn graduate), she told me about the many neuroscience-based reform initiatives the Bank is pursuing in developing countries. The social and economic costs of ignorance cannot be overstated.

This book's neuroscience-based ideas on memory are based on scientific evidence. I suppose I could just tell you what to do, but then you would have to take my word that they could work for you, and you may not be convinced enough to try them out.

Some readers may object to finding science in a "how-to" book. But the necessity was explained by Sonja Lyubomirsky in *The How of Happiness*.[4] She, like me, is a researcher writing for a general audience. Rather than hide or gloss over research, she and her publisher embraced it. On page 4, she writes, "Every suggestion that I offer is supported by scientific research ...Notes and references are provided for all theories, statistics, and original sources. ... Why should readers care whether the advice they read holds multiple advantages over anecdotal or clinical observations? By applying the scientific method, researchers have the ability to disentangle cause and effect and to study a phenomenon systematically, without biases or preconceptions." In her book, she summarizes the actual experiments supporting the advice and supplies end notes, organized by chapter, as I do in this book.

This is exactly why I will refer to learning and memory experiments in this book. I want you to understand my advice, not follow it blindly. Condensed descriptions of the underlying research provide meat for the bare-bone assertions. Thinking people do not just blindly accept whatever any so-called expert tells them. Savvy readers will want credible support for the assertions I make in this book.

Some of this research was done with animals, but that doesn't render the conclusions invalid. Neuroscience discoveries made using animal subjects typically apply to humans as well. Researchers simply prefer using animal subjects, for a number of reasons:

- Experimental variables are much easier to control in animal studies.

- Researchers can do things with animals that humans wouldn't volunteer for, or would insist on being paid for.

- Animals are less costly to keep than humans.

Animal brains work with the same general principles as the human brain. Science has been teaching us how to improve human learning and memory for almost a hundred years— ever since Pavlov showed us that dogs were four-footed furballs of conditioned reflexes.

<br>

**Memory Myth Buster**

*What is learned about how animals learn and remember is not very applicable to humans.* WRONG. Most of what has been learned about animal learning has been verified in humans.

Learning and memory change the physical and biochemical properties of the brain. Experience sculpts and reinforces the connections between and among nerve cells ("neurons"). Learning experiences cause neurons to organize themselves in multiple circuits, providing multiple ways to learn, memorize, and recall information. Learning promotes the formation of new junctions (synapses) between neurons and creates new circuitry. Long-term memory has to be stored, and the storage occurs in an altered microanatomy of synapses and circuitry.

## Learning and Memory Relationships

Throughout this book, I sometimes speak of learning and memory almost inseparably, because, once again, learning and memory are like two sides of the same coin. Learning is the acquiring and understanding of new information or skills. Memory is the retention of what was learned. You can't have memory without learning. You can, of course, forget something you have learned.

Learning involves at least five major processes:

- Registration
- Memorization

- Understanding
- Integration
- Learning to learn

It all begins with **registering** new information. This is the stage where one detects and encodes information. Paying attention obviously facilitates the registration process.

**Memorization**. You can remember things just long enough to use them (called "working memory") or you can have information stored permanently in your brain for use (recall into working memory) any time you need it. In either case, you understand and integrate information that is in working memory.

**Understanding**. You can, as I did, pass college calculus by using the right formulas for given problem types and still not really understand what is going on with the equations. It is vastly more useful to grasp the concepts involved; this allows you to use the information in different ways. To understand, you need to answer such questions as: Is this consistent with what I thought I knew? What is missing or still confusing? What can I do with this information? What else does it apply to? How can it be extended? What is predictable?

Learning is not complete without understanding. Understanding also creates a basis for generating insights and creative syntheses, and these in turn advance the depth and rigor of the original learning. Insights typically come from deduction or induction. Deduction is the Sherlock Holmes process of using general facts or observations to lead logically to a specific conclusion. Induction is the Charles Darwin process of using multiple, apparently unrelated, facts or observations to make a synthesis that integrates them into a broader understanding.

**Integration**. The brain likes to classify, categorize, and organize its information. Thus, new information has to be fitted into an existing learned framework. This is the stage where associations are made with existing memories. Brains are very good at detecting and constructing relationships. If a given relationship is not immediately obvious, the brain may still figure it out and remember it. Constructing such relationships is an integral part of the learning process.

Associations can be constructed subconsciously. If two things happen at the same time or go together in some other way, even the simplest of brains can learn the association. Cueing of relationships can produce what is called conditioned learning. Recall what was said earlier about Pavlov's dogs and classical conditioning, even in primitive animals like flatworms.

But what I most want to emphasize is that associations are even more powerful when they are consciously constructed. This is the stage where you ask yourself such questions as: Where does this information fit in with what I already know? How does this relate to other things I could learn about? What value do I place on this information? How invested in using or remembering it should I be?

Finally, there is **learning to learn**. This is the process of learning the paradigm, the "rules of the game," when it comes to absorbing and retaining new information. This allows you to transfer one learned capability to new but related learning situations. This is the point at which one has reached the threshold where the more you know, the more you can know.

*Memory makes us who we are.*

It should be obvious that what you learn and remember can also change who you are as a person. Memory is often dismissed as a mindless process, simply holding onto information just long enough to meet some immediate need. However, what we remember accumulates over the days and years to change who we are. That can be for better or worse, depending on what we choose to experience and learn. As Aristotle said, "We are what we repeatedly do."

What we attend to is what we actually experience, and therefore what is available to form into memory. Without memory, we would not know who we are. We would not remember our name, our address, our loved ones, or anything about the events that have shaped our lives. Who we are reflects what we have remembered explicitly or implicitly, and what we have learned on purpose or by accident.

In his book, *The Created Self*, Robert Weber makes this point: "We see that memory itself is an important selector, definer, and preserver that goes far beyond sheer storage as it exercises its preferences and aversions. What memory selects to encode and value serves to define the self." Weber goes on to explain there are at least three ways our memories "define the self."

1. We interpret our current experiences based on the store of memories that have created our biases, emotions, and storehouse of knowledge.
2. We rely on our memory to interpret and re-interpret our storehouse of existing memories.
3. We sculpt our personality, attitudes, and abilities by deciding what we want to remember and what we want to forget.

Unless your memory is failing and causing you clear problems at work or in your personal life, you probably take your memory for granted. You may think it would be nice to have a better memory, but why bother? People don't realize how much time and effort they waste trying to compensate for or re-learn things they have forgotten. Some have claimed that a typical person wastes about forty days a year in this way. Even more time is probably wasted by people in high-density training situations, as in school.

You may well believe you can't do much about your memory. Wrong! Would it help to have a testimonial about how I learned the benefits of improving my memory? In school, I almost flunked the fourth grade. As I explained earlier, things turned around in the seventh grade. In high school, my interest in power learning grew even more, because by then I had a lot of interests besides school (girls, sports, clubs, activities, etc.). Yet, I still wanted to make good grades, a drive instilled in me by my parents. So, to excel in school without abandoning my extracurricular interests, I had to learn to study efficiently. That meant learning how to memorize efficiently, preferably during class, so I wouldn't have to study as much in my free time. After learning a few memory tricks I was able to memorize most things in class each day, and the rest I memorized on the bus ride home.

I was busy with lots of things, from raising my farm animals to becoming involved in numerous clubs (I was president of four, and School President for two years). My evenings were filled with dating, "dragging Main Street," and listening to St. Louis Cardinal games. My next big memory motivation came when my father was a recruiter for the Dale Carnegie leadership course. He got me to participate, and I learned the memory tricks that were taught in the course. I turned out to be pretty good at them, and they decided to show off my skills at recruitment meetings. At the start of each meeting, they would tell the audience: "Here is the latest issue of *Life* magazine. Billy Klemm is a sixteen-year-old who has taken the course and he will demonstrate to you the powerful memory techniques that are a part of this course. Thirty minutes from now, Billy will have memorized this magazine. He has never seen it. Yet he will be able to tell you what every page is about, in any order. Or, you can tell him what is on a given page, and he will tell you the page number."

Sure enough, after 30 minutes, I had memorized the magazine (I really hadn't seen it before!). The audience was astonished that I could tell them—at least in general terms—what was on each page, or the number of any page that they described to me. I was astonished too! That's heady stuff for a sixteen-year-old. It certainly motivated me to care about memory. Later, in Chapter III, I'll introduce you to the techniques that enabled me to perform this feat of memorization. There are people who train intensively on these techniques and compete in national and international contests.

About the same time, I developed an interest in becoming a veterinarian. Getting into veterinary school was (and still is) very competitive. Back then there were only 19 such schools in the whole country, and they all had smaller classes than they do now. The only veterinary college I could go to without paying out-of-state tuition was Auburn, which had a contract to take only ten students from each of the states surrounding Alabama. Thanks in part to the memory skills

I'd cultivated, mine was the top-ranked application, and I got accepted by Auburn.

Later, as a veterinary student, I discovered just how difficult that curriculum is. People do not realize just how much there is for veterinary students to memorize, yet there is, and admission standards are commonly higher for veterinary school than medical school. Veterinary students take all the standard medical courses (anatomy, physiology, pharmacology, microbiology, pathology, public health, etc.), each of which deals with multiple species. In addition veterinary students take surgery courses in both large and small animal species. Well, my memory skills paid off, allowing me to graduate fifth in my class while at the same time contributing a weekly column for our national award-winning Auburn university newspaper and being active in campus politics—and enjoying courting my wife-to-be, Doris. The four guys ahead of me didn't have much of a life outside of study.

A few years later, I found myself working as a professor, first at Iowa State University's College of Veterinary Medicine, and then at Texas A&M University, first as a professor in the College of Science and then in the College of Veterinary Medicine. For almost fifty years now, I have had ample opportunity to observe student performance, both good and bad. There are many wrong ways to learn, and students seem to find most of them. Not many years had to pass before I realized that the biggest problem that most students have is poor memory skills. Time and again, students would complain about how hard they worked, without seeing corresponding good results on tests. They taught me many lessons about what not to do in studying.

I spent at least half of my time as a professor doing research, mostly on neuroscience. Inevitably, some of my research involved memory functions of the brain, ranging from consolidation of short-term memories to the way the brain's electrical activity behaves during memory recall.

The upshot of all these experiences motivated me to share with others what I have learned about how to enrich one's life through a better memory.

# Core Ideas about Learning and Memory

## Where Is Memory?

Memory is stored in the form of enhanced function at the junction points (synapses) between neurons. These synaptic changes occur in the chemical communication systems and in their fine structure. You could say this is the brain's hard drive for memory storage. In simple brains, such as a mollusk's, scientists can locate where the memory is physically "contained." But in higher animals, like humans, it is not possible to identify with any great precision where in the brain the memory is. That is because, as one prominent scientist, E. Roy John put it, memory is "not a thing in a place, but a process in a population."

In higher animals, memories are distributed as fragments in several places on both sides of the brain. Many years ago, Nobel Prize-winning research showed that sensory information is broken down and registered in widely scattered neurons. Information is not only detected in this fragmented way but seems to be stored in the same scattered fashion. Think of our brain as a highly fragmented computer hard drive, which apparently does not need to be "defragged." We know this from observing changes in the brain's electrical activity, or in brain scans as subjects form and recall memories.

## Kinds of Learning and Memory

Amnesic human patients reveal there are different kinds of memory, and the brain uses them in different ways. A person can have perfectly normal memory for certain kinds of things and terrible memory for others.

It therefore is not enough to say we have a good or bad memory. Memory improvement often requires focus on specific memory problems rather than some vague notion about memory capacity in general.

There are new memories and old memories. Another category of distinction is that memories for facts and memories for skills appear to involve different processes and parts of the brain.

**Declarative (Explicit) Memory**. A major category distinction is whether or not you are consciously aware of a memory—many memories operate subconsciously. Remember when you were in school, and the teacher asked you a question about a homework problem? Whether you got the answer right or not, you were consciously trying to recall the answer and provide it to the teacher. In such cases you were declaring, either orally or in writing or some equivalent way, what you had remembered. This kind of memory is called declarative memory or sometimes explicit memory. Such memory typically deals with facts and events of which a person is consciously aware.

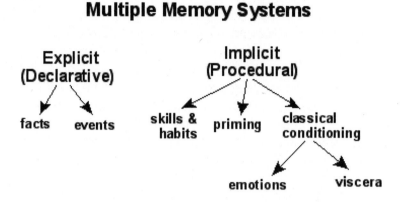

Because declarative memories require consciousness, it is useful to ask about the function of consciousness in memory. We traditionally view the conscious mind as exerting direction and influence over the subconscious. It has "veto power" and, short of that, can guide the subconscious mind's thinking processes. Conscious mind programs the subconscious mind by its conscious choices. Conscious thinking can also provide a starting point for learning and, with rehearsal, can drive learning into an automated underground where the task can be performed without conscious thinking.

**Implicit (Procedural) Learning: Conditioning.** The automated or implicit learning of new things can occur in a couple of ways, and these are typically referred to as "conditioned learning." Such learning occurs when information is readily related and repeated often. At some point, the learning "sinks in" without conscious effort.

Do you touch type? Remember how you learned? Some teaching systems have you memorize, consciously, the location of the keys: A, S. D, F, G on the middle row for the left hand and H, J, K, L on the middle row for the right hand. Then after you deliberate on these locations and practice them until your mind and your fingers know where the right keys are, the lessons move on to the top row's left and right hand keys. When this is learned, you do the same thing with the bottom row. After you have practiced these key strokes for many months, the process becomes automated—i.e., implicit. Ask most typists to describe the keyboard layout and they can't tell you. Their brain just knows (and doesn't bother to tell them about it). This is what is meant by the saying "practice makes perfect." Well-learned skills and habits of all kinds (such as riding a bicycle, swimming, hitting a golf ball, playing a musical instrument, or dancing) fall into this implicit category. Such seemingly unconscious learning is also often called "procedural," because it involves the performance of physical or mental tasks.

Many scientists and philosophers argue that everything we use to control our behavior is implicit learning. The idea that we use what we know consciously is considered an illusion. They say we don't have free will. I have challenged this argument in my other recent book, *Atoms of Mind*.[5]

Actually, I think this illusory free-will theory undervalues consciousness in personal responsibility, but this is a topic of another book of mine, called *Blame Game: How To Win It*.[6] That aside, there is no doubt that willful effort to learn is the most effective way to do so. But regardless of where one comes down on the issue of free will, there is absolutely no doubt that conscious mind directs the formation of memory. Even for those memories that have been driven underground in the subconscious (as in implicit memory), the hidden brain machinery running these operations typically learned what and how to do things by being consciously programmed.

In implicit memory, you remember without consciously trying to remember. You might call these "underground memories," because they are buried beneath the level of consciousness. When such memories are unearthed, they prove you can learn without realizing it. This subconscious learning is the kind that can just sink in while you are thinking about something else.

---

**Memory Myth Buster**

*People are aware of most of their memories.* WRONG. Most memories are probably buried in the subconscious. Constant rehearsal of consciously formed memories may drive them into the subconscious, making them automated and implicit.

---

What's the point of subconscious learning? Why learn things if you don't know you know them? Freud would have argued the subconscious brain absorbs things so it can hide them from the conscious mind. Now, neuroscientists are starting to think subconscious memory may be more efficient, or at least provide an alternative, parallel path for learning so more total learning can occur. It is also likely that the interactions between the conscious and the subconscious mind reinforce the memory processes of both (more about that later, especially in the sleep sections of Chapter IV).

Spatial memory usually qualifies as implicit memory. Your brain knows where you are in space without having to call the information up into conscious awareness. Nonetheless, implicit spatial cues can be helpful for recalling learned material. For example, it has been observed that students perform better on examinations if they take them in the same classroom where they learned the information than they do if the exam is given in another room. Later in the book, I will explain some memory tricks that rely on using spatial location as anchors to help memorize things.

How spatial memory works was elucidated in the early 1970s, when several different labs using rat subjects showed that certain neurons located in a part of the brain known as the hippocampus behave as "place" cells. They discharge impulses only when the rat is located at certain places. Spatial learning seems to take place via these hippocampal cells. This is important to note because, as I will explain in a later chapter, humans with brain damage in this area have great trouble in forming lasting memories. The hippocampus is also a common target for strokes, which notoriously impair memory.

Implicit learning often involves Pavlovian conditioning, a process discovered in Russia by Ivan Pavlov in the 1890s. This kind of learning develops when two or more stimuli are presented at more or less the same time. One stimulus always elicits a response, even in the absence of learning, while the other stimulus is initially novel. In the case of Pavlov's dogs, the unlearned stimulus was the sight and smell of food, which naturally made his hungry dogs salivate. Such a stimulus is called an unconditioned stimulus (UCS). But if a bell is rung consistently before the presentation of the food over a long enough period of time, the dogs will eventually start salivating at the sound of the bell, even if no food is present. They have learned (i.e., have been conditioned) to expect food when they hear the tone. The tone in this case is called the conditioning stimulus (CS), because the learning was conditioned by that stimulus.

Pavlov chose the single best species for studying conditioned learning. There are two definitions for a dog. One is that it is an animal always on the other side of the door. The relevant definition here is that a dog is a conditioned reflex machine. Most of what a dog has learned reflects conditioned reflexes. You may think that your Fido is a four-footed genius, but the fact is that he has just accumulated an elaborate set of conditioned reflexes. They come easily to a dog.

Dogs can even turn the tables on Pavlov and condition humans. For example, my dog Zoe has conditioned *me* to bring her a bone treat after she finishes dinner. Zoe has always had to eat on the porch. It used to be that when she was finished, she'd push open the sliding glass door I would leave ajar for her and come find me for her treat. Now, she just pushes the door, knowing I hear it, and rushes back to the porch and sits to await my arrival with the bone. It works! I am trained now. I wonder if she feels smug about it.

A common example of conditioning that we all experience is advertising. Television commercials and advertising in general aim at getting potential customers to make a Pavlovian association with the advertised product or service. Repetition is central. This is a main reason you see the same ads over and over again.

Advertisers also like to use gorgeous women or celebrities in the ads. The idea is to associate somebody you really like with a product you have not yet learned to like.

A fundamental error made by many advertisers today is that many commercials are so clever, funny, or otherwise engaging that the customer does not make the intended association. What they remember is the clever shtick. If the product is not tied in closely, the association is never made.

Another practical application of conditioned learning is to try to teach humans to alter their visceral function. I cover "Visceral Learning" in the context of psychosomatic disease in Chapter IV.

A related kind of implicit learning, called operant conditioning, is the common way for training work animals and circus animals. Whenever an animal accidentally does something close to what you want it to do, you give it a little reward. For example, if you want a dog to go sit in a corner of a room, you give a cue, such as a hand signal; every time it accidentally moves toward that area, you give the dog a little treat. Once the task is partially learned, you raise the stakes. That is, the dog has to move still closer to your desired spot before you give the reward. You continue this succession until the final learning goal is achieved.

A popular method many dog trainers use to improve such learning is to use a little metal clicker to reinforce the event. Suppose they want the dog to sit in response to a hand signal, such as thrusting the arm with a closed fist. At first this gesture means nothing to a dog, but when it accidentally sits in a confused response to such a signal, the trainer may click the sound and give a little treat. The clicker helps the dog make a more immediate and precise association between the desired behavior and the reward. After a few such trials, the dog learns to sit in response to the hand signal alone. All operant training procedures involve this "successive approximations" approach to learning.

Even animals usually considered less trainable than dogs can learn this way. I have seen these principles used to teach a parrot in its cage to turn to the left, climb up a ladder, ring a bell, climb down the ladder, and walk to the front of the cage. Though the animal may not understand exactly what it is learning, its behavior has been re-shaped and reinforced into a new set of learned behaviors.

The secret to success is strategically delivered positive reinforcement. That is, you get a reward when doing the right thing, or some approximation of it. The reward reinforces the behavior, and the expectation of reward increases the occurrence of the desired behavior. Experiments with animals reveal that the best results occur when the reward is given at unpredictable intervals rather than every time the desired behavior is performed. For example, a rat learns to press a lever for reward if he gets a food-pellet reward for several lever presses, not a pellet for every lever press.

Interestingly, operant conditioning is not commonly applied to humans. Maybe that is because it smacks of manipulation. Good classroom teachers, however, use versions of operant conditioning to motivate their students. This conditioning is less effective than it could be because teachers don't usually use systematic ways to apply operant conditioning to students.

**Priming.** Another learning sub-type is priming, which occurs when information is temporarily or only partly absorbed. While the information isn't actually learned, priming makes it easier to learn later on. This is the reason students are often encouraged to skim a textbook chapter for main points or headings before reading more closely;

the mind is primed to absorb the information more readily, since it already has associations it can link new information to. More practical applications of priming are explained in Chapter III.

**Recognition Memory.** Recognition is a form of passive memory that is much easier to achieve than active recall. Think of all the times you said, or heard others say, "I'd recognize it if I saw it." Multiple-choice questions on student examinations are a good case in point. It is much harder for a student to generate an answer than to pick one from a list of choices, where the correct answer may be recognized once the student sees it. Students will score some 10-40 points lower on the same exam when the questions are converted from multiple-choice to short-answer or fill-in-the-blank questions.

Active recall often requires the assistance of cues that were associated with the memory at the time it was first registered. For example, when you meet a new person, remembering their name is easier if you make visual or verbal associations of the name with certain obvious characteristics of the person. If "John" is bald, you might picture a commode (or "john") and imagine yourself shaving hair off the seat—absurd, of course, but very memorable. Or if "Mary" is always smiling and laughing, you might associate her name with her being "merry." The hairy toilet seat and the merry girl serve as cues to help you dredge up the name. Chapter III provides many tips on how to optimize such associations.

**Basic Memory Processes.** Here is how many scientists think memory works: information comes in from senses and gets encoded as nerve impulse patterns on a virtual scratch pad. After some brief rehearsal, the memory acquires short-term storage and may reside in what we call "working memory," which can be recalled and put to use for a short time. With still more rehearsal, particularly if there is no distraction or new information, the memory gets "consolidated" into a more lasting form, where it can be recalled at later times.

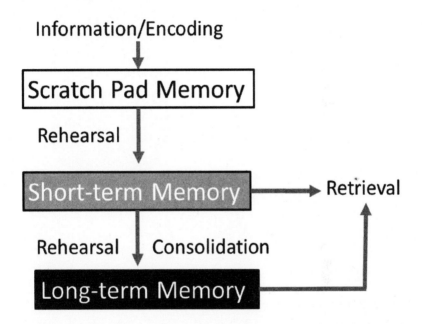

It should be self-evident that what gets encoded on the scratch pad is a limiting factor for what can be stored in your long-term memory. Not registered, not remembered. The effectiveness of this initial encoding step depends heavily on focus of attention and how deeply you think about the context of the situation and associational cues. Whether the initial encoding becomes consolidated into a longer-term memory depends on the processes illustrated in the next diagram.

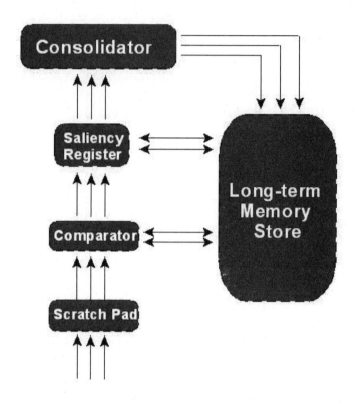

This diagram summarizes memory formation. Sensations and thoughts are put on a virtual scratch pad, which holds the thought or information in a temporary working memory form. This information is then compared in brain circuits with other information, both new and older, long-term memories. Then the mix of new information and stored memory is evaluated for its significance, which may involve biological, emotional, or cognitive salience. This salience evaluation requires testing against what is already stored in long-term memory. Finally, if no sensory or cognitive disruptions occur, the new temporary memory and its contextual associations may be "consolidated" and added to the long-term memory store.

**Brain "Work" and Complex Learning.** These memory processes engage widespread regions of the brain. For all but the simplest kinds of learning, the brain commits huge amounts of its resources to new learning tasks. Because different stimuli are processed by different and often widely separated neurons, we suspect that these neurons form temporary networks to link the distributed information. Recent brain electrical recording studies indicate that widely distributed neuronal populations synchronize at specific oscillating frequencies when they process a complex stimulus or situation. The more demanding the learning, the higher the electrical frequencies seem to become, ranging from around 40 electrical waves per second to several hundred.

Recordings from individual neurons show that their firing rates decrease when a given stimulus is repeated. Likewise, a decrease in activity as learning progresses is a common observation in brain imaging studies—which use blood flow or oxygen consumption to measure neuronal activity. As the brain acquires mastery over a task, fewer brain areas seem to participate and those that do show less metabolic activity. The common interpretation of such observations is that the brain has to work harder to learn something than it does to process things it already knows. No wonder people have always said that "learning is hard work."

One interesting illustration on brain "work" comes from the experiments of Dr. Büchel and collaborators in London.[7] They performed MRI imaging of brain activity as human subjects learned and recalled the association between ten simple line drawings of real-world objects and ten locations on a screen. As expected, activation in specific cortical areas decreased with time as learning progressed and correlated with individual performance at any given point in the training. Thus, it seems that the early stage of learning is hard work because the brain has not had a chance to teach itself how to recruit and coordinate help among different neural circuits. It is as if the brain learns by organizing itself to parcel out components of a learning task to different areas and by becoming better able to orchestrate these areas to work together on the task.

Is there anything we can do to help our brain improve its self-organizing ability? Certainly through willed discipline, our minds can train our brain to accept the hard-work challenge of new learning. The brain isn't going to get any better by being a "couch potato." Anyone who has ever interrupted their schooling for long enough (taking a few years off to work, maybe, or serving in the military) before going back to college knows that the brain gets "out of shape" when it is not used. I have seen the phenomenon in my students after summer break. It takes a few weeks in the Fall for students to get their brains back in high gear. The same thing happens to schoolchildren during their long summer break, which is an obvious argument for re-structuring the school year.

Another general point is that the mental work is harder when trying to learn things separately rather than collectively. It is analogous to trying to complete a jigsaw puzzle piece by piece without ever looking at the picture of the completed puzzle. For memory tasks, you should embed what you are trying to remember in its larger context. This is an extension of the idea explained in Chapter III about memorizing items by category.

# Key Ideas from Chapter One

1. Learning and remembering open the doors to new experiences, careers, accomplishments, and opportunities. Our world becomes larger and more fulfilled.

2. Scientific research shows us practical ways to improve learning and memory.

3. Learning effectiveness depends on several things: a) degree of interest and enjoyment, b) paying attention, c) thinking about what you are trying to learn, d) active engagement, e) continuously improving learning skills, f) knowing memory principles and tricks, g) confronting challenging learning materials.

4. Experience matters. The more you know, the more you can know.

5. Learning occurs in a hierarchy, from lowest to highest: Knowledge, Comprehension, Application, Analysis/ Evaluation, and Synthesis.

6. Learning is not complete without understanding.

7. Knowledge is power, and it's available to everyone who knows how to get it.

8. Learning and memory involve at least four major processes: registration, integration, understanding, and learning to learn.

9. Learning any task is associated with implicit learning capabilities that can generalize to other related learning situations—i.e., learning to learn.

10. Higher levels of learning make it easier to memorize.

11. Learning and memory are two sides of the same coin.

12. Don't take your memory ability—however limited—for granted. You can make major changes in your ability to learn and remember.

13. We are what we remember—including what we know that we don't know we know.

14. Memory is not a thing in a place. It is a process in a population, a distributed network involving different parts of the brain.

15. There are two basic kinds of memory: declarative (memory for facts, events) and procedural (skills and habits, priming, conditioning).

16. You can learn many things without realizing you are learning.

17. People can be good at learning some things and not at others.

18. The brain is a biological computer that can build and program itself.

19. We train our brain, frequently by conscious effort.

20. Implicit spatial cues can help you remember, even if you don't realize it.

21. Implicit spatial cues can be crucial for recalling learned material.

22. To be remembered, a stimulus or learning event has to register in the brain, be temporarily available as working or "scratch pad" memory, compared with existing memory, evaluated for meaning, and rehearsed.

23. The more knowledgeable you become in a certain area, the easier it is to pay attention. In other words, the more you know, the more you can know.

24. Go beyond recognition memory to the point where you don't require external cues (e.g. multiple-choice quiz questions). Recognition memory is the weakest form of memory.

# II. LEARNING STRATEGIES

When confronted with a learning task, do you have a strategy or do you just jump in? Learning should be thought of as a challenge that puts the learner in a position of needing to win the challenge. Think of learning demands as a form of competition, like a sport in which you compete with others for better grades, better job, career advancement over others, etc. Learning can also be a competition with yourself, as in improving your golf game, learning a new language, playing a musical instrument, etc.

The odds of winning in any contest increase when you have effective plans and strategies. In this chapter, we explore some of the strategies that make learning success more likely. Here you will find specific suggestions for how you should orient to and approach learning tasks.

## Experience Matters

Everybody learns ways to learn and remember as they go through life. Too often, they learn ineffective ways. In any case, life experience determines not only what you learn, but how you learn.

One enormous social problem is that children from low-income culturally deprived families do less well in school. This book is not the place for arguments over the cause of this distressing reality, but this is a good place to consider the substantial role that environmental enrichment has in learning and memory. Some classic experiments in rats revealed environmental effects on early development, including the ability to learn at later ages. Mark Rosenzweig and colleagues reported a large series of experiments on young rats revealing many beneficial effects on brain development from raising rats in stimulating environments.[8] Brains developed better learning ability when young rats had opportunities to explore novel objects, to exercise, to live in social groups, and to "play." In terms of memory performance, such rats had better ability to solve difficult memory problems such as mazes and visual discrimination reversals.

There are all sorts of implications to experiments on environmental enrichment. Society accepts the premise that early childhood experiences can create life-long benefits or handicaps depending on the "richness" of those experiences. Project "Head Start" is the public-policy initiative that grew out of research like this. Head Start does produce academic gains, although studies show these are lost after the first two years of school. I suggest that this backsliding occurs because the home environment has not changed. Biologically, the brains of children are constantly being re-built.

Social and educational environmental effects can also operate on adult learning capability.[9] There are numerous examples of people with impoverished childhoods (think Abe Lincoln) who acquired great mental capacities as an adult. In many ways, an even more inspiring "rags to riches" story is that of the 19th century famed biologist, Thomas Huxley, who grew up in the slums of London, with no family and no education.[10] If you are one of those short-changed by your childhood, you should take heart from such examples.

## Why the Smart Get Smarter

The reason experience can determine smartness is that the brain is a biological computer that can build and program itself. The more input the brain gets, the more able that brain is to sculpt an extensive library of circuits and associations among circuits to process information. In short, the brain learns how to learn.

As an example, consider the circuitry in the cerebral cortex devoted to processing sensory experiences from the arm. We know about this sensory cortex because experimenters have placed electrodes over different cortical areas in anesthetized monkeys and recorded sensory cortex responses to electrical stimulation of the various nerves in the arm. The arm has three main nerves (radial, median, and ulnar), and specific cells in the cortex respond to electrical stimulation of each of these nerves; experiments in monkeys by Dr. Michael Merzenich and colleagues show that cutting the median nerve in the arm causes a functional shriveling of the amount of cortex that normally responds to median nerve stimulation. Since these cells are no longer needed for the input from the median nerve, they get recruited into circuitry used by input from the two other nerves in the arms. We know this occurs because the amount of cortical tissue that responds to sensory input from those other nerves expands greatly with time after the median nerve is cut.

So, remember this when I and other memory experts try to convince you of your learning capabilities. Your brain can even re-wire itself. In the process of creating new circuitry, the brain creates new capacities for learning.

## Learning to Learn

As the brain re-wires itself from experience, it can change the capacity for learning. This is especially true for certain kinds of learning skills. Learning occurs at several hierarchical levels, ranging from simple knowledge to higher levels of comprehension and incorporation, where knowledge is applied to solving problems and creatively applied to new situations. The formal way of categorizing different kinds of learning is based on the "Taxonomy of Learning"[11] theory as developed by Benjamin Bloom.[12] This scheme designated three domains of learning: thinking, feeling, and doing. All three, of course, involve memory. Moreover, as I will explain later, using memorized information at one level influences how well the memory develops on a lasting basis. Using facts at all levels leads to the expert's schema that I explain in the next section.

Bloom identified six types of learning, arranged in a hierarchy. The "lowest" form is **Knowledge**, which is information recognized and at least temporarily memorized. The next level up is **Comprehension**, which entails understanding. Next is **Application**, in which the learner can apply what he or she knows to the real world. The fourth level is **Analysis**, wherein one can use the three lower levels of learning for such purposes as criticizing, comparing, contrasting, discriminating, and other analytical approaches. Next is **Synthesis**, in which what has been learned can be re-organized and re-formulated in creative ways. Finally, there is **Evaluation**, which is not much different from Analysis. If I were making a hierarchy of my own, I would combine

Analysis and Evaluation, and place Synthesis at the highest level of learning.

These different levels of learning all involve memory. None of the levels can be accomplished without what is called "working memory," which is the temporary memory one thinks with.[13] Working memory has to be fed either with re-exposure to the original knowledge or recalling it from permanent memory stores. In Chapters III and IV, I will explain how working memory is essential for each of the higher domains of learning.

What I wish to stress here is that each of these higher domains of learning contribute greatly toward mastering the long-term memorization required in the lowest level of Knowledge learning. In Chapter III, I have a section on "consolidation," in which it will become clearer how developing lasting (consolidated) memories is facilitated by rehearsal strategies that engage the higher levels of learning. In short, I contend that knowledge memory and the higher levels of learning are mutually supportive.

The brain also learns a hierarchy of emotional responses to enrich the awareness and growth of our attitudes and feelings. This hierarchy of levels begins with **Receiving and Responding**, which refers to paying attention and reacting to emotional stimuli. Next there is **Valuing**, in which the learner attaches salience and emotional significance to an object or idea. Finally, there is **Organizing and Characterizing**, which Bloom considered separate but which I am combining for our purposes. This highest level of emotional memory occurs as learners accommodate various emotional responses into their own emotional schema to such an extent that the learning now becomes a personality characteristic. A common example is attitude adjustment, wherein a person changes biases to create a new way of responding emotionally to a given set of stimuli.

What was incompletely considered in the original formulation of emotional learning is the influence of emotions on the memorization process. This is discussed in several places in this book, but especially in Chapter IV.

Psychomotor learning is the progressive acquisition of physical skills, as might occur in sports, piano playing, and the like. Even though this kind of learning is quite different from thinking and emotional learning, there are some common denominators. In this book, I will show how some of the discoveries about memory processes are applicable to improving psychomotor learning. You might even be able to develop a better golf swing.

When a person knows a body of knowledge across all levels of the learning hierarchy, we can call them an expert. What makes an "expert"? In most any field, the experts have a hard time telling you what it is that has made them an expert. Often they are unable to tell you how they solve problems or generate new insights. The reason is that expertise develops over time, and much of that learning has become so well learned that it is automatic. Moreover, experts have developed what some call an implicit capacity in the form of what others have called a learning style, or template, or schema.

Mental templates or schema put the brain on autopilot, enabling it to accomplish tasks without much effort. This feature of learning is especially prominent in the elderly— most of whom have significant degeneration of the brain but are still able to perform at seemingly normal mental levels. I remember being stunned at seeing the shrunken brain in the brain scan of my dying elderly father. His mental functions were not nearly as diminished as the scan would suggest.

Schema manifests in other ways too. You may wonder why some people seem to become more competent as they get older, at least up to a point. I like to think that at 78, I am at the top of my game. Even though my brain has probably deteriorated, I compensate with the lifetime schema acquired over the years.

Learning experiences help develop the capacity to learn. Part of that capacity likely results from a better ability to absorb contextual cues and to make associations among various cues. Rich experiences during development also increase the likelihood of developing a more extensive repertoire of learning skills.

It is possible to teach people how to learn to learn. Though we have very little theoretical understanding of what is involved, it is generally a primary purpose of formal education to teach to some degree how to learn to learn. One of the first experimental demonstrations of the learning-to-learn phenomenon was by H. C. Blodgett in 1929.[14] He studied maze behavior in rats, tracking how many errors they made while navigating a maze for a food reward. The control group ran the maze and found the food, with the number of errors decreasing slowly over successive days as they learned where the food was. Experimental groups ran the maze daily for three or seven days without any food reward. Naturally, they made many errors each time, because there was nothing to learn. However, when they were subsequently allowed access to a food reward, the number of errors dropped precipitously on the very next day's trial. In other words, the rats had been learning about the maze—its layout, number of turns, etc.—during the initial explorations, even when no reward was available. The learning just wasn't being put to use.

The idea was expanded and formalized some 20 years later by the famous physiological psychologist Harry Harlow.[15] Harlow studied monkeys, testing their progress on visual problems and other tests of discernment. Training on a series of different but related problems accelerated their rate of improvement. Increasing the number of problems on which monkeys were tested led to the observation that the monkeys' general learning competence improved over time.

Harlow developed the prominent "learning set" theory, which posits that learning any task is associated with implicit learning capabilities that can generalize to other related learning situations. These days, educators think of this as "transfer," where learning one task may make it easier to learn another related one. Typically, this learning set is acquired subconsciously as a by-product of experience.

One practical illustration of learning-set theory is language learning. Many people who learn a foreign language find it easier to learn a second language—even a third language, or more—if they are related, as in Romance languages. Learning how to set up equations to solve a math problem can make it easier to set up equations for other math problems. Learning how to play one song on a piano can make it easier to learn other songs. Learning how to play one musical instrument makes it easier to learn another instrument. In other words,

*The more you know, the more you can know.*

Ever wonder why some people can learn like sponges, soaking up information in great gobs, while others struggle to learn? Learning sets provide an explanation. It is akin to the rich getting richer, while the poor get poorer. The "more you know" axiom is especially heartening for learners who struggle early on mastering a given learning task. They will get better if they stay with it and don't get discouraged.

But then there is the typical case that most people just rock along with whatever learning abilities they have, making no effort to change basic learning and memory skills. Improving your memory capability requires you to make a conscious effort to use the ideas and techniques that are explained in this book. Just knowing what to do accomplishes nothing if you don't act on that knowledge. Yet making any kind of change is often hard for many people to do. It has always been hard for me to understand, for example, why students especially seem reluctant to use these memory principles and techniques. They have what I would think a compelling need to improve their memory abilities. I wrote about my frustration in a *Psychology Today* blog post. Fellow college professors have reported similar observations. One professor posted this observation: "I used to try and help college students to improve their learning skills, but sadly very few truly were interested. For the most part, just getting them to study at all was a big issue. I learned to ask about their 'study' environment—which often included non-stop text messaging interruptions, sometimes multitasking with Facebook and listening to overly loud music."

Why the reluctance to improve learning and memory skills? One explanation might be hubris. A teacher commented on my blog post as follows: "Contrary to what you might expect, the students who were by far the easiest to teach were the poorly educated, sometimes not particularly literate ones. These students knew their own limitations and were happy for all the help that they got in study, literacy and life skills. At the opposite end of the spectrum, all the really difficult students I ever had in my classroom were university students, particularly those doing higher degrees." In my own classrooms, students seem to think they know best how to learn. After all, they perfected their learning style enough to get admitted into a competitive university.

Another possible explanation for resistance to improving learning and memory skills is doubt—many students lack confidence in their learning ability. Adults sometimes think (and even perversely revel in) the affirmation that they are who they are and they can't or don't need to change.

Another reason might be that people are just too busy. A posted response from a college student explained it: "As a college student myself I can say that training our memory is just not my top priority. We feel so stressed and busy with trying to keep up on school, studying, work, and relationships that any time we would get to train our memory we just want to catch up on sleep." Here was my response: "Hey, don't give me that. I was a harried, overwhelmed college student too—until I used good memory principles and techniques. Think of it this way: college is like a very steep mountain that takes four years to walk up the road to the top. Consider how much easier the trip would be if you took two weeks to learn how to ride a bike. That's about 1% of the total time. And, when you get to the top, you have a huge set of learning and memory skills you can use to make your work life easier and more productive.

Bottom line: people use all sorts of excuses to resist improving learning-to-learn skills. They should read my book, *Blame Game: How to Win It.*[16]

# Be Strategic

Learning to learn should begin with a strategy. There are many aspects of learning skills that can be manipulated as part of such a strategy.

## State-Dependent Learning

One aspect of manipulating learning strategy is to take into account the physical and mental state at the time of learning. Learning occurs in context, and it helps to be aware of the situation and contextual cues in which one is learning a given task. The environment and physiological condition provide important contextual cues at the time of learning. Peter Russell, author of *The Brain Book*,[17] explains the memory storage mechanism this way: "Memory is not like a container that gradually fills up, it is more like a tree growing hooks onto which the memories are hung." Memories hung on the same branch are linked to each other.

In other words, the situation and context of a learning event are inextricably associated with the learning event. The memory formed can include many aspects of the conditions under which learning occurred.

Likewise, duplicating the original state of learning affects the recall of a formed memory. A drunk, for example, may remember events that occurred during drinking better when he is drinking again than he can when sober.

Here is another example. Duncan Godden and Alan Baddeley conducted an experiment in which groups of scuba divers listened to a list of words underwater and also while sitting on the beach.[18] The divers recalled the most words when they were retested in the same place as they initially heard the words, whether it was on the beach or under water. Since memories are a web of associations, the learned words are strongly associated with specific visual cues, and mutually reinforcing. The words in the study above were not memorized in isolation but in a context wherein remembering any one part of the situation or scene helped to recall the rest.

State-dependent learning might also help explain déjà vu, where various cues in a place or situation trigger related memories, making you believe you have been there before.

So how do these illustrations of location effect apply to practical situations? One common example that some teachers know about is that students will score better on tests given in the same room as the instruction than if the test is given in another location. This suggests that multiple cues associated with what we are trying to learn are important. The cues can reinforce each other and enhance learning, because the cues are being faithfully registered.

Pairing where-we-are information with what-we-are-supposed-to-learn information can produce synergism, both during learning and during the need to recall. Because both kinds of information can be faithfully and independently encoded, they can reinforce each other or interfere with each other during recall, depending on whether or not the learning and the recall situations are identical.

To actively capitalize on the potential of state-dependency, I suggest two things: 1) when a need to recall occurs, try to be in the same state as when you first learned it, and 2) pay more conscious attention to the location and situation present when you are trying to memorize.

## Learning Styles

Everybody has a certain learning style that can be altered and improved. You should be aware of the style that works best for you, but don't be so sure that is the best style. One widely recognized problem among education professionals is that too many children are one-mode learners. Educators classify students as visual learners, auditory learners, and kinesthetic learners. The latter group learns best by moving around and engaging physically to perform learning tasks.

Unfortunately, in my view, the educational community puts the emphasis on adapting curriculum rather than on adapting children. Today's approach is to structure curriculum in several ways: one way for visual learners, another for auditory learners, and so on. This reflects the typical educational mind-set of teaching "stuff" to kids rather than teaching them how to learn. This is especially regrettable in the early grades, where the brain of a child is still plastic enough to learn multiple styles of learning. Superior learners should be able to learn in multiple ways.

We should devise ways to increase the learning-skill repertoire of children so a kinesthetic learner, for example, is no longer handicapped by only being able to learn well in that one mode. I use this example because hyperactive kids are often accepted as innately limited to kinesthetic learning.

This stance may seem to conflict with the idea of building on one's strengths. But here we are talking about young children, who still have the capability of readily developing multiple learning strengths.

---

### Memory Myth Buster

*The best way for schools to be more effective is to customize curriculum for the needs of each student.* WRONG. The best way is to teach each child how to adapt to various learning requirements. Teach them how to learn under a variety of circumstances. Current practice is to adapt curriculum to a student's "learning style." Strong learners are not handicapped by just one learning style.

---

Even though people have preferred learning styles, they can learn new ones. This is especially important for children, whose developing brains can learn multiple styles when they have that opportunity. Neglecting this "window of opportunity" can consign a child to a crippling limitation. By catering to a kinesthetic learner, for example, you deny that child the opportunity to fully develop other styles. The real world of experiences does not always come in a convenient package that matches one's learning style.

For adults, it might be a different matter. It is harder for adults to build a new learning style. For them, being more aware of their optimal learning style allows an adult learner to build on strength. They may be better off by using their optimal learning style for new tasks.

## Executive Functions

Manipulating learning style takes conscious effort. You might think of this as part of an executive function of the brain. Children typically have poorly developed brain executive function and are limited in their awareness of what they are feeling, thinking, and doing. This makes self-control more difficult for them, and learning suffers as a result. Impulse control is a cardinal feature of brain executive function. Factors that influence the development of EF in children include social acceptance, deliberate practice, emotional intelligence, and stress-coping capabilities. I have specific advice for these factors elsewhere in the book. The point here is that executive functions govern the ability to actively monitor and control attempts to learn and memorize.

Executive functions depend on the prefrontal cortex (PFC), which is the last part of the cortex to mature. The PFC reaches its peak development in a person's late 20s, and declines thereafter in most people. Obviously, certain diseases or aging-related deterioration of the PFC result in diminished executive function.

In young children, readiness for school is primarily judged on the basis of their executive function capability. Sometimes, development of this capability is impaired by well-meaning parents who over-manage young children, controlling their environment so rigorously that the children do not get much chance to think, feel, and act on their own. As adults, such children often show poor judgment and make foolish choices.[19]

Educational research on developing executive function is in its infancy, but that is a pressing objective in neuro-education research. Educational strategies for doing this remain to be developed, but at the moment, some claims for success are made for "Tools of the Mind" and Montessori schooling.[20] The over-arching issue is on discovering the teaching strategies that develop EF. Inadequate development of EF confines a child's capacity to benefit from school. This conclusion reinforces my life-long cynical conviction that "education is wasted on the young."

Executive functions not only include conscious self-awareness, but include the capacity for deliberately guiding how one approaches learning tasks. Every learning strategy should include specific tactics. "How should I approach this learning task?" is the question you ought to ask. The answer, of course, depends on the nature of the task, what you already know, and on your own learning strengths and weaknesses.

There are certain approaches you can implement to promote learning and memory that get you a lot farther and faster than passively trying to "soak up" knowledge. In the last few years of teaching college students I have noticed they are increasingly passive learners, tending to operate in an "entertain me" mode. This is no doubt due to an "electronically-manufactured attention deficit" as one Wall Street Journal letter writer put it. More than that, our TV, movies, YouTube, and other media provide the illusion that learning can be absorbed by osmosis and does not benefit from active engagement.

## Break Learning Tasks into Small Chunks

A major application of executive function to learning is to develop strategies for learning. One of the most important learning strategies is to organize learning materials in small chunks, so that the brain is not overloaded. Such "chunking" of learning material promotes long-term memory.

Acronyms are an example of chunking, where one word is substituted for many words. Of course, most of our learning tasks can't be captured in acronyms. For such tasks, we need to limit material in chunks that we can accommodate in terms of our attention span, and mental fatigue limits.

## Spread Out Learning

Part of a learning plan should be to arrange learning so you can spread it out over time. Don't try to learn everything at once. Spread it out, with repetitions spaced in time. Many studies have established that memory results improve when specific learning tasks are repeated at delayed intervals than if they are grouped together.[21]

Of course, what happens during the intervals is important. Especially immediately after a learning session, you should not jump into a different learning task or intensely demanding mental activity. That can interfere the learning you are carrying around temporarily in working memory. Recent learning takes a while to "sink in," and distracting stimuli can interfere with that process (I'll explain this concept further in Chapter III).

The best practical solution is to study in short sessions (15-30 minutes), using the time between sessions to rehearse and apply the new information. For example, if you are studying a technical manual, read the instructions for twenty minutes or so and then take a break, at which point you could start on the first steps, get your tools together, etc. If you have a golf pro pro teach you a new swing, listen and watch his instruction first, then take a while to practice what he showed you.

## Put Items to Learn in Categories

Executive control of learning should include arranging learning materials into categories. People love to classify things. Examples are numerous, and include size, color, form, shape, function, etc. Placing a new idea or concept into the appropriate category facilitates the learning process. Our brains just feel more comfortable placing people, objects, and events into categories. We group together items that share common properties.

For example, we naturally group living things into groups, such as people, animals, plants, etc. Then for each group we create sub-groups: humans can be categorized by race, gender, class, etc.; animals fall into kingdoms, phyla, classes, and species. Apparently the brain finds this mode of operation an easier way to remember things. Categorization is an extension of association. The brain wants to associate like things together, so that when it comes time to remember them, the associations are already in place, which helps the recall process.

Why is this propensity built into our nervous system? Some people think it has to do with language. Putting objects and ideas into categories makes it easier to apply labels to them. On the other hand, if the linguistic ability to assign labels is our more intrinsic capability, maybe young children find it easier to remember the names of things if they assign them verbal category labels. But this phenomenon may involve more than just language. To illustrate the value of categories, the author of *Peterson Field Guide to Birds of North America* showed that bird species were easier to recognize and remember when he placed together pictures of birds that had similar features.[22] Whatever the mechanism, it is certainly true that we learn the advantages of putting things in categories in the process of growing up. Learning to learn is in part learning to categorize.

This may say something about learning and memory in older humans. We have all observed that people tend to become set in their ways as they age; hence the saying, "You can't teach an old dog new tricks." I call this phenomenon the "hardening of the categories." This may explain why the elderly can have amazing recall for things learned in their youth and still struggle to retain new memories. It is important to add that if seniors use the ideas of this book, they can learn and remember better than youngsters who do not.

To learn and remember new things, we should work with our brains the way they are designed to work. We can actively promote categorization of things we are trying to learn. For example, to illustrate how you might memorize some key ideas you will learn as you go through this book, let me list 25 buzz words in scrambled order. How long do you think it will take you to memorize this list?

*state dependency, think, motivation, acrostics, exercise, classical conditioning, multitasking, deliberate practice, consolidation, story chains, attentiveness, working memory, priming, belief, cues, acronyms, interference, stress, concept map, categorize, association, images, self-testing, sleep, peg systems*

Now suppose we group these ideas into four simple categories: attitude, lifestyle, memory principles, and mnemonic "tricks." Now see how much easier it is to remember these 25 items when we group them in these categories. Only "Memory principles" might be difficult to memorize.

**Attitude:** motivation, belief

**Lifestyle:** stress, exercise, sleep,

**Memory principles:** state-dependency, attentiveness, cues, categorize, classical conditioning, priming, working memory, think, consolidation, deliberate practice, interference, multitasking, concept map, self-testing

**Mnemonic "tricks":** acrostics, acronyms, images, peg systems, story chains

Notice the information is now organized so that instead of 25 unrelated things to remember, you only have four sets of related things. The next memory trick is to visualize the items—NOT think about the words.

So, for example, what comes to mind to represent "Attitude?" It might be a sound-alike, such as "altitude." Imagine you are at high altitude in a plane and you jump out without a parachute but your partner has jumped out with one. You have enormous "motivation" to steer over and hang on to the partner. You have the "belief" that you will die if you fail to hang on and may well survive if you do hang on.

For "Lifestyle" you might think of the fun life of having your own sailboat. See yourself in the boat and a storm comes up, causing great anxiety and "stress." You work like crazy to get the sails down. That is a lot of "exercise." You are now exhausted. See yourself lying down in the boat's hold to "Sleep."

I will skip developing scenes for the rest in the interest of brevity. The point is that the memory task is greatly simplified by grouping and by imagining mental pictures of the items in the group. All these scenes are ridiculous, but that's what promotes memory. We remember associated things best when they are distinctive. In case you have lingering doubt, try thinking about Daffy Duck, Road Runner, and all the other cartoon characters you watched years ago as a child; chances are you still remember them pretty vividly today, in large part because of how over-the-top and ridiculous they were.

Using categories can help resolve the common problem of forgetting where you put things. People are most likely to forget where they stored important things when the items have been put in an unlikely place. Storing items in logical and likely places makes it easier to make associations. You always, for example, can easily associate your car keys in the side pocket of your purse, or your wallet in the top left drawer of the dresser, or your grocery list stuck on the refrigerator door. But as soon as you depart from these associations by putting such items in unlikely places, you lose your association handle. So why do people put things in unlikely places? First, they may be unorganized people. Secondly, some people truly believe that putting things in unlikely places makes them more memorable. Wrong. Without good associations, memory becomes less likely.

## Map the Concepts

Brains are built to map the environment in time and space; i.e., they keep track of where things are and the associated times.[23] The brain informs itself that way and uses that information to guide planning and behavior appropriately. Such mapping can occur implicitly, but the executive functions of consciousness allow us to experience, manipulate, and apply the information in the maps.

So, if the brain wants to map its information, why don't we help it along by consciously mapping what we want to learn and remember? A common tactic for more effective learning is called **concept mapping** or **mind mapping.** In such mapping you write key ideas inside a circle and draw lines among circles that indicate relationships. Sometimes, you may write a little text along connecting lines to indicate the relationship. Many web sites and several books are available to show examples.

Concept maps assist learning in several ways. They:

1. Require mindfulness. You have to think about the learning material to construct a useful map.
2. Boil down information to its essentials, reducing the amount that has to be actively learned.

3. Group information in meaningful categories and relationships.

4. Promote understanding, and new insights may emerge.

5. Display information in a spatial array, which in itself facilitates memorization because the same part of the brain that forms memories is also the part that forms mental maps of spatial relationships.

Maps can be hand-drawn or created with any of a number of computer programs; some are free to download. In general, I prefer hand-drawn maps because each map can be made to look unique. Hand-drawn maps should be in pencil to allow erasure. Computer-drawn maps tend to come out all looking about the same, which makes them harder to memorize. Computer mapping programs do make it easier to move items around and alter the links.

Memorization of a map can be hindered if there is too much clutter in the map, especially if there are many key ideas and too much text. For large amounts of information, I suggest having more than one map: one an overview map showing key ideas and their primary sub-head topics, then a more detailed map for each sub-heading.

Too much text creates a major problem. Text is hard to memorize. One advantage of computers is the ease of adding clip-art images, which—if they represent ideas in a vivid, meaningful way—make them much easier to memorize than text.

The best way to study mapped information is to self-test. To self-test mapped information, re-draw the map from memory, check for errors, and then re-draw again from memory.

# Practice Deliberately

Deliberateness is another executive function. Learners benefit from having a strategy for rehearsing what they are trying to learn. The best learners do much more than just repeat the learning material. They bring conscious design, awareness, analysis, and correction of error to their memory rehearsal. Another key component of deliberate practice is that the standard of excellence keeps getting raised in small steps as one achieves mastery at a given level. "Memory athletes" use this kind of memory practice to rise above their own innate memory capability, which is usually not much better than anyone else's capability. This is the kind of practice performed by superstars in any field: music, art, business, sports, science (and by straight-A students throughout their education.). Geoff Colvin in his book, *Talent is Overrated*,[24] argues that superstars in every field don't emerge because of some special talent. Their success comes from deliberate practice sustained over many years.

His book summarizes basic principles that enable individuals of ordinary talent to achieve excellence. In every field Colvin surveyed, ranging from business, to music, to sports, to activities, we wrongly assume that excellence was achieved not by talent but by what is commonly called "deliberate practice"— with emphasis on the word "deliberate." I call it working smarter. Superstars reach that level of achievement by:

• Working hard at their craft with **smart, intentional planning** to improve their basic competencies in very specific ways. Applying the "learning-to-learn" lessons of this book to enhance work skills is an example.

- Having the passion, resources, and time to learn their craft. This means **making a commitment** to becoming a better learner.

- **Raising their goals** to new and more challenging goals. Learning a foreign language is an example.

- Structuring practice in ways that **provide constant and detailed feedback.** Self-quizzing is an example.

- Continually **expanding their knowledge base**. This includes learning the tactics others use successfully in study.

- Focusing on **improving weaknesses**. This means, for example, things such as improving reading handicaps or deficient communication skills.

- **Seeking encouragement and help from others.** This means developing a circle of friends and mentors who value achievement, as well as people to compete against.

# Learn from Mistakes—Yours and Those of Others

The saying that the "rich get richer" has the corollary of the poor getting poorer (at least relative to the rich). Of course there are exceptions, but these correlations happen often enough to indicate there is some truth to the saying. I never heard anybody explain this, other than to whine that life is just unfair. But there is an explanation.

---

### Memory Myth Buster

*We learn best from our mistakes.* WRONG. Some people keep making the same mistakes. Most everyone learns best from their successes. They focus on what it takes to win, and learn to do that consistently.

---

Why do so many people keep making the same mistakes? I suspect that habit and emotional factors have a lot to do with it. Compulsive gambling and drug abuse are classic examples of repeatedly doing what you already know is wrong. Failure to learn from mistakes is self-defeating.

My parents always told me to learn from my mistakes. Actually, I found it was more efficient (and less painful) to learn from the mistakes of others. The bottom line is to be aware of mistakes, no matter who makes them, and use your brain's executive control to reduce the chances that you will make these mistakes.

Failure to learn from mistakes eventually corrodes one's attitude towards learning. This can produce "learned helplessness," the "I give up" attitude that is so easy to develop after repeated failure. The problem is compounded by the stress that develops from frequent failure, which in turn impairs your ability to learn from your mistakes, increasing the likelihood you will continue to make bad choices.

How does one "learn from mistakes"? Somebody else's mistake is easier to confront than one's own. The more insecure one is, the harder it is to face one's limitations. And that creates the vicious cycle of continuing to make the same mistakes, which in turn reinforces the sense of inadequacy and insecurity. Break the cycle with courage to confront your own weaknesses as well as learn from others.

# Strive for Deep Analysis and Insight

In addition to having well-defined learning strategies, it is also important to develop the habit of thinking deeply about what you are trying to learn. For example, we can extend the idea of categorization by thinking hard about how to organize learning materials in rational ways. In particular, it is important to distinguish the information that you must memorize from the information that you can deduce. This helps you to use core principles and logic to arrive at answers and thereby reduces the amount of information you have to memorize.

*Never memorize anything that you can figure out.*

Let me give an example of how thinking can reduce the memory load. Suppose you had to memorize the upper arm's muscles, what those muscles do, and which bones they attach to. First, think of the joints, which muscles either flex or extend joints. The joint of interest in our example is the elbow joint. An extension of the elbow joint which straightens the arm can only occur by contraction of muscles on the back side of the arm. To extend the elbow, the muscle must span it; i.e. be anchored at one end on the upper arm bone (humerus) and on the forearm bones (radius and ulna). Similar logic applies to muscles that flex the joint, only these obviously have to be located on the front of the arm.

So now you are left with having only to memorize the muscles' names and, plus perhaps some details about the specific areas on the bones to which they are attached. You start with biceps and triceps, which most people already know are located on the front and back, respectively. You may have to memorize that the "bi" and "tri" parts of the words refer to two or three points of origin. Both span the elbow, and therefore must attach on the forearm bones, radius and ulna. Think about this: when you flex the elbow, it can also twist. This makes it easier to remember that the biceps must attach to both bones. But extending the elbow cannot twist it, so the triceps must attach on only one forearm bone (the ulna). The triceps must obviously attach at the other end to the upper arm bone (the humerus). You might be tempted to think the biceps attaches on the front of this bone, but think about this: when you lift something heavy with your arm, it typically involves also the shoulder. That is explained by the attachment of the biceps to the shoulder blade (scapula).

Think about this: you can make lots of movements involving flexion of the elbow, from unscrewing a cork in a wine bottle to throwing a baseball so it will curve. One muscle can't do all that. There are two other elbow flexors, and they are hidden under the biceps (as are their "hidden" functions in complex arm movements). These subtle functions don't have to involve the shoulder, so they arise on the humerus and, to support complicated elbow flexion, one muscle attaches to the radius (the one called brachioradialis) and the other to the ulna (simply called brachialis).

My point with this explanation is that by thinking logically about your learning material, you can greatly reduce the amount of brute memory required.

In addition to thinking about how to plan learning, we should also think hard about the learning material itself. Analytical thinking enables a deeper level of learning. Because analysis forces us to rehearse the new material, it also intensifies the extent and the durability of what we remember.

The ability to reason varies widely. Most people may not know that reasoning ability can be improved through specific teaching strategies. Specific options are currently a hot topic among neuro-educators. Learning to decipher visual analogies seems to be one promising method for training reasoning ability.

Everyone can learn to be more analytical. Some might think this is not possible, that one is either born with intellect or not. Wrong! The main difference in IQ is the speed at which one solves a problem (IQ tests are timed). Moreover, several new studies show that IQ can be changed by consistent and intense mental activity over time.

I used to believe I was stuck with my limited intellect, until the day a research professor one day had this to say about my lab report, "Klemm, you are very industrious. But you need to strive for insight." My first reaction was that he was insulting me, implying I am not smart enough to meet his standards of intelligence. Neither he nor anybody else had taught me how to be more insightful. Maybe such a skill is not even teachable in the usual way of teaching. What I discovered, however, was that just striving for insight was enough to produce more insight.

Young children are less insightful than older ones, and we become more insightful as we grow. Any elementary school teacher will tell you that some children have very poor thinking skills. One cause is growing up in culturally impoverished houses. Bad teaching is also a major factor. Many parents and some teachers think it is bad to challenge children's thinking, even when it is flawed. They think that such challenges are a confrontation that damages self-esteem.

*The reality is, if a person lacks faith in their ability to learn, it becomes a self-fulfilling prophecy.*

High-stakes state testing aggravates the mental shackling. Students are trained to look for the one "right answer." Many students are actually afraid to think for themselves. The conformity of schools has drilled students into a submission that interferes with analytical and creative thinking. The typical multiple-choice format of testing can be especially unfair to creative students who get confused because they think of valid answer choices that are not available for a test question.

## Build on What Works

Successful people are especially adept at learning from their successes, while the unsuccessful often fail to learn from their failures. T. Boone Pickens, who has made (and lost) several fortunes, recalls the teaching from his basketball coach in high school: "Never dwell on your losses." Sure, learn what you did wrong, but focus on what it takes to win and learn how to do that.

The human brain is wired to learn better from success than from failure. It all has to do with the positive reinforcement (reward) system in the brain.

I remember trying many times to quit smoking. I only finally succeeded when I took up jogging, which is accompanied by the positive reinforcement of endorphins. Jogging felt good, and the pleasurable association was reinforced by noticing that the time it took me to catch my breath after a jog was shortening by the day.

The most obvious example of the role of positive reinforcement and learning is how animals are trained for circus performances, and how dogs are trained to sniff out drugs or corpses, etc. Animals learn more effectively and faster when they receive positive reinforcement after doing something right than when they're punished for doing something wrong. Psychologists say the same principle holds for people.

We can speculate that humans find successes to be more informative than failures. When you fail, you typically already know why, but might be afraid to confront the underlying causes. When you succeed, it is easy (and rewarding) to ruminate, at length, on why things worked out well.

There is a biological explanation for why you learn more from success than from failure: the brain has a "reward system" that promotes memory. This system releases neurotransmitter chemicals norepinephrine, dopamine, and endorphins, all of which have a direct biological influence on memory formation. For example, recent experiments show that dopamine affects long-term storage of memories. Rats were trained to remember a fearful experience. Injecting a dopamine blocker into the hippocampus, where the memory formation process begins, erased the long-term memory if given 12 hours after the original fear-inducing stimulus.[24] This suggests that the normal release of dopamine can promote memory, which is not surprising since dopamine promotes the formation of proteins used in synaptic junctions of neurons. This may explain why memory deteriorates in Parkinson's disease, which is caused by insufficient dopamine.

The ongoing release of dopamine in the course of just living may help form lasting memories, regardless of the nature of the memory. This raises questions that scientists have not studied yet. It may be that dopamine helps us remember both the good and the bad. And maybe it is one reason why bad memories are hard to erase (see comments of post-traumatic stress disorder in Chapter III).

## Key Ideas from Chapter Two

1. An intellectually rich environment, especially in childhood, helps develop mental competence, including learning and memory ability.

2. Learning experiences help develop the capacity to learn.

3. Pavlovian (classical) conditioning is altered responding that occurs when two stimuli are regularly paired in close succession. The response originally elicited by the second stimulus becomes associated with the first.

4. Operant conditioning produces behaviors that tend to continue because they have been repeatedly positively reinforced. Those behaviors that are punished or are not reinforced tend to gradually end.

5. Positive reinforcement promotes learning faster and more effectively than negative reinforcement, but both can work.

6. State-dependent learning and remembering is based on the physiological and mental state of the organism.

7. Educators classify students as visual learners, auditory learners, and kinesthetic learners. Good learners learn to operate in all modes.

8. Breaking learning tasks into small chunks, with a short rehearsal after each chunk, facilitates memorization.

9. Spread out rehearsal of learning chunks over time.

10. Strive for deep analysis and insight.

11. "Habituation" (one type of forgetting) sets in when learning tasks lose their significance. Refresh continually the importance of what you are trying to learn.

12. Your location and condition can affect what you learn. You will recall better in the same environment in which the original learning took place.

13. Effective learners have a "deliberate practice" strategy for learning new material, and use content-specific tactics.

14. Brains like to categorize information. This helps both learning and memory.

15. Don't memorize what you can figure out. Organize what you do need to remember in small chunks.

16. Mapping concepts and their relationships in visual displays promotes both understanding and memory.

17. Most people learn best from their successes, not their failures.

18. Repeated failures can lead to "learned helplessness." Success requires breaking this cycle.

19. Too many people take the wrong lesson from their failures: they believe that they are the failure, when another strategy might have led to different results.

# III. MEMORY TACTICS

Can you memorize the gist of what is on every page of a document, by page number, in the time it takes you to read it? Can you memorize the sequence of a deck of cards in 30 minutes? Well, so-called "memory athletes" can do astounding feats like this, and they have annual contests to see who are the national and world champion memorizers. But their basic memory capabilities are not much better than yours. They do it because they use certain memory tactics, which are explained in this chapter. The chapter explains all of the typical "peg systems" and the system for memorizing numbers that the athletes use. Getting the most out of these tactics requires hard work and repeated practice at using these tactics, as memory athletes do when they train.

You can use some of these tactics in a casual way, but of course you would not perform the amazing feats of memory athletes. Not to worry. This chapter also provides numerous, less mentally strenuous, tactics that we all can use without brain strain. The chapter gives specific advice on how to become better organized, how to manage an information load, how to improve attentiveness, how to make helpful mental associations to promote memory, an explanation of the role and importance of working memory, how to convert what is in working memory to more lasting form, the role of mental imagery and how to make images more powerful memory aids, how to self-test, how to cope with tip-of-the-tongue problems, and a host of other tips. Finally, there is even a section on how to forget the bad things, as in post-traumatic stress syndrome.

## Get Organized

Probably the first thing you want to do with complex learning material is to organize it. Want less of a memory burden? Get organized![25] Organizing your life simplifies it. You don't forget as much. You become less stressed. You don't make so many mistakes.

Lack of organization leads to generalized forgetfulness. You forget where you put the car keys. You forget appointments. You forget to do important tasks. You may even be thought of as absent-minded. Take it from an old professor: this is a stigma you want to avoid.

Adhering consistently to an organization plan promotes habit formation, and you don't even have to think about where something is. I will give some examples of how I try to organize my life. I have a bedroom bureau organizer that has compartments for keys, coins, pens, etc., and electrical connections for cell phone, electric shaver, etc. I use vertical document holders for storing bills, envelopes, TV schedules, and all sorts of things. Actually I have several of these for different kinds of documents. I am absolutely dependent on file cabinets. I have five in my home and five more at work. Each drawer has its own category of items, such as one drawer for financial records and one for personal records (insurance, car registration, receipts, and so on). In addition, I have a huge number of computer files stashed in folders synchronized across several computers.

Here is a summary of a few basic ideas everybody can follow to simplify their lives:

- Develop routines. You don't have to think about your habits, you just do them—this takes some of the burden off of your memory.

- Have a place for everything, with everything in its place. Put important items back in the same place each time, such as bills, car keys, purse, wallet, the daily mail, etc.

- Use lists, on scrap paper or your smartphone if you have one.

- Use sticky notes to write yourself reminders. Put them where you know you'll see them and, if possible, somewhere relevant to the task. For example: put a note reminding you to make a dental appointment beside the phone, rather than, say, on your dashboard.

- Get a filing cabinet (or two, or whatever it takes) and label the files in whatever way is most meaningful and useful to you.

- Use the One-Minute Manager technique of deciding in one minute what to do with every new piece of paper (act on it, throw it away, or file it).

- Keep a calendar and check it each day. Make it a habit.

- Have a tote bag or briefcase that always has in it what you need for the day. At home, put in it what you need to take to work. At work, put in it what you need to work on at home.

While following this book's advice should make your brain stronger and more effective, no one can recall every detail with perfect accuracy. Why put all that strain on your mind? Here are some popular tools utilizing today's technology to help you organize, prioritize, and remember the little things, so your poor brain doesn't have to:

**Evernote.** Evernote is a popular note-taking tool that helps you keep all sorts of notes well-organized. Since it's web-based, you can access it anywhere there's an internet connection.

**UberNote.** Use UberNote to email or IM notes and online bookmarks.

**Stickies.** Use this tool to jot down notes on stickies that stay on your computer desktop.

**Jott.** Leave yourself a note, add an appointment to your calendar, and even have your voice mail transcribed, all with a phone call.

**Google Calendar.** Google fans love this calendar that helps you track events, set reminders, and import appointments straight from Gmail—and it's all shareable with others.

**Remember the Milk.** This dynamic to-do list keeps all your tasks organized, reminds you of important due dates, and works with Google Calendar.

**bitBomb.** bitBomb sends you text message reminders of your tasks.

**Agatra.** If you have a hard time remembering all those passwords for gaining entry to websites, use Agrata–an encrypted, secure tool–to keep track of them all.

# Get the Clutter Out of Your Life

You can't be organized if your mind is cluttered. So get rid of clutter. Everybody knows that to remember something the information first has to register. For example, it is hard to remember names of multiple people you meet all at once at a party. The names often do not even register in consciousness.

The same thing can happen for other kinds of stimuli, such as visual scenes. Experimental verification of this finding is technically difficult, but common sense suggests that seeing a lot of clutter all at the same time should make it difficult to focus and register the information you may need to memorize. It is akin to multitasking, that great enemy of memory that I discuss in the "Memory Consolidation" section of this chapter.

A recent study is very relevant, even though it did not address memory as such. The researchers found that when the eyes look at a cluttered scene that contains multiple stimuli present in the visual field at the same time, brain-scan imaging showed that the brain circuits compete for neural representation of the images. The competition suppresses responsiveness throughout the visual cortex, because the brain cannot efficiently handle the sensory overload. Memorization effectiveness would likewise have suffered had it been tested.[26]

The stimuli did not elicit much of a brain response when subjects' concentration was disrupted by having to perform a complex letter-discrimination task. But when objects in the scene were presented one at a time, robust brain responses developed. In an attended situation where subjects had to focus on the objects and perform a task on those same images, visual cortex responses were, not surprisingly, greater than in the unattended case. Presumably, paying attention evokes more activity because more visual features are being processed and consciously perceived. How much attentiveness enhanced brain responses depended on how much clutter was evident in the stimuli.

What's the practical application? What this suggests is that the amount of visual clutter interferes with stimulus registration in the brain. Moreover, this interference can be somewhat offset by deliberately paying more attention. Clutter creates distraction and interference for formation of long-term memories. We instinctively know this. When you walk into an office to visit with an executive whose desk is clear, you tend to be impressed. This person must be well-organized and have "his act together." He or she is also likely to register and remember more of what the two of you say.

Another example can be found in a typical elementary- or middle-school classroom. The classrooms I visit are filled with visual clutter: vivid posters and pictures all over the walls, assorted stuff hanging from the ceilings, etc. The idea ostensibly is to keep kids stimulated. Is that one reason there are so many ADHD kids in schools? I think the clutter distracts children from instruction. No wonder teachers complain about having to repeat the same instruction again and again.

Another common example is found in computer slide shows, which often have too much information on a given slide. The problem is compounded when the information is presented in multiple lines of bullet points. Effective presentations use fewer words and more pictures or clip art (graphics need to be relevant). Authors of slide shows may be tempted to present too much information in the show—that need should be satisfied with separate handouts. The purpose of a slide show is to stimulate interest, motivate, entertain, and engage the audience. There are much better ways to distribute didactic information.

## Less Can Be More

Having too much to learn makes it difficult to organize and reduce clutter. Remember my axiom stated earlier: Never memorize anything that you can figure out. This fits the current theme that the less you try to memorize, the more effective your memorization can be. Try to focus on key points to memorize and "ad-lib" the rest. This will see you through most tests, speeches, or other challenges to your memory.

The reason overloading your memory is counterproductive involves many things to be explained later, such as limits on working memory, interference effects, and stress.

## Prime Your Memory Pump

After learning material is reduced and organized, the next thing to do is to get an overview of it in your mind. This produces priming, a subconscious conditioning effect in which exposure to a stimulus promotes memory of the stimulus the next time it occurs. In typical priming experiments, subjects may be asked to complete fragmented words or identify a word or a picture after a brief exposure. Priming is evident when the subjects can complete or identify items that they recently saw or heard faster or more accurately than items for which there had been no prior exposure. Healthy volunteers exhibit priming of new associations in a word-stem completion test only when they are aware that they are producing words from a study list to which they were previously exposed.

Research on priming is usually done with either words or images. For example, subjects may be asked to name or to complete a fragmented form of information such as to complete the word fragment, (ele.....) after having been primed by looking at pictures that included one of an elephant. With picture priming, subjects may be primed with brief glimpses of a set of pictures and then be asked to name them or to name pictures with missing elements that are gradually re-introduced.

The importance of awareness during learning has been studied in an intriguing study comparing the explicit and implicit processes by Robert Clark and Larry Squire at University of California, San Diego.[27] They varied Pavlov's famous conditioning technique in humans and used eye blinking as the conditioned response. Here is how it works: if you blow air into the eye, the eyelids blink. This is an unlearned (unconditioned) response. But if you precede the air puff with some other stimulus, such as a tone, after many such pairings, the eyelid will blink as soon as the tone is heard—before the air puff. Blinking to the tone is an implicitly learned (conditioned) response.

They compared this kind of learning in normal subjects and in amnesic patients who had damage to the hippocampus, the part of brain that converts scratch pad memory to long-term memory. In one condition, they evaluated conditioned learning where the tone cue (CS) was on continuously until presentation of the air-puff "unconditioning stimulus" (US) was presented. They compared this situation with one where the cue was on briefly, followed by a delayed interval between CS and US.

The design made a big difference in the results. Normal subjects became conditioned readily under both situations. However, brain-damaged amnesiacs never acquired conditioning when the cue was on only briefly. This phenomenon may contribute to the well-known memory problems of the elderly.

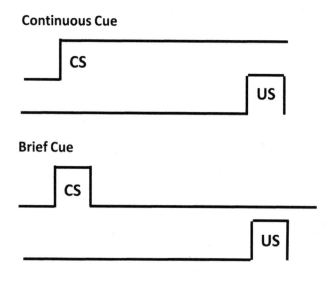

**Continuous Cue**

**Brief Cue**

Two kinds of conditioned learning designs. In the continuous cue design (top half of diagram), the conditioned stimulus (CS) is sustained until the unconditioning stimulus (US) is delivered. In the brief cue design, the CS is not on all the time.

The CS is a priming cue. When it is on only briefly, an otherwise implicit learning situation acquires some kind of explicit expression that normal subjects use to help achieve the learning. A debriefing session after the experiments revealed that only the normal subjects who were consciously aware there was a delay between CS and US were the ones who acquired the learning. None of the amnesiacs had such awareness, and none of them became conditioned when the priming cue was not continuous.

This is not as arcane as you probably think. You remember better if you make it a point to be consciously aware of the subtle cues present in the learning environment and situation. What is important is awareness of the timing relationships between them. For example, suppose you wanted to condition your nervous system to lower blood pressure. First, you have to identify a short stimulus that lowers blood pressure, acting as a US. Such a stimulus might be looking at a restful picture (a beach, or mountains, or forest). Then, you pick another stimulus to serve as CS, preferably one that occurs frequently during the day. It might be looking at your pencil. The idea is to build up a conditioning relationship between looking at your pencil and looking at your favorite restful scene and an implicit memory of the association will develop. Eventually, you would hope to lower blood pressure by looking at the pencil, which you have to do many times a day anyway. The experiments mentioned above indicate it would work best if your training trials used the continuous conditioning design. You would want to look at the pencil continuously and then look at the restful scene, preferably both in the same field of view. If that is not practical, you need make it a point to be aware of the time lag between the cue and the US.

This kind of implicit priming can cause biased attitudes. For example, a classic study by Bargh and colleagues[28] implicitly primed subjects with words related to the stereotype of elderly people (example: Florida, forgetful, wrinkle). Upon leaving the testing booth, the subjects walked more slowly than normal. Similar tests showed that those primed with rude words were more likely to interrupt an investigator than those primed with neutral words, and those primed with polite words were the least likely to interrupt.

Priming most assuredly helps to create bias and prejudice in which subjects do not consciously realize their attitudes are being changed by the priming stimuli in their culture. Indeed, priming is a huge factor in creating distinctive cultures.

Priming can be a good thing if we consciously use it to facilitate learning and memory. We ought to get implicit priming and explicit learning to work together and reinforce each other. If you need to memorize something, it helps to be consciously aware of the potential cues present in the learning environment and situation.

A priming effect may be a factor in the "total immersion" approach to learning a foreign language. Even though at first you do not remember many foreign words swirling around in your head, having heard them before makes it easier to remember them as the need becomes more compelling.

Another practical application of a "mere exposure effect" is in shaping the attitudes and preferences of children. For example, if you wanted your kids to appreciate classical music, jazz, or whatever, you should expose them to it when they are young. It is well established that if kids are exposed to a home in which parents read and in which parents read to the kids, the children are more likely to grow up appreciating books.

---

## Memory Myth Buster

*Learning without remembering is wasted effort.* WRONG. While it is of course desirable to remember what you learn, the mental exercise involved in learning is valuable in its own right. Also, even forgotten learning has a "priming effect," making it easier to re-learn the material the next time.

---

The idea of priming also applies to forgetting things you once knew. Can there be any value in learning something you don't remember? Even when you don't remember something you once learned, there can be value in the learning experience. One benefit of learning is it gives you something to think about. Thinking provides a backdrop for gaining understanding and insight. Whether or not you remember your understanding and insights is another matter, but the mental exercise has some merit in its own right. You might generate a creative idea and remember it, even though you don't remember what information made that possible.

If learning does not form lasting memories, you will have to learn all over again. Consider the case of H.M., a man who had both temporal lobes of the cortex surgically removed. The major structure removed is known as the hippocampus, which you may remember I said helps to form memories. After the surgery, which was performed to stop out-of-control epilepsy that originated in the medial temporal lobe, H.M. could no longer learn anything new. Every new learning experience had to be repeated, and it was never remembered. Things he had learned before the surgery were remembered. This problem lasted all the rest of his life. Thus, scientists came to suspect that the hippocampus was necessary for memory consolidation, which has been amply confirmed in subsequent animal experiments and human clinical observations.

H.M. revealed something else. They gave him a game to play each day. Every day, they had to teach him the rules of the game again; he always had to ask to be reminded of the rules. Yet over time, he got better and better at playing the game. This suggested two kinds of memory, one explicit and consciously realized, and another implicit or procedural, operating subconsciously. The hippocampus is essential for explicit, but not implicit memory. This distinction has become well established through subsequent research under a variety of learning and testing conditions.

Fortunately for the vast majority of readers of this book, the hippocampus is still intact and you can form lasting explicit memories if learning is approached in the right way. Showing how to do this is the purpose of this book.

The second thing learning without remembering is good for is that re-learning is easier than initial learning. Ever have the experience of learning a language, not using it for a while, and then having to re-learn it? If so, you know what I mean. The second time, the learning goes faster. The reason is some of what you learned the first time was subconsciously remembered.

Scientists call this implicit memory, as opposed to consciously recalled explicit memory. In the case of re-learning situations, the initial learning is a "priming" event that expedites subsequent re-learning and may in fact contribute to creating lasting memory. A good practical example of priming is what happens when you skim a book before reading it. Looking at the table of contents, headings, and pictures will increase the amount of material you will remember after reading the text.

## Pay Better Attention

Implicit priming may be a useful first step, but to achieve mastery, you have to make a conscious effort to remember. To do that, you have to pay attention and focus. As you go through each minute of each day, you construct your reality from what you pay attention to. The more attentive you are, the more you experience. What did you get to experience and perhaps remember because you paid attention to it? What did you not remember because you weren't paying enough attention or were distracted?

I can illustrate the point from an incident during my recent vacation in Guatemala. I was sitting in a restaurant and saw a mural. I noticed a couple of round mounds, one looking like a human breast. I also saw a trapezoidal shaped piece of stone with a ball on top. When I quizzed myself about what I saw, that was all I remembered. Then I looked again and noticed many little things in the painting: ears of corn, slices of melon, slices of lemon and lime, peas, a few coffee beans, and bananas. There was a broad swath of greenery in the background and lots of flowers spread around throughout the mural. Then I realized the mural was telling the story of the country. The rounded mounds represented the unique geological formation around the city of Flores, where I had been the day before on my way to the Mayan ruins at Tikal. The piece of stone represented Tikal's pyramids, administrative buildings and plazas. The ball stood for the ball courts found in all the Mayan ruins that dotted the country. The corn and various foods told the story of Guatemala's agriculture. The greenery and flowers represented the lush vegetation of the country, and its weather, especially that of the jungle in the northern part of the country.

See how much I missed by being so inattentive when I first just glanced at the mural? Best of all, attending to these symbols of the country automatically triggered a flood of remembered associations of my trip to Tikal, scenes of the countryside and small towns while riding in cabs and vans, the various restaurants and their food dishes. One picture captured so much of my vacation in a way that will be lasting. I won't have to look at all my many digital photographs to remember.

Many people, most of the time, don't pay close attention. They just passively respond to whatever grabs their attention, as I did when I first looked at the mural. Developing a focusing habit of mind must come from active, intentional sources. It needs to be a mental top-down process where you decide what to pay attention to and for how long.

The other day, I was attending to a bird foraging on the ground for food. The bird had no doubts about its intent: finding food. It was totally focused on scanning every inch of ground. The only things that grabbed its attention were items that might have food value. I notice how its whole body and tail twitched every time the bird saw something of potential value. Of course, some of the items were shining rocks, pieces of paper and the like that were only discovered irrelevant when picked up and inspected. Nonetheless, the bird kept on task. Hey, if a bird brain can sustain focus, so can we.

On the other hand, in due course another bird of the same species flew over, and this bird got distracted and flew away with the other bird. How often such distractions have a similar effect on us and break our concentration.

Life, for bird brains and for ours, is filled with constant demands for our attention. Distractibility is a special characteristic of children. We are supposed to grow out of that. I don't think our current generation, being brought up multitasking on cell phones, Facebook pages, video games, MP3 players, etc., will be able to grow out of their short attention spans. I see such distractibility in today's college students, and every professor I have discussed this with confirms my opinion that today's students have shorter attention spans than students a decade or so ago. Regardless of attention span as a youth, as we get older, most people lose some of their ability to pay attention and become more distractible.

The ability to focus is a learned skill, and if you are deficient in this area, there are ways to improve. First, know that the human brain is wired to be selective in what it attends. The brain does not have the capacity to pay attention to everything at once (people who multitask don't do an optimal job on any of the tasks).

The good news is that you get to decide what to attend to at any given moment. Sometimes, however, things grab your attention, perhaps even when you did not want to notice (as in bad experiences). This brings up the point that some people have disciplined attention selectivity where they choose most of the time what to focus on, while other less fortunate people respond passively to whatever grabs their attention.

People have a natural tendency to be more attentive to the first and last pieces of new information. This is the so-called "serial position effect." If, for example, you are trying to memorize a list of items, you will tend to remember the first and last items in the list. The practical implication is, of course, that you have to pay attention more and work harder to memorize items in the middle of the list.

Of course, once you have identified what needs your attention, discipline is needed to stay focused and not let the mind wander or be distracted by other things. Later, I present some tips on how to train yourself to be more attentive.

Attentiveness is the cornerstone of good memory. Memory begins with registering the information in the first place. The brain will encode it, but memory forms only if you pay attention and actually register it via the appropriate sensory system.

The role of emotion in attentiveness is captured in the observation of Charles Darwin: "Pain is increased by attending to it." The principle applies to everything. One school of thought is that we pay more attention to negative feelings, such as anger, sadness, or fear, simply because they are more powerful than pleasant things.

On the other hand, positive emotions such as joy, curiosity, and contentment cause us to reach out to explore the world, and such reaching entails paying attention. Research demonstrates that attentiveness goes up when people make it a point to put themselves in a good mood. I now realize why listening to jazz music seemed to help my learning when I was going through veterinary medical college. The jazz put me in a good mood. Other people like to study when listening to classical music. Of course, whatever music one listens to, it must not be distracting, such as lyrics that will grab your attention away from what you are trying to learn.

Being more attentive not only gives you a richer experience in the now, but it also increases the amount of experience you will remember.

## Attentional Blindness

When you focus attention on one thing, it can make you blind to other things. When you have something specific to learn and memorize, devote focused attention to it. There is a price to pay, however, because when focused on one thing you fail to see or hear other things. This is called "attentional blindness" and occurs because the brain has a marked limit on perceptual carrying capacity. This was demonstrated in a classical video you can still see on the web at www.invisiblegorilla.com. Investigators filmed a group of six people passing a basketball to each other and were instructed to count how many times those in white shirts passed the ball. In the middle of this activity a man dressed in a gorilla suit slowly walked through the group and turned to the camera and thumped his chest. Astonishingly, about half of people who take this test never see the gorilla. You can test your friends at the YouTube video of this experiment. The discoverers of this phenomenon were Christopher Chabris and Daniel Simons, and they have described this and other similar attentional blindness experiments in their book, *The Invisible Gorilla*.[29]

Why do I bring this up when I am trying to convince you that focused attention is a good thing for learning? It is because multitasking is so popular today, and people think it makes them more productive. I develop this theme later in the sections on "Working Memory" and "Memory Consolidation," but for now the point is that the brain can only hold a few thoughts at one time. Multitasking generally makes you less effective at each thing you are trying to do at once.

## Stop Mind Wandering

Attention fades when you lose interest, and you lose interest when a learning event loses its significance. A basic mode of operation of all animals, even lower animals, is the phenomenon known as habituation. That is, when a novel learning event is presented repeatedly, you get used to it and start to ignore it. You get in the "habit" of no longer paying attention. Actually, you are learning to unlearn. Numerous animal experiments have clearly shown that learning ceases when habituation sets in. If the stimulus is changed, then "dishabituation" can occur, and you may start paying attention again. The practical application for memorization is that you may have to repeatedly refresh the information you are trying to remember, such as thinking about it in different ways or applying it to different situations.

You can think of habituation as learning to ignore. The practical applications for human memory are that we remember associations where the conditioning stimuli are relevant, that is, paired with some meaningful event. Once the meaningful event stops appearing, we soon come to ignore the stimuli with which they were paired. The learning to ignore of habituation should not be confused with "extinction," which is equivalent to learning to forget.

## Don't Divide Your Attention

Have you noticed how many television programs refresh the story line after commercial breaks? Script writers intuitively know that the commercial distracts one's attention from the story line and that the viewer has to be given some reminders.

Distractions seem to arise from everywhere, causing most people to have a hard time sustaining focus. They have much greater problems if they try to divide attention. Whenever I drive somewhere with a passenger and start talking, my passenger often comments that the car slows down. It is not just my brain that has trouble doing two or more things at once. It is basic biology for all of us. The brain seems to operate best if it can focus.

Recently there has been a big flap about car accidents being caused by cell phone users. Many state governments have made it illegal to talk on a cell phone while driving. The problem is that the brain has to divide its resources for the separate tasks of talking and driving. Scientists have actually seen this effect by using brain imaging studies. In one study[30] the brain was scanned while volunteers performed two tasks separately and when they performed the two simultaneously. During separate-task performance, the task that was verbal lit up the image over the lateral part of the cortex (that is, there was more blood supply there because cells in that area process language). Then during a visual task, the back of the brain lit up (vision is processed in the rear of the brain). But when both tasks were performed at the same time the amount of activity in the verbal area and the vision area were both suppressed. In other words, the brain just could not respond optimally to both tasks at the same time.

When attention is divided by multitasking, information is not registered well and thus less likely to be encoded and learned. Later, I will explain the devastating effects of multitasking on converting temporary memories into long-lasting form.

## Learn How to Pay Attention

Even if you have attention-deficit disorder, you can learn how to focus better. One of the things that sets professionals apart from amateurs is their ability to focus on their area of expertise. For example, in a recent experiment performed at Wake Forest Baptist Medical Center, brain imaging studies of 20 non-musicians and 20 musical conductors showed that the brains of both groups diverted activity from visual areas of the brain during musical listening tasks.[31] Activity increased in auditory areas of the brain, while it fell in visual areas. But during more complex music, brain activity changes were less marked in the conductors. The conventional interpretation is that when the brain focuses, it becomes more active in the areas that are processing the subject of the focus. In well-trained subjects, such as conductors in this case, their brain doesn't have to work so hard to pay attention to music, so there is less need for the brain to be more active in the auditory areas. So what this suggests is that ability to focus is a learned capability that derives from an actual lasting change in the brain.

The leader of the study, Jonathan Burdette, said "This is like closing your eyes when you listen to music." That is, you can pay attention to the music better when your brain is not being distracted by visual stimuli. He went on to make this analogy: "Imagine the difference between listening to someone talk in a quiet room and that same discussion in a noisy room—you don't hear as much of what's going on in the noisy room."

It is not enough to say we need to pay attention better to remember better. The trick is in learning how to focus and be more observant. Below is a list of general principles that can help. Many of these are elaborated at various other places in the book.

## Thirteen Ways to Improve Attentiveness

When you were a child, like all children, you were told numerous times to "Pay attention!" That alone should tell us that attentiveness is a learned capability. If by now you are a Senior, you may have an inattentiveness problem again. Aging processes make many Seniors as inattentive as they were as children. Few people have the temerity to tell a Senior to "pay attention," so you may have to be your own taskmaster.

Everybody from first-grade school teachers to Ph.D. candidates knows that to learn and remember things you need to pay attention. The trick is how to make yourself more attentive and focused. A great book on this topic has been written by Winifred Gallagher called *Rapt Attention and the Focused Life*.[32]

The implied assumption in all this is that people learn to focus and have to be reminded often in order to master the ability to concentrate. Over the years people can improve their ability to concentrate. The ability to focus is a habit of mind, one that must be acquired through years of being reminded and of doing it. If this habit has deteriorated, it is not too hard to re-learn it.

Of course, with today's school children, it is a different matter. Any experienced teacher will tell you that kids' attention spans are terrible, and much shorter than was typical a generation ago. The problem, presumably, is our new age of multitasking, where constant flitting from texting, to phone calls, to Web browsing, to video games, and the like makes our kids scatterbrained.

What does one do to improve the ability to concentrate? It takes the discipline of frequent self-reminding. You learn to focus by making yourself do it—again and again, until it becomes a habit, a way of thinking. Here are some specific tips:

1. Value attentiveness. All of us get much less out of life than we could because we are not paying attention.

2. Live in the now. You can correct past weaknesses and mistakes and reduce their likelihood in the future, but it has to be done in the now.

3. Be more aware. Consciously attend to what you are doing, why, and how. Be aware of your emotions and adjust to make them serve learning objectives.

4. Notice the little things. Develop an eye for detail.

5. Notice the small pleasures of life. It teaches you how to focus and makes you happier. Target things that are fun and provide positive reinforcement.

6. Set goals, monitor progress, make needed adjustments.

7. Identify targets for aiming your attention. Choose challenging targets of attention, ones that push you to the edge of your ability to focus.

8. Shut out distractions. Don't be sidetracked by interruptions or mind wandering.

9. Don't multitask. This is the arch enemy of attentiveness and profoundly interferes with the ability to learn and especially to remember.

10. Fight boredom. Make targets of attention more engaging by creating competition or making them into some sort of game, but don't let it become a drill.

11. Make emotion work for you. Develop a passion for what you experience. Both negative and positive emotions work. The kiss of death for learning is to be bored and detached from what you are trying to learn.

12. Practice attentiveness. Acquiring good concentration ability is little different from developing a good golf swing.

13. Learn how to meditate. Yoga, for example, not only relaxes, it teaches attentiveness.

## Learn from Media that Promote Attentiveness

We live in a multi-media world. Usually, this is a distraction that disrupts attentiveness, especially varying with the kind of media. For example, a recent brain imaging study showed that going online stimulated larger parts of the brain than the relatively passive activity of reading a novel or non-fiction book. This was interpreted to indicate that Internet browsing is better for brain development than reading books.[33]

But before you tell schools to throw away the textbooks and let the kids browse away, you should know this: when a brain lights up in many places, it means the brain does not know how to deal with all the stimuli. It has not mobilized or focused its neural circuitry to deal with the stimuli efficiently and effectively and therefore has to recruit large expanses of circuitry to process the information. In most imaging studies I have read, when a brain knows how to cope with a task, FEWER areas light up because the brain doesn't need to use as many of its resources. In other words, a brain works best when it can focus its resources. If you want your kids to learn how to be more scatterbrained as they grow up, put them on the Web. If you want them to develop better attentiveness and improve critical-thinking skills, have them read good books. Their brain will thank you. The sad truth is that teachers tend to reduce assignments that require reading because so many school kids are so far below grade level in reading.

## Make Associations

The disruption of distractions can be reduced by making a conscious effort to create mental associations for what you are trying to remember. Think about anything you know. Notice that you also thought of associated things. Memories are formed—and recalled—as clusters of associated items. Forming and recalling memories works best by associating something new with something we already know. The hardest and most inefficient way to memorize is by rote. Here I wish to stress that the original encoding of new information is enriched by making meaningful associations that will prove valuable in later processes of memory and retrieval.

Think of memory like a fish net—no, not the holes in the net. Focus on the knots. Each knot can be thought of as a node in a network of linked memory associations— like cues, any one of which can help you connect with the whole of the memory. Most explanations of memory associations involve a chain metaphor, with the idea that each new idea links to an existing link. But in the reality of the brain, the linkages spread out in four dimensions.

Memories with lots of cues are easier to memorize, because the cues magnify the associations that can be made. The value of cues is more evident in recall, where cues can help drag out the primary linked memory. If you go fishing for a buried memory, hooking a cue can drag along the memory you are looking for.

For typical human memory tasks, various contexts exist, such as where you are or what you are doing while trying to memorize something. What kind of mood you are in might be a cue. Are you stressed or embarrassed because you find it difficult to remember? Or are you confident you went about learning in the right way and your memory will work for you? Whatever the emotion, consciously make it part of the memory as you try to form it and as you try to recall it. All of these things can be usefully associated with what you are trying to remember.

## Working Memory

A key aspect of memory is the amount of information you can hold in conscious awareness long enough to use it. An everyday example is holding a telephone number in conscious awareness long enough to dial the number. Ever wonder why there are seven digits in phone numbers? It is because at one time, psychologists thought the typical working memory capacity was for about seven serially ordered items. We now know it is only four or less. Earlier tests did not provide controls to keep from chunking digits and using sequential patterns.

---

**Memory Myth Buster**

*The typical working-memory span is for seven items.* WRONG. For most people, it is four or fewer independent items.

---

Physicians like to evaluate working memory because it is usually the kind that is most vulnerable to brain dysfunction. A typical test is to recall a string of digits that are presented in random order, such as 4,6,3,2,5,0,1. The longer the strings you can recall, the better your working memory. A more challenging example is a recently introduced Digit Ordering Test, in which a person not only has to remember the string of digits but also has to reorder them, in either ascending or descending order.[34]

*"My short-term memory is not as sharp as it used to be.*

*Also, my short-term memory is not as sharp as it used to be."*

—*Bill Harper*

Ever walk into a room and suddenly ask yourself, "What was it I came in here for?" The nerve impulse pattern that represented the working memory of what you went in there for got obliterated by some new and distracting thought. The new thought created its own working memory representation.

## How We Think When Conscious

Working memory does much more than affect how we memorize. It affects how we think! Working memory is used for comprehension, reasoning, planning, and problem solving. As such, anything one can do to improve working memory is certainly worth pursuing.

During memory recall, working memory contains a temporary memory of the current experience and also holds chunks of memory that have been stored as long-term memory. Whether the working memory chunks are new information or information retrieved from storage, the memory is central to the thinking process.

When we are thinking consciously, our current thoughts are held in the "real time" of working memory. Think of working memory operating during thinking as a place holder for a succession of the elements of thinking. Each element is what is held on the scratch pad at any given moment.

As long as you have your learning in what is called "working memory," you can think and solve problems with it. If you are thinking about solving a math problem, for example, each step is successively brought into working memory, used as input for a "thought engine" that uses the succession of input from working memory to solve the problem.

Think of it like streaming audio/video, where "thought bytes" move on to the scratch pad where they are used in the thought process and then moved off the scratch pad to make room for the next thought byte. The thought bytes of working memory and the "thought engine" operate via the impulse neural representations of the respective information.

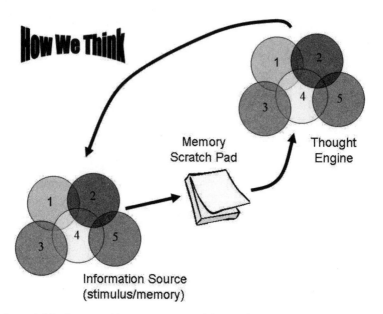

**How We Think**

Memory
Scratch Pad

Thought
Engine

Information Source
(stimulus/memory)

A model for how working memory participates in the conscious thinking process. Elements of thinking are numbered in sequence from 1 to 5. Successive elements of thought, which may come from current stimuli, memory stores, or sources generated internally from elsewhere in the brain, are successively routed via the working memory "scratch pad" into the "thought engine" circuits that accomplish the analysis and decisions involved in thought. Think of the pad as a frame in a movie or video in which thought elements stream through the pad. Similar processes could also operate subconsciously. The capacity of the scratch pad limits thinking power.

How profound and sophisticated one's thought capability is must be affected by how much "stuff" can be held on the working memory scratch pad. As long as you have your learning in what is called "working memory," you can think and solve problems with it. This reminds me of what a Special Ed middle school teacher once told me about her students. She said her special-needs kids "can do the same math as regular students, but they can't remember the steps."

The scratch pad is crucial for conscious thought, because the scratch pad is a virtual way-station that momentarily freezes the information for the conscious mind to reflect on and use to make decisions about how the information might be applied, altered, or ignored. Most importantly, consciousness allows the mind to know what is on the scratch pad and integrates it with what was just on the pad and what is about to be put on the pad.

It does seem reasonable to me to suspect that same process of feeding small chunks of information sequentially into a "thought engine" would also be an effective way for "thinking" to occur subconsciously. One possibility is that the same processes operate subconsciously except that what is on the scratch pad and running through the thought engine is not accessible to consciousness and cannot as readily process a stream of thought frames through past, present, and future.

We do know that thinking and use of working memory occurs in our sleep, most certainly during dreaming. During sleep, our subconscious mind is allowed to work without all the interferences that our conscious mind picks up during the day (see explanations on sleep in Chapter IV).

A recent study, not explicitly concerning memory, sheds some important light on how subconscious thinking affects the quality of thought. In this study, the researchers examined how people make the right choices. They compared the quality of choice that resulted from conscious thinking with that resulting from subconscious thinking. They found that the best choice does not necessarily come from conscious deliberation, although that is what most people would expect.[35]

An alternative way of making choices is to "mull it over," or "sleep on it," letting the subconscious mind work on the problem while you pay attention to other things.

Here is how they studied this issue. In one study, subjects were given information about the attributes of four hypothetical cars, and they were to decide which was the best car based on the attributes assigned to each car. Analysis conditions were either simple (based on only four attributes) or complex (based on 12 attributes). After reading about the attributes, subjects were assigned to one of two groups: conscious analysis or to a subconscious thought condition. In the conscious condition, they thought about the attributes for four minutes before making a choice. In the subconscious condition, subjects were told they would have to make a choice in four minutes, but they were distracted during that time by solving anagrams.

Not surprisingly, when only four attributes were involved, subjects in the conscious-thought condition made the best choice of car. But when the complex condition of 12 attributes was involved, results reversed. The best car was chosen most reliably in the subconscious-thought condition.

In a second study, one change was made. Instead of choosing the best car, subjects were asked about their attitudes toward the four cars. Again, conscious thinkers made the clearest distinctions among the cars when only four attributes were considered, but the opposite occurred when 12 attributes had to be considered.

In another experiment, two stores were selected, one that sold complicated items and the other a department store that sold simple products. As people left the store, shoppers were asked questions about what they bought, why they bought it, how costly it was, and how much they thought about making the choice. The buyers were categorized as either "thinkers" (those who spent a lot of time consciously making a decision) and "impulse buyers" (who did not spend much time consciously thinking about the choice). Several weeks later, these same people were called to check on how satisfied they were with the purchase. As expected, more post-choice satisfaction was found in the conscious thinker group, but only for the simple items in the department store. For the complex choices, the subconscious thinkers expressed the most satisfaction with their purchases.

What all this implies is that simple decisions are best made by careful conscious thought. But for complicated decisions, the best choices may result from "deliberation without paying attention," that is, letting the thinking be done by the subconscious mind.

## Working Memory Capacity Correlates with IQ

Very compelling evidence for the IQ connection has been provided in a study of 128 young adults given a battery of working memory tasks and general intelligence tests. Data revealed a clear correlation between IQ and working memory.[36]

J. R. Flynn first noted that standardized intelligence quotient (IQ) scores were rising by three points per decade in many countries, and even faster in some countries like the Netherlands and Israel.[37] For instance, in verbal and performance IQ, an average Dutch 14-year-old in 1982 scored an astounding 20 points higher than the average person of the same age in his parents' generation in 1952.

These IQ increases over a single generation suggest that the environmental conditions for developing brains have become more favorable in some way.

What might be changing? One strong candidate is working memory, defined as the ability to hold information in mind while manipulating it to achieve a cognitive goal. Examples include remembering a clause while figuring out how it relates the rest of a sentence, or keeping track of the solutions you've already tried while solving a puzzle. Such abilities would certainly affect performance on IQ tests.

Flynn has pointed out that modern times have increasingly rewarded complex and abstract reasoning. Differences in working memory capacity account for 50 to 70 percent of individual differences in IQ.[38] (abstract reasoning ability) in various meta-analyses, suggesting that working memory is one of the major building blocks of IQ. This idea is intriguing because working memory can be improved by training.

## Use Working Memory Training to Raise IQ of Children

First, let me challenge the common assumption that IQ is fixed. It is not. It improves dramatically in the early school years for all children. Moreover, a recent study shows that both verbal and non-verbal IQ can change (for better or worse) in teenagers.[39]

Educators have known for some time that it is possible to train ADHD children to have better working memories, and in the process improve their school performance. The idea that working memory capacity might be expanded by training normal children has not yet caught on. Test-driven teaching in U.S. schools teaches students what to learn, not how to learn.

Researchers in Japan recently tested whether a simple working memory training method could increase the working memory capacity of children.[40] While they were at it, they tested for any effect on IQ. Children ages 6-8 were trained 10 minutes a day each day for two months. The training task to expand working memory capacity consisted of presenting a digit or a word item for a second, with one-second intervals between items. For example, a sequence might be 5, 8, 4, 7, with one-second intervals between each digit. Test for recall could take the form of "Where in the sequence was the 4?" or "What was the 3rd item?" Thus students had to practice holding the item sequence in working memory. With practice, the trainers increased the number of items from 3 to 8.

After training, researchers tested the children on another working memory task. Scores on this test indicated in all children that working memory correlated with IQ test scores. That is, children with better working memory ability also had higher IQs. When comparing children who got working memory training with those who did not, investigators found that children who got the working memory training performed better than controls on the working memory test did. When first graders were tested for intelligence, the data showed that intelligence scores increased during the year by 6% in controls, but increased by 9% in the group that had been given the memory training. The memory training effect was even more evident in the second graders, with a 12% gain in intelligence score in the memory trained group, compared with a 6% gain in controls. As might be expected, the lower IQ children showed the greatest gain from memory training.

## Use Working Memory Training to Raise IQ of Adults

We could expect working memory capacity and IQ to change in youngsters. But lasting change can be produced in adults too. I recently found a paper revealing lasting improvements in brain function were produced in healthy adults by only five weeks of practice on three working-memory tasks involving the location of objects in space. Subjects performed 90 trials per day on a training regimen (CogMed). MRI brain scans showed increased activity in the cortical areas that were involved in processing the visual stimuli. Brain activity increases in these areas appeared within the first week and grew over time. Similar results have been reported by other investigators. In a few cases, where different kinds of stimuli were used, memory training induced a decrease of brain activity in certain areas, which is interpreted to indicate the trained brain did not have to work as hard.[41]

Another study provides strong evidence that increasing adult working memory capacity will raise their IQ.[42] The subjects, young adults, were trained on a so-called dual N-back test in which subjects were asked to recall a visual stimulus that they saw two, three or more stimulus presentations in the past. As performance improved with each block of trials, the task demands were increased by shifting from two-back to three, then three to four, etc. Daily training took about 25 minutes.

Intelligence tests were periodically given based on visual analogy problems of increasing difficulty. This kind of testing measures what is called "fluid" intelligence, which refers to the ability to reason and solve new problems independently of previously acquired knowledge. The investigators found working memory training improved scores on the intelligence test. Moreover, the effect was dose-dependent, in that intelligence scores increased in a steady straight-line fashion as the number of training sessions increased from 8 to 12 to 17 to 19. Working memory capacity presumably transfers to visual analogy tasks because you have to hold many visual features in working memory while you try to identify which pattern is missing in the matrix.

Advances in this arena of raising IQ in teenagers and adults may come faster now that we have so many published reports indicating that working memory capacity can indeed be expanded by training. The trick is in finding which approaches work best. Currently, we believe that working memory can be expanded by attentiveness training, music, and such tests as the "N-back" test and certain game environments. One study by Verhaeghen and colleagues showed that memory span could be increased from one to four steps back with 10 hours (1 hr/session) of N-back training.[43]

Perhaps you have heard of so-called brain-fitness training, typically packaged as computer games that stimulate the brain. A whole cognitive enhancement industry is flourishing. The idea of brain fitness software is that playing mentally challenging games will make you smarter. This is not necessarily true. Several recent reviews suggest that such games do little to increase IQ. I can only recommend with some certainty those games that are confined to expanding working memory capacity, and even here, one should not expect too much. I know about three such programs, MindSparke, Cogmed, and Jungle Memory. I have no personal experience or financial interest in any of these, but each has the potential to be helpful, especially for kids or adults with attention deficit.

Fundamental changes in working memory capability can be achieved by playing rigorous working-memory games. You can play these games for any length of time and repeat as often as you like. Performance is automatically scored for each game session. See http://brainworkshop.sourceforge. net/, http://www.soakyourhead.com/, or http://cognitivefun. net/test/5 and pick the game you like best. You may have to install a plug-in for your browser.

The basic idea is that the computer presents you with a string of items (numbers, geometric images, etc.) and quizzes you to see if you remember the item that was presented n-steps earlier. You can set the difficulty level. For example, once you master remembering the immediately preceding item (1 – back), you can tell the computer to require you to recall the item two steps back, or three, or more.

A more challenging modification is to play the game in dual mode ("dual n-back"). In this variation, two independent items are presented simultaneously such as sound and a number or image. The task is to remember for both strings when an item was presented n-steps back in time. Dual n-back training has a multitasking feature that may make it less effective than single n-back training. A comparison study is needed.

## Reduce Working Memory Load

Obviously, you can make your working memory more effective if you don't overload it. As I mentioned, paying attention is prerequisite to learning, and the ability to pay attention seems to be affected by how much information (load) is being carried in working (scratch pad) memory. These principles have been elucidated in human experiments testing the assumption that attending to relevant details in a learning situation requires the details to be held in working memory. Having other, non-relevant, information in working memory at the same time serves as a distraction, lowering attention, and interfering with memory formation.[44]

In one experiment, participants performed an attention task requiring them to ignore distracting pictures of faces while holding in working memory a string of digits that were in the same order (low memory load) or different order (high memory load) on every trial.[45] The test thus was one of multitasking, one task being holding the digits in working memory and the other task being identifying whether a name flashed on the screen was of a famous politician or a pop star, while a contradictory face was projected. For example, the name Mick Jagger would have the face of Bill Clinton superimposed, and the task was to know Mick Jagger is a pop star, not a politician.

The attention performance degraded severely with high working memory load. That is, the distracting faces created confusion when subjects were also required to hold mixed-order digits in working memory at the same time.

The point is simple. It is hard to think about two complicated things at once. Recall the earlier explanation on how working memory contributes to thinking. If the working memory load is too high, thinking becomes inefficient. Especially relevant is the fact that simultaneous tasks create memory interference effects. The growing trend, especially among young people, to multitask may seem wonderful. Social culture in industrialized countries is creating a whole generation of young people who have poor attentiveness. This all started with television, which of course created the added problem of filling kids' minds with mush. In more recent years, the problem is being compounded by technologies that encourage multitasking (cell phones, text messaging, Web surfing, iPods, video games, etc.).

---

**Memory Myth Buster**

*Multitasking is a wonderful capability.* WRONG. Maybe sometimes it is efficient for undemanding tasks, but it adds unacceptable load to working memory, which interferes with consolidation.

---

Multitasking interferes with retaining what is on the working memory scratch pad in two ways: 1) something distracted you and put new information that displaced what was in your working memory, or 2) something that was on your mind beforehand impaired your ability to hold the item in your working memory.

We are learning that there is such a thing as "proactive" interference. That is, working memory is impaired by previous material that was in the working memory. This is why, for example, you sometimes forget why you opened the refrigerator door—some immediately preceding thought corrupted your working memory. You probably don't remember the disruptive thought, because it never got consolidated in memory because it was erased off the scratch pad by the thoughts associated with opening the door. One study by Jonides and Nee[46] indicated that forgetting from working memory would be minimal if it were not for proactive interference.

The notoriously low capacity of working memory is largely due to proactive interference. Just practicing demanding working memory tasks for more items may actually increase memory span, and that effect might be due to unintended training to resolve proactive interferences. When faced with serious memory tasks, get in an environment that does not supply irrelevant information. Force yourself to think only of things that are relevant to what you are trying to think about and remember. Concentrate!

# Train Working Memory to Feel Good

Training working memory not only helps thinking ability, it makes you feel good. Biological reward comes from the release of the neurotransmitter dopamine. Dopamine release is promoted by performing working memory tasks,[47] which suggests that working memory tasks are actually rewarding. In the study of human subjects by Fiona McNab and colleagues in Stockholm,[48] human males (age 20-28) were trained for 35 minutes per day for five weeks on working memory tasks with a difficulty level close to their individual capacity limit. After such training, all subjects showed increased working memory capacity. Functional MRI scans also showed that the memory training increased the cerebral cortex density of dopamine D1 receptors, the receptor subtype that mediates feelings of euphoria and reward.

Students who make good grades feel good about their success. Likewise, people who are "life-long learners" have discovered learning lots of new things makes them feel good.

## How to Help Your Working Memory Capacity

If the demands made on working memory could be lessened, better thinking and learning would result. Certain strategies can help to reduce the load on working memory. Learners should be encouraged to employ the following devices:

- Provide help, such as using cues, mnemonics, reminders.

- KISS (Keep It Simple, Stupid!) (example: use short, simple sentences, present much of the instruction as pictures/diagrams).

- Organize information in categories, in small chunks.

- Don't try to learn so much material at once. Less can be more.

---

**Memory Myth Buster**

*The size of one's working-memory capacity is fixed.* WRONG. You can increase working memory capacity with training.

---

# How to Promote Long-term Memory Formation

Memories that are temporary can be a blessing in that they keep our minds free of useless junk we would not use very often anyway. But obviously, temporary memories are a curse if you need to have the information memorized permanently. For these cases, the trick is to get temporary memories converted into permanent ones. Scientists call this process consolidation.[49]

## Protect Recent Memory from Interferences

Reducing interference is the best way to promote long-term memory formation. Experiments over 100 years ago made it clear that distractions or other kinds of brain-function interference can prevent humans from consolidating new learning into lasting memories.

The oldest and best-known disruptive effect is head trauma. Depressant drugs, such as alcohol, interfere with consolidation, whereas stimulant chemicals may indirectly enhance consolidation. The positive effect of stimulant drugs can be duplicated by voluntary arousal and focused attention. In other words, just trying hard to consolidate memory can work.

Many kinds of distractions can interfere with consolidation. You don't have to be knocked in the head to interfere with learning. Any distraction occurring between a learning event and when consolidation is occurring can interfere with the consolidation.

Interference effects are about the same in everyone. People with low IQs and people with high IQs have similar requirements for new memories to consolidate. Moreover, everybody has a similar need to rehearse material they want to memorize. For example, when we learn a new word, most of us require a repetition on that same day and on each of the next several days in order to get useful command of the word. How much rehearsal and how close the spacing needs to be depends on other variables I discuss throughout the book, such as the motivation to remember, the emotional impact of the event, whether or not the event was imaged in the mind's eye, and what happens immediately after the learning event.

Temporary memory usually has to be kept "on-line" for many minutes in order to facilitate consolidation. For example, a revealing experiment on spatial learning of a food foraging task in rats showed rats could maintain an unusually long and accurate spatial working memory. One explanation is that the working memory was kept intact and viable by response strategies and the use of olfactory cues in addition to visual cues. The basic principle seems to be to use multiple senses during and immediately after learning. Also, as they went about their continual foraging, the rats were "thinking" about and applying task-relevant response strategies immediately after the training trial.

Using multiple senses focused on a single task and applying a sustained effort of performing the task constitutes a powerful form of rehearsal we humans can surely emulate to enhance our own memory ability.

## What Life Is Like Without Consolidation

Damage to certain brain areas creates a state where nothing new can be consolidated. Learning can still occur, but lasting memory of what was learned does not occur. The first clues about which brain areas are important in consolidation came from clinical studies in humans with brain lesions. I mentioned earlier the classic case is that of "H. M.," a man who had both temporal lobes of the cortex surgically removed to stop out-of-control epilepsy that originated in the medial temporal lobes. The major structure removed was the hippocampus, a C-shaped structure on both sides of the brain lying within the temporal lobes of each cerebral hemisphere.

After the surgery, H. M. could no longer remember any new learning. Every new learning experience had to be repeated. Things were learned, but never remembered. Things he had learned before the surgery were still remembered, presumably because they had already been consolidated. Thus, scientists came to suspect the hippocampus is necessary for memory consolidation, and this has been amply confirmed in subsequent experiments and clinical observations.

Studies of H. M. over the years have firmly established three things about memory: 1) memory formation is a distinct brain function, separable from other brain abilities, 2) the medial temporal lobe of the brain, where the hippocampus is, is necessary to form declarative (but not procedural) memories, and 3) the medial temporal lobe is not the final storage place for memories.

Most sensory information, such as what you see or hear, goes first to the neocortex, that outer mantle of the brain that evaluates and acts on the information. Then, the information goes from the neocortex to the hippocampus. At the same time, input can arrive in the hippocampus from the emotion-generating part of the brain via another pathway involving a structure known as the septum. Through some pathways not yet discovered, memory gets saved in a distributed fashion in many parts of the brain. A diagram of some of the relationships is shown below:

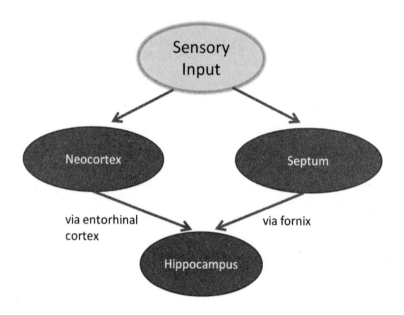

Paths through which sensory information reaches the hippocampus for subsequent memory consolidation.

The neocortex and septum structures act as a feed-forward information filter, taking information that has been processed and routing it to the hippocampus. Note that the information has been processed rationally in the neocortex and emotionally in the "emotional brain" structures that feed the septum. This system of structures is not necessary for preservation of long-term memories, once they already exist.

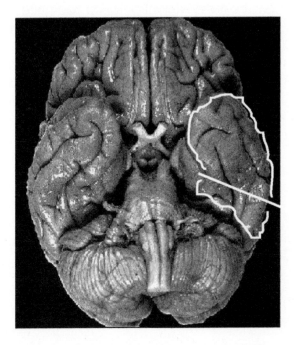

View of the human brain as it would be seen from below. The structure outlined in white is the temporal lobe. The white line points to the area known as the parahippocampal gyrus. The other memory structures and the hippocampus itself are folded underneath the temporal lobe where they are not visible from this view.

## Brain Areas Working Together to Form Memories

More recent evidence indicates consolidation also involves the part of the prefrontal cortex that lies along the midline of the front part of the brain. This part of the brain is crucial to conscious thinking and it is uniquely developed in humans. Neuronal impulse activity in this part of the cortex becomes selective during consolidation. Stimulus-specific neural activity emerges when stimuli are reliably associated, and is sustained during the interval between two paired stimuli but not during the interval of two unpaired stimuli. The firing pattern IS the working memory. This selective firing can become more prominent over several weeks after learning, even without continued training. That is almost like the brain teaching itself what to remember. When selective firing can be re-created long after initial learning, we say the memory has been consolidated.

There is a practical consequence. Complex thought occurs in the prefrontal cortex. The more you think intensely about what you are trying to memorize, the better the hippocampus and prefrontal cortex can work together to consolidate the memory. In other words, the best rehearsal for memorizing is not rote repetition, but hard thinking.

## Don't Multitask. It Is the Archenemy of Memory Consolidation

People today, especially young people, seem very adept at doing many things at once. We older adults tend to be awed at how young people can multitask. They seem to text message on cell phones, watch TV, listen to music, play a video or computer game, carry on a conversation, read and post to Facebook, and maybe even study their school lessons with apparent ease and do it all simultaneously.

Multitaskers are programming their brains to be more distractible, rather than learning how to focus. Nobody should be surprised that people who multitask a lot are easily distracted. It could well be that they multitask a lot because they are so distractible and less able to focus. Rather than do any one thing well, they do them all poorly.

According to a Kaiser Family Foundation study last year, school kids in all grades beyond the second grade committed, on average, more than six hours per day to TV or videos, music, video games, and computers. Almost one-third reported that "most of the time" they did their homework while chatting on the phone, surfing the Web, sending instant messages, watching TV, or listening to music.[50] And we wonder why test scores on standardized tests don't improve?

Youngsters think that this entertainment while studying helps their learning. It probably does make homework less tedious, but it clearly makes learning less efficient and less effective. Multitasking violates everything we know about good memory practices.

We have objective scientific evidence that multitasking impairs learning. A recent study by K. Foerde and colleagues[51] had college-age students learn a task under two conditions, one with no distractions and the other while listening to high- and low-tone beeps, attending to the high ones. In this situation, total amount of learning was superficially the same in both conditions, but with distractions the learning was stereotyped and learners had difficulty in applying what they learned to other contexts and situations. The study also used brain scans under test conditions, and the data indicated that the memory task and the distraction stimuli engaged different parts of the brain and that these regions were probably in competition with each other.

Many adults, and even teachers, encourage multitasking because they think it is good stimulus for the brain and is a useful skill. But multitasking prevents the focused attention and reduction of distractions that are necessary for good memory. Basically, every task demands its own piece of our attention. Every task has its own requirement for space in the memory we use to think with, i.e., working memory, and working memory has very limited capacity. So, in other words, every task acts as a distraction. Distractions interfere with both memory formation and recall.

Worse yet, the repeated multitasking is re-wiring the brain to perform multiple tasks at once, which has the effect of training the brain to be distractible and incapable of focus. A research group at Stanford[52] performed an experiment proving that multitaskers do not pay attention, control their memory, or switch among tasks as well as those who are used to completing one task at a time. The research put about 100 students through three tests which revealed that the multitaskers were easily distracted by everything. The researchers began with the belief that multitaskers have superior mental capabilities. What they found was the opposite. They weren't even good at task switching.

You would think that experienced multitaskers would be better at task switching because they do it all the time. The explanation may be that they have re-programmed their brain to deal superficially with information.

Another study found similar memory interference effects in young adults and, when memory was tested in older adults, memory performance was more impaired by task interruptions compared with young adults.[53] Brain scans showed that brain activity in all subjects switched to attend to the disruptive stimulus, but older adults showed evidence of more difficulty in switching brain resources in response to stimuli.

The study did not directly examine ability to memorize, but there surely must be a significant difference, given that memory formation is enhanced by sustained attentiveness and focus. There may be some undiscovered benefits of multitasking, but memorizing cannot be one of them.

*Multitasking violates everything we know about good memory practices.*

Nor is intelligent thought likely to benefit from multitasking. Multitasking bombards working memory with scrambled and unfocused information and probably keeps the brain from learning how to optimize focus and orderly sequence thoughts through what I call the brain's "thought engine." Several studies that I have summarized earlier show that intelligence correlates with working memory capacity, which under the best of circumstances is limited and easily overloaded by multiple simultaneous informational input.

Frequent multitasking programs the brain to become more distractible. This has serious negative consequences for the way people understand, think, remember, communicate and socialize. The multitasking mind skims through life instead of engaging it deeply. Multitasking drives subconscious, procedural parts of the brain, whereas top-down attentiveness drives the declarative memory processes of the hippocampus to form memories that we can use in conscious and high-level processing.

There is another downside to multimedia multitasking. There is no down-time; it goes on 24/7. Where is there time for introspection, for savoring life? Parents need to intervene with their multitasking children: 1) take away the smartphone and use only a plain cell phone; 2) limit access time to the TV, video games, the Internet, and MP3 players.

And think about this possibility: all this entertainment that kids access could be programming them to be mentally lazy, passive observers of life. As I mentioned before, I and other professors think we see this in many of today's college students.

## How the Brain Fools You Into Thinking You Are Really Multitasking.

Our brain fools us into thinking it can do more than one thing at a time. It can't. Recent MRI studies by P. E. Dux and colleagues at Vanderbilt prove that the brain is not built for good multitasking. When trying to do two things at once, the brain temporarily shuts down one task while trying to do the other.[54] Their MRI images showed a central bottleneck occurs when subjects were trying to do two things at once, such as pressing the appropriate computer key in response to hearing one of eight possible sounds and uttering an appropriate verbal response when seeing images. Activity in the brain that was associated with each task was prioritized, showing up first in one area and then in the other—not in both areas simultaneously. In other words, the brain only worked on one task at a time, postponing the second task and deceiving the subjects into thinking they were working on both tasks simultaneously. The delay between switching functions can be as long as a second.

Two behaviors that might seem distracting may actually be helpful for memory. One may surprise you: gum chewing. According to folk wisdom, chewing gum is supposed to help you concentrate. If so, then chewing gum ought to help you remember. This idea has been formally tested in experiments at a university in England.[55] Keith Wesnes and his colleagues divided young-adult subjects into three groups and had them perform memory tests during: 1) gum chewing, 2) sham gum chewing (pretending to chew gum by making the appropriate jaw movements, and 3) control, where no chewing or chewing movements were performed.

Subjects were tested for picture recall, spatial working memory, numerical working memory, delayed word recall, word recognition. Several measures of attention were also assessed to check for evidence that gum chewing improved attentiveness. These tests included a simple reaction time test, a choice reaction time test, a digit vigilance test, and heart rate measurement. A cognitive load test was also conducted in which subjects subtracted by threes (repeated subtraction of three from a randomly generated starting number) and by sevens.

A clear memory improvement from gum chewing occurred for spatial working memory, numeric working memory, and longer-term memory involving immediate and delayed recall.

There was no evidence for improved attentiveness. In fact, the sham chewing group revealed an impaired simple reaction time score, compared to the control and the gum chewing group. Presumably, this reflects a need for the sham chewers to think consciously about making the sham movements, which diverted some brain resources from participating in the reaction-time response.

The authors suggest that perhaps the increased heart rate of the gum chewers increased blood flow to the brain.

Another group of investigators had reported earlier that chewing increased blood flow to the fronto-temporal regions of the cortex that are involved in memory tasks. It is also possible that gum chewing increases insulin release, which perhaps could affect the availability of glucose to brain cells. Maybe the rhythm of chewing has some effect.

The second possible exception is listening to music while trying to memorize. We all know that students like to listen to music while studying. There is a Web site that gives an overview of what little research has been done in this area. There has been interest in the so-called "Mozart effect" in which listening to classical music is supposed to help memory. The results are conflicting.

Whether or not music helps memory is surely a function of how distracting the music is. If one pays attention to the music, then it would interfere with what you are trying to memorize. Music with a lot of lyrics is probably bad for memorizing, because the words would interfere with the words you are trying to remember. Rap music would be an example of the worst possible case. Instrumental music played as background might help memorizing because it puts you in a good mood. Maybe it was the rhythm of jazz that helped me learn veterinary medicine. Maybe the rhythmic beat of the music is akin to the rhythm of gum chewing. I don't know if listening to music with strong rhythm is for everybody. It could be distracting. The matter might warrant formal investigation.

## Test Yourself

Tests do more than just measure learning. Tests are learning events.[56] Testing forces retrieval of incompletely learned material and the very act of retrieval is a rehearsal process that helps to make the learning more permanent. Testing, and not actual studying, is the key factor on whether or not learning is consolidated into longer-term memory.

Why does forced recall, as during testing, promote consolidation? Much more about this is presented later, but when a memory is retrieved, it is a repeat of the original learning and the brain will try to consolidate it again. Repetition strengthens consolidation.

A recent report from researchers at Washington University in St. Louis examined the role retrieval had on the ability to recall that same material after a delay of a week.[57] In the experiment, college students were to learn a list of 40 foreign language word pairs, manipulated so the pairs either remained in the list (were repeatedly studied) or were dropped from the list once they were recalled. This design is like studying flash cards: one way is to keep studying all the cards over and over again; the other way is to drop out a card from the stack every time you correctly recalled what is on the other side of the card. After a fixed study period, students were tested over either the entire list or a partial list of only the pairs that had not been dropped during study. Four study and test periods alternated back-to-back. Students were also asked to predict how many pairs they would be able to remember a week later, and their predictions were compared with actual results on a final test a week later.

The initial learning took about 3–4 trials to master the list, and was not significantly affected by the strategy used (rehearsing the entire list or dropping items out as they were recalled). On average, the students predicted they would be able to remember about half of the list on a test to be given a week later. However, actual recall a week later varied considerably depending on learning conditions. On the final test, students remembered about 80% of the word pairs if they had been tested on all the word pairs, no matter whether they had studied multiple times with all of them in the list or if they dropped correctly recalled words from the list in later study trials. However, recall was only about 30% correct when correctly identified words were dropped from subsequent tests, even though all words were studied repeatedly. In other words, it was the repeated testing and associated recall, not the studying, that was the key factor in successful longer-term memory.

This study also showed the subjects could not predict how well they would remember, which is consistent with my years of experience as a professor. Students are frequently surprised to discover after an examination that they did not know the material as well as they thought they did. If I were still teaching, I would give more tests. Students would hate it, of course. And I would encourage students to use self-testing as a routine learning strategy, something one study revealed to be a seldom-used strategy. The repeated self-tests should include all the study material and not drop out the material the student thinks is already mastered.

Self-testing with flashcards can be very useful, especially for vocabulary or foreign language learning. Create flashcards with the information you are trying to learn and drill yourself to help make it stick in your mind. A web site helps you create, study, and share flash cards on any topic you choose: http://www.flashcardmachine.com/medical-mnemonics.html.

I suggest creating some "extraneous" flash cards. In a given stack of cards, you can randomly slip in a couple of the novel ones. In fact, the novel cards can have legitimate memory items on them, but you don't review these particular cards every time you go through the deck. A variant of this idea is to separate cards into stacks based on how well you have learned them. When rehearsing a stack that you know fairly well, insert a few of the cards from the stack that you have not memorized.

## Act on What You Just Learned

The idea is to apply what you just learned in some way before it gets erased off your working memory "scratch pad." How you "act" will vary with the learning task and the situation at the time of learning.

You can write down the gist of the new information, make drawings, construct a peg-system image, or any of a number of ways to apply what you are trying to remember. The key point is to DO SOMETHING with the information right away. Sometimes it will suffice just to stop and think about it. Whatever you do, quiz yourself. Don't assume you remember. Put yourself to an honest test.

## Don't Over-train: You Can Learn Too Much

Experiments have revealed human memory performance unexpectedly deteriorates if learning sessions were increased to four 60-minute sessions at regular intervals on the same day. In other words, the more the subjects were trained, the poorer they performed. However, this effect did not occur if subjects were allowed to nap for 30-60 minutes between the second and third sessions.[58] I will have a lot more to say about sleeping and naps later in Chapter IV.

---

## Memory Myth Buster

*You can never study too much.* WRONG. Over-learning can be counterproductive and actually interfere with recall.

---

Over-training disrupts performance, perhaps because too much repetition lessens perceived importance and produces habituation. Also I suspect that as training trials are repeated, the information starts to interfere with memory consolidation, perhaps because of boredom or fatigue.

All this suggests memory consolidation would be optimized if learning occurred in repeated short sessions with intervening naps and on different days with regular nighttime sleep. In other words, repeating long study periods in the same day on the same task can be counterproductive. This is yet another reason why students should not cram for exams. Learning should be optimized by rehearsing the same learning material on separate days where normal sleep occurs each night.

## Reconsolidation and Unreliable Memory

One thing people don't think about much is that long-term memory has to be maintained by the brain. Permanent memory is stored in the form of the chemicals and anatomy of synapses, and these undergo continuous change over the years. So how does the brain remember what it has remembered? The answer must lie in genetic coding. That is, the synaptic changes associated with learning must influence expression of genes, so that as memories are destroyed over time, they can be re-built by way of new gene expression. It is a wonder we can remember anything for long periods if the memory is continually being destroyed and re-built. It also is not surprising that memories that do persist can degrade and get corrupted in all this process.

We also know that any time a stored memory is recalled, a subconscious reconsolidation process also occurs. This actually is useful when updated information needs to be incorporated into the original memory. But as the updating consolidation is occurring, it is susceptible to disruption by mind wandering, other stimuli, distractions, etc.

Such reconsolidation involves a new round of protein synthesis in brain cells, similar to that which is needed to make the initial learning a lasting memory. Therefore, a reconsolidation process must be protected from disruptive or corrupting influences if the updated information is to be integrated correctly and consolidated with the original learning.

Each time you recollect, something new can happen. When you recall something you have remembered, as in rehearsing

---

**Memory Myth Buster**

*Once learned, once remembered. That is, what you remember about an experience stays the same each time you use that memory.* WRONG. Each time a memory is recalled it is subject to corruption by mind wandering, other stimuli, distractions, etc. It may well get reconsolidated into a different memory.

---

a memory, that memory can be changed. Usually, we don't want the memory to change—we are rehearsing in the first place to make the memory stick.

Everyday experience reveals how commonly people remember things wrongly. Discuss with most anybody what each party said in a past argument or controversy, and it is usually the case that different people recall the same events in different ways. Nobody has the whole story.

There are three kinds of falsehood: omission, commission, and misremembered. If any of these occur intentionally, they are lies. Unintentional misremembering occurs all the time, and it is especially prone to happen with the passage of time. This is a special problem when adults try to remember childhood experiences. For details, see Daniel Schacter's book, *Memory Distortion*.[59]

Some formal experiments show that accurate recall may be no better than chance. This raises a dilemma: how can we be certain of the justifications for our prejudices, grudges, and animosities that we harbor toward the parents, teachers, and children we knew while growing up? What about the validity of the ideas, opinions, and beliefs we developed as children?

"False memories" commonly contaminate eye-witness reports of accidents and crimes. False memories can be created that feel just as valid as real ones and cannot be distinguished from real memories. Our legal system has not really come to grips with false memory. But there is a growing trend for courts to be skeptical of uncorroborated eye-witness testimony. It is increasingly hard to get a conviction if the only evidence against the accused is a single eye-witness report. Perhaps, in the interests of justice, that is best.

Social conflicts often arise and fester from false memories. The more one dwells on past affronts and offenses, the more distorted they may become with each reconsolidation. The is a main justification for the old adage to "bury the hatchet." Life is simpler and happier when people are willing to try a fresh start.

People who have fallen out with one another need to consider:

- There may be a biological reason that is causing a person to act badly.

- The person who feels justified in his or her wrath should know he or she could likely be remembering things incorrectly.

To help reconsolidation strengthen rather than corrupt memory, stay focused during rehearsal on the things you are trying to remember. Make certain there are not distractions or extraneous information or emotions being inserted into the reconsolidation process.

There are of course situations where you would prefer to modify a memory by changing its content during reconsolidation. I explore this later in this chapter in connection with Post-traumatic Stress Syndrome.

Many memories, especially if they involve the emotions, are like knee-jerk reflexes. When someone insults us, it can trigger a flash of anger. The punch line of a joke propels a laugh. An act of kindness can elicit our appreciation or love.

Emotions are also learned, triggered by memories of past events we perhaps no longer consciously recall. Emotions also affect our ability to memorize new experiences. Memory ability is impaired by stress, anxiety, fear, or depression. In all my years of teaching college students, I have learned that when a student's grades suddenly fall, it almost always reflects an emotionally traumatic event. If feelings interfere with memory, changing the feelings will be rewarded with better memory.

Rebecca Rupp described an experiment on memories of elderly people who were screened both before and after admission to nursing homes.[60] After institutionalization, their memories turned sour. They now had more unpleasant memories involving pain, loss, loneliness, and death. As Rupp puts in, "The remembered past was a function of the experiences present."

Memory ability is facilitated by good emotions, such as confidence, contentment, and happiness. Emotions and memory are inextricably linked. One example: psychoactive drugs are emotional crutches that not only hijack our natural emotional coping mechanisms but also impair our ability to remember. Emotions and memory are even processed in the same parts of the brain.

I could have begun this section with illustrations from my childhood, but I don't remember much about my childhood. What I do remember are the events that were associated with profound emotions, such as: watching the gamecocks I helped my dad raise peck each other to death in cock fights; steering my dad's car as I sat on his lap driving from

Naples to Miami through the Everglades; embarrassing myself while learning to ride my new bike by driving it into the nearest telephone pole; trying to become "teacher's pet" of a teacher I had a crush on; the two fist fights I won; and so on. I may have repressed a lot of other memories that were too unpleasant, perhaps for example, the fights I lost.

Well, the point is emotion often has profound effects on memory, making it more likely the event will be remembered, but also likely to be distorted. That is the reason for the common finding that eye-witness testimony about crime scenes is often wrong. Even happy memories can be exaggerated. That's why the fisherman's catch tends to get bigger with each telling.

## Use Images

Whoever said that "a picture is worth a thousand words" could have been a memory expert. All "memory athletes," the card counters at casinos and participants in formal memory tournaments rely almost exclusively on mental-image representations of what they want to remember. But regular folks can benefit from this technique as well. One experiment with college students has documented that they learned chemistry much better if the instruction was provided in picture form than if done verbally.[61]

Visual memory has astounding capacity. A study by T. F. Brady validates the conclusion that ordinary humans have astounding memory capacity for visual (but not auditory) memories.[62] In this study, young adults viewed a succession of object images, one every three seconds, and told to remember as much as they could. After about each block of about 300 images, they were given a 5-minute rest break.

After 10 such blocks (total images seen = 2,500; total time about 5.5 hours), they were tested with probe images and asked for each one if it had been seen before. Performance accuracy was remarkably high for all conditions, respectively 92%, 88%, and 87% accuracy. Remembering 2,500 images with this level of recognition accuracy is truly astounding.

As comparison, a related study M. A. Cohen's group showed that auditory memory was markedly inferior.[63] When subjects listened to sound clips (conversation, animal sounds, music, etc.) and then asked to distinguish new from old clips, under all conditions performance was systematically inferior to visual-memory performance.

Apparently, everyone has a degree of photographic memory. Certainly, the odds of recognizing that you have seen something are very high, at least under conditions where the image is a simple object. With complex images that contain multiple details, the details can serve as useful cues or could even become confusing distractors. It is also not clear, if the visual-image capacity is limited to recognition or whether it applies to generating a recall without an image probe. Even so, it is a good bet that memory performance will be optimized if memory items are converted to mental images.

Why are pictures so effective? The explanation lies in the fact that the sensory systems and brain devote far more nerve cells to vision than to any other sense. To compare vision and sound, scientists have counted the number of fibers in the nerves that convey vision (optic nerve) and sound (auditory nerve) in humans. The estimates of fibers in the optic nerve range from 730,000 to 1,700,000, whereas the estimates for auditory nerve fibers only range from 28,000 to 30,000. The counts are estimates based on hand counts of samples of each nerve under a microscope. At a minimum, 24 to 57 times as many nerve fibers are devoted for vision than for sound. No wonder we remember pictures best! A similar difference exists when you consider the vast difference in human cerebral cortex that is devoted to vision and sound.

## Visual Memory Has Astounding Capacity

People with outstanding memories, such as so-called memory athletes who compete in memory contests, create mental images of what they are trying to remember. This is what is usually meant by the term "photographic memory." Now, a formal scientific study validates the conclusion that ordinary humans have astounding memory capacity for visual (but not auditory) memories. A picture may not be worth as much as a thousand words, but it is worth more words than you can remember.

---

### Memory Myth Buster

*"Photographic memory" only exists in a few lucky people.* WRONG. Anybody can learn to memorize with mental images, which are much easier to remember than words.

---

## Create Powerful Images

Several key principles apply to making visualization effective:

1. Use as many senses as possible. Images should be colorful, in three dimensions, and be associated with sound, rhythm, and touch.

2. Create an organized sequence of images. The ordering can be done on the basis or logic or by using numbered "peg systems" (see below).

3. Exaggerate. Making images ridiculous or absurd makes them memorable.

4. Keep it simple. The association needs to be direct and clear-cut.

I use the acronym AVENUE to remind everyone of the features that make a memory image memorable and put you on the avenue to a power memory. The idea is that if you use these elements, it is more likely you will remember your image. Applying this acronym to your images will make them much more memorable:

AVENUE

A = action

V = vivid

E = exaggerated

N = noun

U = unusual

E = emotion

Think of yourself as being on the avenue to a great memory.

Here is a story to illustrate the point: Do you know what the capital of Nevada is? No, it is not Las Vegas, but that is probably the first thing that comes to mind. The capital is Carson City. To remember this, you could visualize the Las Vegas strip of casinos, because that is the first thing most people think of about Nevada. Pretend you are a car and your older son is also a car (CAR + SON = Carson). Picture the cars in a vivid way (they are purple Volkswagen Beetles). You have this wild exaggerated story line of the two cars driving into the CITY to cruise. You and your son drive the Beetles through the plate glass windows, smashing into gaming tables. Chips fly all around. Patrons are enraged, call the cops, and chase you two out of the casino into the city. Your race back out into the street to escape. Note most of the items are nouns, easy to visualize. The action is pronounced. And you are a key part of the story, emotionally engaged.

I bet you will never forget the capital of Nevada.

# Use Traditional Mnemonic Devices

## Use Sound-alikes (Audionyms)

Most of the things that are hard to learn, such as strings of numbers, nonsense syllables, or scrambled words, are hard to remember because they are hard to visualize and there is little to associate with the items.

Sometimes, the problem is handled by using "sound-a-likes" (audionyms). This memory tip involves changing the sound of the item you are trying to remember into a sound-alike that you can use to generate a mental image. The audionym approach can be used for a variety of purposes: remember such things as names of people or countries and labels for objects and structures.

A word or a person's name that cannot be imaged may be made easier to remember by associating it with something that sounds similar. Let me illustrate this technique by showing how to memorize the names of Presidents 11 through 20. "Polk" sounds like "poke," so you can envision a President poking someone in the eye. Now build up a chain of associations to reproduce the actual sequence of Presidents. Number 12 is "Taylor," which sounds like "tailor," so visualize a tailor at a sewing machine being poked in the eye. Next is "Fillmore," which sounds like "fill more." Now you can see our one-eyed "tailor" stuffing (filling) more and more stuff inside the suit he is sewing. He doesn't like the result so he "Pierce's" the suit with a knife to empty out the stuff. The suit still looks a mess so he blows it up with a cannon, the kick of which bucks him off (sounds like "buck from the cannon" ... Buchanan). The next President is Lincoln, which sounds like "links." So the tailor builds a chain-link fence out of all the pieces of the blown-up suit. Then he uses the fence to make an outhouse, "John" for "Johnson". Standing outside is a doorman to the outhouse who grants (Grant) permission to go in and ceremoniously ushers him in. The first person to go in is "Hayes" in the form of the sound-a-like bale of "hay." Next to go in is the cartoon character, "Garfield" who uses the hay as kitty litter. Of course this is ridiculous! It is also probably why you might have just learned President's 11-20—in one trial. Similar "short stories" of pictured sound-a-likes could be used for the first ten Presidents and Presidents 21-30. Notice also that another principle operates here: "chunking." Items to memorize are grouped in small chunks.

Here is another example: if you wanted to remember the names of the planets of the solar system you could image making a mark (Merc, Mercury), a vein (for Venus), an ear (Earth), a Jeep vehicle (Jupiter), a swampy marsh (Mars), an urn (Saturn), rain (Uranus), a napkin (Neptune), and a plate quibbling here, but Pluto is a dwarf planet (now, anyway). Then, if you wanted to remember all of the planets, in order, you could construct an image composite, such as painting a red mark on a vein of the ear, while you are riding in a Jeep that makes a sudden lurch to a marsh and falls into a giant urn. The urn breaks as a result and you have caused it to rain from the urn onto a napkin that has been laid onto a plate.

This example introduces the idea of chained story telling in which a series of mental images are linked together into a composite. If you develop the composite image in a series of discrete steps, as done in the above example, you can remember sequential order.

## Use Acrostics

Acrostics are short sentences wherein the first letter of each word  represents a word you are trying to remember. Consider the following examples.

1. Music learners remember the notes on lines of sheet music as  "Every Good Boy Does Fine" (E, G, B, D, F) and spaces as "FACE"  (F, A, C, E).

2. One acrostic for remembering the names of cranial nerves and the order from which they emerge from the brainstem is well known to medical students: On Old Olympus Towering Tops, A Famous Vocal German Viewed Some Hops (Olfactory, Optic, Oculomotor, Trochlear, Trigeminal, Abducens, Facial, Vestibulocochlear, Glossopharyngeal, Vagus, Spinal Accessory, Hypoglossal). What makes this acrostic so effective is the ease with which you can make a mental picture. Moreover, all the elements can be contained in a single picture. You can make it more memorable by incorporating action: you can see and hear the German standing on the mountain singing an operatic song.

3. First presidents—Washington And Jefferson Made Many A Joke [Washington, Adams, Jefferson, Madison, Monroe, Adams, and Jackson]. Picture founding fathers sitting around a table laughing.

4. Geologic time periods—Camels Often Sit Down Carefully. Perhaps Their Joints Creak. Persistently. Early Oiling Might Prevent Permanent Rheumatism. [Cambrian, Ordovician, Silurian, Devonian, Carboniferous, Permian, Triassic, Jurassic, Cretaceous, Paleocene, Eocene Oligocene, Miocene, Pliocene Pleistocene, and Recent]. Picture a creaky old camel trying to sit down carefully, with a geologist oiling their joints.

Obviously you can string small acronyms together. For example, for the 10-11 Presidents mentioned above, the first acronym could be Presidents Treasure Fun Breaks and the second and related acronym could be Lewd Jokes Give Hearty Giggles.

There is a Web site that helps you create acrostics for any situation. You just type in key words and the program spits out an acrostic (http://www.joglab.com/default.aspx).

## Use Acronyms

Acronyms are words where each letter is the first letter of a word. The letters in AARP, for example, are associated with the Association for the Advancement of Retired People. Words that are already familiar were used to create the title. The acronym thus is easy to remember, because the words they stand for are familiar. And the context of an association for retired people makes it pretty obvious what the RP stands for. The military is notorious for creating acronyms. They use so many it is almost like a language of its own.

## Check out these examples:

1. U.S. Great Lakes—HOMES [Huron, Ontario, Michigan, Erie, Superior]
2. DNA—deoxyribonucleic acid
3. RIM—cell cycle of Rest, Interphase, Mitosis
4. NASA, NATO, USDOE, etc.

In these examples, I hope you recognize how much easier these acronyms would be to memorize if you went beyond the word representation to add also visual imaging. For the Great Lakes, for example, picture your house and those of your neighbors (HOMES) floating on a lake.

Clearly, acronyms might work even better if you make up your own, because ones that you make up will be more likely to involve the associations that you most readily call to mind.

## Use Story Chains

Both examples just given illustrate the principle of using images in sequentially ordered story chains. The approach can be used with all kinds of mental images, not just those derived from sound-alikes.

## Use Peg Systems

Want a photographic memory? People who compete in memory contests seem to have such memory, but actually their basic mental abilities are not much different from those of you and me. "Memory athletes" use special mental-image association techniques that make them look like mental giants. Maybe you could become a "memory athlete" and compete in memory contests. Remember the earlier story of when I was a teenager showing off my skills to recruit members to the Dale Carnegie course?

How did I pull off such amazing feats of memorizing in 30 minutes what was on every page of a magazine? I created pictures in my mind that represented what was on each page. These pictures were associated with pictures that corresponded to page numbers. Page 11, for example, was coded as a goalpost, because 11 looks like a goal post. Then the contents of page 11 were linked in picture form to my image of a goalpost. If the page was about Elvis' childhood in Mississippi, I would picture Elvis in a cotton field on the Mississippi delta, with the cotton field laid out like a football field with goal posts at each end. Other details on the page would be plugged into this visual scene.

Peg systems involve use of one imaginary image that serves as an anchor or peg for other images that you want to remember. The peg image is something you already know from past experience or from deliberate memorization of the pegs. The memorization action requires that you stick the image representing what you are trying to remember to the peg image or you integrate both images into one. The basic idea has been implemented in several ways.

Peg systems of various sorts have been developed. No doubt you have seen or heard about people who put on stage shows of astonishing memory and win memory contests. Some people think that these experts just have natural talent. They all use peg systems, but their natural talent enables them to use peg systems more effectively than most people. It is a matter of how well they have developed their skills at imagining images.

The idea of mental pegs is attributed to Simonides, a Greek poet who lived around 500 BC. Remember, in those those days very little was written and knowledge was passed around by oral tradition. There was a high social premium placed on being able to remember well. So, it was not surprising that the ancients became expert at finding shortcuts and devices to help them memorize.

## Numbered Memory Pegs

The pegs in this system are images representing the numbers. In Chapter IV, I present a well-known coding system for memorizing numbers based on the idea of converting digits 0-9 to a consonant letter and then making a visualizable word by adding vowels. If you memorize the simple rules, it becomes easy to make up words for any number and use these words to create an image peg.

For example, the word for 1 could be "tie." Thus, whatever you wanted to memorize, in the number one position of a list for example, would be converted into an image involving a tie. For example, a grocery item, string beans, could be seen as bundling together a batch of string beans with a necktie. Now, that grabs one's imagination and makes it easy to remember string beans. This is the system I mentioned earlier that I used to wow people with my ability to memorize magazine content in a few minutes.

Here is a list of words (mostly nouns, because nouns are easier to visualize) that are gleaned from various memory-tip books. Look at these and refresh your memory of the word-forming rules.

| 1 | tie | 26 | nacho | 51 | lot | 76 | cage |
|---|---|---|---|---|---|---|---|
| 2 | knee | 27 | neck | 52 | lion | 77 | cake |
| 3 | maw (mother) | 28 | knife | 53 | lime | 78 | cave |
| 4 | rye | 29 | knob | 54 | lure | 79 | cap |
| 5 | law | 30 | mice | 55 | lily | 80 | fez |
| 6 | jaw | 31 | mat | 56 | leash | 81 | foot |
| 7 | key | 32 | moon | 57 | log | 82 | phone |
| 8 | ivy | 33 | mummy | 58 | lava | 83 | foam |
| 9 | bow | 34 | mower | 59 | lip | 84 | fur |
| 10 | toes | 35 | mule | 60 | cheese | 85 | file |
| 11 | tot | 36 | match | 61 | sheet | 86 | fish |
| 12 | tin | 37 | mug | 62 | chain | 87 | fog |
| 13 | dam | 38 | movie | 63 | jam | 88 | fife |
| 14 | door | 39 | mop | 64 | cherry | 89 | fob |
| 15 | tail | 40 | rose | 65 | jail | 90 | bus |
| 16 | dish | 41 | rat | 66 | judge | 91 | bat |
| 17 | dog | 42 | rain | 67 | check | 92 | bone |

| 18 | dove | 43 | ram | 68 | chef | 93 | bum |
|----|------|----|-----|----|------|-----|-----|
| 19 | tub | 44 | rower | 69 | ship | 94 | bear |
| 20 | nose | 45 | roll | 70 | case | 95 | bell |
| 21 | nut | 46 | roach | 71 | cot | 96 | beach |
| 22 | nun | 47 | rock | 72 | coin | 97 | book |
| 23 | name | 48 | roof | 73 | comb | 98 | beef |
| 24 | Nero | 49 | rope | 74 | car | 99 | pipe |
| 25 | nail | 50 | lace | 75 | coal | 100 | daisies |

If some of the words aren't easy for you to remember, make up your own word, just so long as it follows the number coding rules. Obviously, you can use these rules to make up image words for any number, though it can take a lot of creativity to do so.

An alternative approach is the so-called PAO system described in Joshua Foer's book.[64] PAO stands for person-action-object. The idea is every two-digit number has a mental-image representation involving a human doing something to an object. For example, 21 might be Peyton Manning throwing a football into a bowl of soup. Such images need to be vivid and weird, and, moreover, you have to rote-memorize an arbitrary action image for every number pair. The system is very effective for "memory athletes" who take the time to build such a mental library. Permutations of this system are used to memorize sequential order of playing cards or long strings of digits.

One problem, not easily solved, is how to un-remember what is on the pegs when you need to tackle a new memory challenge. After all, you use the pegs over and over again for different items. Actually, this did not seem to be a problem back when I was memorizing magazines. Memory athletes say they don't have a problem erasing peg lists when they move from one contest to another. Clearly, this system works best only for items you just want to remember for a short while, like grocery lists.

## Body-part Pegs

One peg system involves body parts: toes, feet, ankles, calves, thighs, buttocks, stomach, etc. Because you already know the body parts and their sequence, you don't even have to memorize these pegs. Memorizing a grocery list of "marshmallows, candy, peanuts, milk, squash, and beans" might be accomplished as follows: you picture marshmallows between your toes. They keep popping out as you walk and you have to stop and put them back in. Then you imagine seeing an ankle bracelet made of candy bars. You want one, but you can't have one because you would have to tear up the anklet. Next you visualize a bag of peanuts stuck in the calf-high stocking. The bag keeps banging into your other leg, and every once in a while you have to stop and put the bag back in the stocking. For the milk, you see yourself standing in a huge carton of milk, up to your thighs. You can't get out, because the top of the container is too high to reach by jumping. Every time you jump, you fall back in, up to your thighs. Next you remember squash because you see yourself sitting down on squash, squashing it with your butt. Finally, you remember beans, because you see beans (navy, naval) squirting out the navel in your stomach. Well, we could go on and on, but you get the idea. You don't need a whole book to elaborate the idea with examples, which is what most memory books do.

## Room Method

Another technique elaborated by most memory books is the room method. These are typically referred to as "memory palace." The principle is that memory is expedited not only by having information represented by images, but having those images anchored in specific locations within rooms. You use familiar objects in a room to serve as memory pegs, again creating mental images for each item to be memorized and then sticking it onto the peg. The approach can be extended to all the rooms in your house or objects in your car, or any structure.

Joshua Foer elaborated this approach and told the story of how he learned the tricks used by "memory athletes," and within one year of practice with the Palace system and other imaging techniques he became the U.S. Champion memorizer.[65]

These techniques allow "memory athletes" to do such astonishing feats as memorize the precise order of 1,528 random digits in less than an hour or memorize the sequential order of two decks of cards in less than five minutes. A memory champion from Malaysia memorized the entire 56,000 word, 1,774 page Chinese-English dictionary. Foer himself learned how to memorize the sequence of playing cards in one minute and 40 seconds, setting a U.S. competition record. Foer spent many days visiting with, as well as competing against, these memory athletes. What he learned was that he and the other memory athletes had just average memories when they didn't use their special techniques.

In the real world, there is not much of a market for memorizing long strings of digits. Nor is card counting all that useful either, given that casinos know how to deal with card counters.

The specific problem with "Memory Palace," is that you either have to have separate buildings (palaces) for each group of things you want to remember, or you have to erase all the old images to make room for new pegged images for each new memory task. Multiple palaces can produce quite a memory burden, and frequent "erasing" means that the memory is only good short-term. This may not be the best way to build lasting memory.

## Numbered Space Systems

Dean Vaughn[66] has a spatial location system that I like, based on using an imaginary numbered cube. This relies on an image of a cube, representing an empty room. Locations in the room are identified by position or number, beginning at one corner and moving around the room (wall to corner to next wall, etc.). Including the top and bottom of the cube, this gives peg anchor locations for 10 items. And if you need more than 10 items, you can create other cubes for 11–19, 20–21, etc.

You can start numbering at any point as long as you are consistent. I like to start with the wall facing me as point #1, because this is the center of the overall image. Here is an example of how I used this system to memorize a speech about writing as a career, given to an English club at Blinn College in Brenham, Texas.

Here is how I do it: I make a computer graphic template of a numbered cube and save it to use any time I want to develop a talk. Then for a given talk, I load the template in

PowerPoint and read in appropriate icons to act as pegs. For example, my writing talk was on the subject "The Who, What, Where, Why, When, and How of Writing." Icons are picked on the basis of what comes to my mind when I think of the word. For example, "who" makes me think of a hoot owl; "how" makes me think of an Indian. Many of the icons are sound-a-likes, or "audionyms." For example, for "what," I picked "hat," for "where" I picked "hair," for "when," I picked hen.

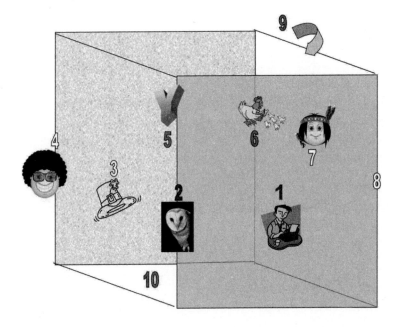

After I print out the graphic, I write in pencil beside or underneath each icon in pencil a few key words and create mental images to represent the ideas associated with those key words. When I rehearse, if I can't recall all the images for a given peg, I look at the key words and reinforce the image or make one that will work better for me.

As the talk's preface, I talk about my writing life, which I represent with the icon of a person (me) typing. Then I attached associated mental images to the real icon on the graphic (my high school, my college newspaper, a sample of my research papers, and a sample of my books). Next in the talk, I wanted to cover the topic of who do you write for. First, I discuss that a true writer writes because he must, that is he writes for himself. So I picture the owl looking at me. Then, I cover the theme that writers should know their audience and market, so I imagined the owl rotating its head as owls do to look away from me to look at a crowd of people. Well, I could go on with elaborations to the point of tedium. I assume you get the drift. The basic idea is to use images that make sense to you and associate them with your information.

After creating my mental images, I had them all memorized after about two to three rehearsals, and gave a 45 minute talk without notes and without even my hard copy of the numbered cube—not bad for somebody my age.

## Memory Image Maps

I have invented another way that may be a little better. I call it "Memory Image Mapping." Like the Palace or cube methods, it uses images anchored in specific spots, but you don't have to erase anything each time you want to learn a new set of information. The method works like this:

A memory map can be constructed from a table, similar to the kind of data tables you are already familiar with. I create a computer template file of such a table which I load whenever I need to create a new image map. An ordinary table has boxes arranged in rows and columns. The information is not in the form of numbers or text, but as images that represent numbers and text. I use clip art for most of the pictures, which I conveniently select from the huge library in Microsoft PowerPoint. In my table the images are put at the intersections of the lines so the table can hold more images. Finally, the lines are dashed so that they are less distracting. Number of cells is easily adjusted to accommodate fewer or more images. You can use the same table template for everything. Just omit images for nodes you don't need to use.

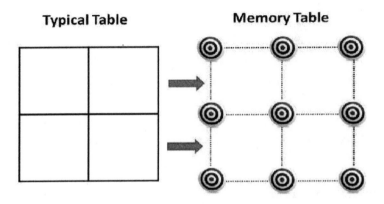

An ordinary data table (left) is laid out in blocks, with empty cells that may be surrounded by borders and data found inside the cells. A Memory Image Map has the same design, but the data go at the intersections of lines—which are target points for pictures that represent items to be memorized. The lines are dashed or otherwise suppressed to reduce distraction. Note that this design also can hold more information. In a 2x2 table, only four items can be contained inside the cells, but nine can be contained at the intersections. Note also, that the information is spatially mapped, and you would read the map in the normal reading fashion (left to right, top to bottom).

Treating items to be learned and remembered this way has the following advantages:

- Facts and ideas are more memorable if they are represented as images.
- Anchor-point targets facilitate focus, and attention is central to remembering.
- Spatial location is itself a memory aid.
- The layout directs navigation from one point to the next and can even be used to specify sequential order of the items to be memorized.

The spatial layout is central for making this mapping strategy effective for one-try learning. Although back when I was a college student I had not invented this memory-image mapping strategy, I knew intuitively that spatial layout really made remembering easier. In my lecture notes, for example, I developed a mental picture of the layout of information on each page. For example, I might know that the page contained a graphic in the top right, a data table in the center, and a cycle of chemical reactions at the bottom. This formed the starting point for self-quizzing. I would begin with generating the mental image of a page's layout, and then quiz myself on the details found in each location. Just remembering what was found in each location would often trigger my memory of the details of the graphic, the table, or the chemical cycle.

I will represent the advantages of this strategy with an example that captures the essence of the image map.

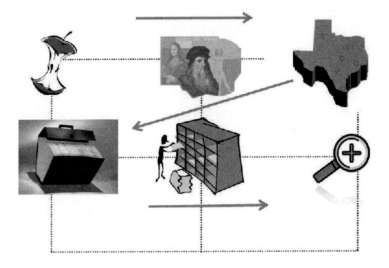

The six mapped images above represent the principles of this memory strategy. Reading left to right: 1) the focus is on core ideas. The principle is to reduce the amount of information load and memorize only what you must. 2) Facts and ideas are represented as pictures, carried in the mind's eye as mental images. The principle is that images hold a great deal of information and are much easier to remember than words or numbers. 3) Information is mapped in space. The principle is that where information is provides important cues that facilitate memory of what it is. Moreover, using the natural reading order of left to right, top to bottom, you can sequence items in an easy-to-remember order. 4) Information is segregated, with a different image acting like a file folder to capture related details. 5) Information is sorted by category. You can put related items on the same row. The principle is that when items are sorted, remembering any one will serve as cues to retrieve the others in that same category. 6) The Memory Image Map can be expanded or shrunk as needed, just by adding or subtracting the number of table cells and the corresponding points of line intersection. Note that in this example, the last three target points were not used because they were not needed.

One issue remains: how do you prevent getting multiple maps all jumbled together in your mind's eye? A learner may have many different maps for facts and ideas within a given academic course and may have maps for several courses. The problem is reduced by the very way the image maps are constructed: as a package. All items are unified inside the same map. So the trick is how to call up any one of multiple maps. The solution is to have a linking image that is so powerful it automatically pulls up the right map.

Every map you or I construct has one or more images that are very powerful and attention grabbing. We can use that image as the linchpin to connect the whole map to a cue image. For example, I give one-hour seminars totally from memory to seniors on "Eight Things Seniors Can Do to Improve Memory." The talk is imaged-mapped to a table with two rows of four images ordered left to right, and when I give the lecture, the topics are presented in that order. To recall the whole map in a seniors seminar talk, I use the first image in the map, which is a pigeon-hole mail box that I use to remind me of what to say about getting organized. The recall link for the map comes when in my imagination I stuff images of elderly people into each pigeon hole. One hole has a person and a cane, another a person in a wheelchair, another with a portable oxygen tank, etc. So, when I think of seniors, I think of this weird pigeon-hole image, and that brings up the whole one-hour lecture.

Here is how I recently used this approach to introduce a speaker (I just hate it when an introducer reads a speaker's background by reading her resume). The table was viewed on as pinned on the speaker's office door, which I see at least once every day. For each cluster of information (former positions, notable achievements, current activities, personal tidbits of interest to the audience, etc.), I represented the cluster with a relevant mental pictures and "pasted" them at each intersection point of the table. Rows in the table were set aside for a common theme (first row: former positions, second: current positions, third row: notable achievements, etc.). During my introduction, I just read off in my mind's eye the pictures from left to right.

# How to Deal with Forgetting

Forgetting is not a defect, it is a normal function. Forgetting serves to filter out information that exceeds our needs or that is no longer needed. Sometimes, forgetting serves the very useful purpose of moving on in life, leaving painful memories behind. However, many of these memories may still exist, lying dormant until the right set of cues uncovers them.

We forget more than we remember. Moreover, most of the forgetting occurs soon after learning. For example, in the late 19th century Hermann Ebbinghaus studied the recall of strings of nonsense syllables (example, xatch, obcur, votuf, etc.). Memory fell off dramatically with time after learning. Within the first few minutes, less than half of the items could be remembered. By 10 minutes later, only slightly more than one third could be remembered, and this level of error persisted out to a month after learning. Of course, in this case, the level of forgetting was magnified because these words made no sense and there was nothing to associate with them. The clutter they created in the mind created interference with memory.

Ever hear the insult, "I have forgotten more than you'll ever know"? Insult aside, we all forget an enormous amount of stuff we once knew. Why is that? Maybe it is more useful to ask, what makes things memorable? All those who were old enough at the time remember the day John Kennedy was shot. Many people say they remember what they were doing at the exact moment they heard the news. Maybe you remember the blurry image of Neil Armstrong as he stepped onto the moon. I'm sure we all remember what we were doing on 9/11 when the World Trade Center was destroyed. We remember these things because they had real impact. They were important intellectually and emotionally. They grabbed our attention and even today evoke vivid, specific imagery.

Remembering phone numbers, grocery items, and the like is hardly as gripping. However, such mundane information can be made captivating, and thus become memorable, but we have to contrive ways to make it so.

Do you remember the names of your elementary-school teachers? How about the name of the bully in middle school? Or names of your friends when you were a kid? These are all things you remembered well at one time and remembered for a long time. But you may well have forgotten by now.

Scientists like to talk about "long-term" memory, but even long-term memory has its limits. Even long-term memories have to get rehearsed once and a while or they may eventually fail to remember. Or if you do remember, there is a good chance that the memory is corrupted and not totally correct. The consequence is that things that happened long ago may be either forgotten, misremembered, or so buried that it takes a great deal of cuing to retrieve the memory.

We lose these memories because they don't get rehearsed. Typically, they don't get rehearsed because there is no need. But such loss does remind us that memories tend to decay, and if they serve a long-term need, you will need to recall them occasionally and get the memory reconstructed.

Failure to remember much about our childhood probably involves other factors too. Some faulty or incomplete memory is perhaps due to repression and trauma; this idea of repression was central to Sigmund Freud's work. But some memories can't be retrieved because you can't recall the contextual cues originally associated with the events. See for yourself: have you ever gone back to visit the home you grew up in years after moving out, peeked inside of your old elementary school, or re-visited any other significant places from your past? I recently did this went I went back to my old college, Auburn. Though most of the buildings were new or refurbished over the last 50 years, there were still so many left-over cues that I was flooded with memories of the original buildings and things that went on there. Chances are you have experienced something similar.

I believe that many childhood memories no longer exist or are false memories because the brain has re-wired itself in the process of growing up. The brain of a child is being continually built and re-built in terms of connections among neurons, the chemical and hormonal sensitivities of neurons, numbers of neurons (at least in a few brain areas), and the number of supporting cells known as glial cells. The circuitry supporting memory is continually sculpted by new experience. Such sculpting must certainly carve away some of the circuitry that had been used to support certain old memories.

# Unlock Hidden Memories

What is really irritating is to fail to recall something that you know you know when it is important to remember. Everyone is familiar with the feeling of grasping for a name or a word that, for whatever reason, is just outside your mind's reach. Students taking a quiz commonly complain that they know the answers to questions they missed, and in fact often recall the answers after they turn in the exam. Many people, even young people, have "senior moments" or "brain freeze" and even sometimes forget the name of someone they know very well.

Picture this scene: you go to a fancy dinner party and spot a very prominent person you met casually a few months ago while jogging. Now you want to approach this person and make a good impression by showing that you remember the name. But you have a brain freeze. You wanted to go over and say, "Hi, _____, remember me? We met when we ran in the 10 k at Andover last Spring." Without the name, you don't have nerve to break into her group. On the way home, after the party of course, it suddenly hits you—"Janice Hopkins! Where was that name when I needed it?"

Why was that so hard to remember? Actually you did remember it you just could not recall it on demand. And "demand" is the operative word. There are two reasons for failed recall here:

1. Anxiety/Stress—You felt pressured to remember. The subconscious mind that you rely on for memory recall does not appreciate having demands made.

2. Unusual Context—She wasn't sweating and wearing baggy running clothes. Indeed, the formal setting provided cues that interfered with recall.

Psychology professor Robert Baker 's book *Hidden Memories*[67] argues that many memories lie buried in our brain and are only brought to the surface under certain, often extreme conditions. Much of the foundational evidence comes from the many studies of Freud, who used hypnosis to uncover buried memories of early childhood. Baker points out that "accurate records of many objects and events will enter our minds completely unaware and can show up in the form of intuition, likes, and dislikes of which we are totally ignorant of their origin." He reminds us of procedural memories that have become subconscious and automatic—like the proverbial "riding a bicycle." The corollary is that we know much more than we realize and that it may affect our behavior in unrecognized ways.

Baker also discusses the fact that we have memories that we do not recognize as such. Sometimes, for example, what we think is an original idea or phrase is actually a buried memory. The déjà vu phenomenon may also reflect a past memory of an actual event that we have forgotten.

Retrieval processes are among the least understood aspects of memory. F. C. Bartlett[68] argues that memory recall is not a matter of retrieval but of reconstruction. This view helps explain several things. In a memory reconstructive process, the original event could be colored by subsequent experiences and rationalizations whose emotional impact made a lasting change to the original memory.

In the book *Between the Lines*, Robert Haskell's central premise is that subconscious memories and thoughts routinely get expressed as "subliteral" meanings in human communication.[69] In other words, much of what we say not only has an obvious literal meaning, but also a less obvious, and sometimes very different, subconscious meaning. This idea applies to body language, of course, but Haskell extends it to encoded talk. The idea is related to such euphemisms as "political correctness," "double-speak," and of course, reading "between the lines."

Retrieving memories is a kind of "mental time travel." Our brain has to go through and reactivate the neural networks that contain the representation of the original memory and its associated cues. How does the brain select among its countless representational networks the network or networks that it needs at that moment?

A leading theory for how the brain searches its memory banks is that memories are indexed by category. This would explain why categorization is so important in learning. The basic idea is that during recall, the brain uses categorical general knowledge as contextual cues for the specific memory being sought. For example, in trying to remember what you saw on a trip to a zoo, you would use your zoo category, that is, your general knowledge of the kinds of animals usually seen at zoos as cues to assist in the recall of animals that you actually did see. As specific details emerge in the recall process, these serve as further cues to refine the search.

This theory has now been tested by Sean Polyn and colleagues in a brain-scan (MRI) study of humans engaged in memory retrieval tasks.[70] Specific patterns of brain activity were associated with specific picture categories. During recall testing, these cortical activity patterns correlated with correct verbal recalls from the category normally associated with that pattern of brain activity. Moreover, the cortical activity pattern preceded by several seconds the verbalization of the correct memory response. Correctness of recall could actually be predicted by the pattern of activity that was seen just prior to recall attempt.

The most common experience of hidden memories is what we call "tip-of-the-tongue" (TOT). Failure of retrieval under TOT conditions is thought to occur when something interferes with the retrieval process.

Interference may occur before the memory is formed (proactive) or afterwards (retroactive). The original studies of proactive interference used a design in which three or four recall tests were given in rapid succession. Stimuli in each trial were similar (setting up the probability of interference). Each trial was separated by a distracter-filled interval. The material was hard to learn, but not if interference was reduced by using less distractive items.

Recall interference can even occur with well-learned material. Most readers have experienced the following problem in a meeting or conversation: You have an "agenda item" that you plan to introduce, but you get so distracted by other pressing items in the conversation that you forget to bring up your agenda item.

Retroactive interference occurs when new information, especially if it is similar to the material to be memorized, is introduced shortly after the attempt to memorize is made. Interference with memory formation is magnified by similarities between the learned material and the post-learning distracters. Some interesting examples in studies of human infants have shown that infant memories are highly vulnerable to interfering information presented while the training memory is still active (that is, before consolidation), but are resistant to interference after being reactivated (after consolidation).[71]

One leading explanation for TOT is that words of similar meaning or sound "block" the path of the word you are seeking. Recent research by Lori E. James and Deborah M. Burke suggest that TOT experiences have to do with weak connections among word sounds represented in memory.[72] The idea is that language retrieval depends on memory of both a word's meaning and its sound.

James and Burke tested the idea that sound is as important as meaning in being able to remember a word by conducting an experiment in which subjects were asked 114 general-knowledge questions. The questions were designed to elicit certain words from the subject, ones identified by the researchers as commonly-forgotten TOT words. For example, people were asked, "What word means to formally renounce a throne?" Answers (in this case, "abdicate") included proper names and other seldom-used words. For some of the trials, participants were asked to read ten priming words before the question was asked; half of these priming words shared at least one sound feature of the target word. For example, when "abdicate" was the target word, "abstract" was used as one of the priming words. When participants pronounced words that sounded similar to the target word, they were more likely to answer the question correctly—to retrieve the difficult "target word."

This research may explain why a word or name that we struggle to remember oftentimes occurs to us later, seemingly out of nowhere. These pop-ups might occur because you have just heard a word that shares a similar sound. That is, retrieval can improve when the recall task is accompanied by phonologically related words. The experimenters found this to be true for both older and younger study participants.

So, as a practical matter, how can people keep their memory recall process from getting rusty? Dr. James suggests that this is a "use it or lose it" situation. Words or names that are hard to recall become more retrievable if you use them once in a while. This would surely be facilitated if you created a new association or memory gimmick. More generally, James suggests that "People should keep using language, keep reading, keep doing crosswords. The more you use your language and encounter new words, the better your chances are going to be of maintaining those words, both in comprehension and in production, as you get older."

Another explanation for these TOT moments is suggested by research conducted by B. A. Kuhl's group who argue that that the problem is actually a failure to forget.[73] That is, you remember too many wrong things that interfere with the recall of what you want. Researchers at Stanford University recently clarified this problem by a study in which subjects were required to recall words from among many similar words that they had also seen. They viewed a succession of word pairs. A given cue word was paired with six associated words; example: ATTIC—dust, ATTIC—junk, etc. During practice and recall testing, a word cue was presented along with the first letter of the missing word in the pair. This design forced subjects to recall in the face of competing memories. For example, they might have to recall ATTIC—d (dust), even though their memories were cluttered with the other five ATTIC word pairs (ATTIC—junk, etc.). Subjects were also tested on how well they remembered the word pairs that they had seen before but not practiced.

Recall effectiveness ranged from about 30 to 80%, with better performance correlating with poor recall of those words that subjects were not supposed to remember. In other words, the better subjects could forget irrelevant information, the better they could recall what they were supposed to remember.

The key to solving the TOT phenomenon is to hit the right cue, the one connected strongly enough with what you're looking for that the association is made and the answer comes to you. But how do you do that? There's no silver bullet. One popular technique for overcoming TOT is to run through the alphabet. Sounding out letters and sounds might just trip the right switch:

"What's the name of that old cigarette-smoking actor? You know, the big famous one? A…..B…..buh…..boh…. Bogo? Beggar? Bogart! Humphrey Bogart!"

It's also a good idea to run through all the associated images or ideas that you relate to whatever it is you're trying to name. For example, I recently had to remember the first name of a graduate student I had some 30 years ago. His last name was Smith. Unfortunately, the only first name for Smith that came to mind was Stan Smith, the famous tennis player. I immediately knew this was not my Smith, and I had to force myself not to think of Stan, because that was blocking retrieval. The next step was to think of all the cues that I did remember about my Smith. I remembered what he looked like (tall, skinny). I remembered the research project we did (hypnotizing rabbits) and the details of our experiments. I soon recalled the title page of the paper we produced, which also listed both of our names. Voila! I suddenly saw his first name: Greg. The right answer just popped into my brain, no doubt triggered by all the cues. By the way, related to the "use it or lose it" idea, after telling this story enough times, I no longer have a tip-of-the-tongue problem with Greg Smith.

The Key Is In the Cue. "Oh yea, now I remember!" How many times have we done that after being given some reminder cue for a memory that we had but could not recall? The memory is there all along, but we need cues to bring them to the surface of consciousness. Why is a cue needed? First, recall that association is a key element in memory, and cues generally remind us of the original associations we used to create the memory.

## Unlock Those Memories with Cues

All sorts of things can serve as cues for recall. One perhaps unexpected source of cuing is odor. Odors may have a priming effect. David Smith at Bishop's University in Canada, compared learning in subjects that smelled either jasmine or a perfume while learning long word lists.[74] They were re-tested some time later, and one or the other odor was present during the recall testing. Best results occurred when the odor during re-test was the same as the odor during learning. This effect of odor is also an example of the so-called "state-dependent learning" that we have described in Chapter II.

Here we see how specific this effect is. It is not just having any odor present when trying to elicit recall of items learned in the presence of odor, but that the best results occur when the odor is the same in both conditions.

Endel Tulving, an experimental psychologist at Yale, has clarified the idea that memories can be enduring, even when we cannot recall them at a given moment. His explanation is that we fail to recall because a critical cue is missing.[75] Tulving and others performed simple yet elegant experiments that illustrate the point. For example, one experiment involved presenting words in pairs of closely related word (bark / dog; for example). Subjects were told that the right-hand members of each pair were the target words that they would be asked to remember during a recall test. Not surprisingly, subjects did quite well, averaging correct identification of 74% of the target words. But on another test, the subjects were given another list of words that were associated with the target words from before but had NOT appeared in the original presentation. Generally such cues failed to trigger recall of the related target words originally presented. These results suggest that recall depends on highly specific cues, even when the memory trace itself has not been lost.

## Cuing Effect on Recall

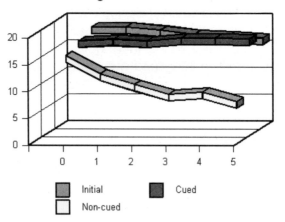

Effect on recall scores at various times after learning word lists when one category of words was followed by learning a second list prior to being tested on the first. The graph shows the disruptive influence of presenting other lists learned between presentation of the original list and the non-cued recall test. The degrading effect was not seen when recall was cued.

What this shows is that the memory was there all along. It just needed appropriate cues to trigger recall. This viewpoint does not preclude the possibility that some forgetting is due to deterioration of a memory trace. The important thing to remember is that we remember much more than we think we do and that appropriate cuing can unveil that.

## Learn to Forget

Forgetting can also be learned. This is called extinction, as was discussed in Chapter II.[76] When a memory is recalled, the memory trace may have to be re-created, during which time it can be susceptible to disruption and even erasure. Whether or not erasure occurs depends on how robust the original learning was and of course on what other events may happen during the rehearsal. Like all forms of learning, extinction involves encoding, consolidation, and retrieval.[77]

Why does this understanding matter? For one thing, extinction learning is the best available therapy for treating Post-traumatic Stress Syndrome, which is explained at the end of this chapter.

Experiments by Mark Eisenberg and colleagues[78] involving conditioned taste aversion in rats and aversive conditioning in fish show that the stability of retrieved memory depends on the behavior controlled by that memory. This study was focused the extinction of a learned behavior after removing the associations that enabled the original learning. For example, fish become conditioned to swim away when they see a light flash because they had been trained by a mild electric shock after the light flash. Then, if the mild shock was eliminated, the fish soon stopped responding to the light. They had now learned to forget the need for the aversive behavior.

For many decades scientists thought this was just simple passive forgetting or unlearning. Now, it appears that extinction is an active process, actually a form of learning to unlearn. The Eisenberg group and others have shown that extinction can be disrupted by such treatments as injection of protein synthesis inhibitors or anesthesia given immediately after retrieval. In other words, learning to forget involves the same basic biological processes as any kind of learning.

## How to Forget the Bad Things

All of us have had bad experiences we would just as soon forget. But some things are hard to unlearn. In a simple Pavlov conditioned learning situation, for example, it is relatively easy to unlearn something that has been conditioned by separating the paired cue and the learned object. Now a study of humans by A. Olsson and colleagues shows a conditioned fear response to faces from a social group different from one's own social group is more resistant to extinction than is a similarly conditioned fear response to faces from one's own social group.[79] This bias appears to be less in people who have had greater experience with the social out-group.

Social behavior may be a product of evolution. Cohesion within a like-group is promoted by built-in tendencies for suspicion toward strangers and a readiness to develop persistent fear of them. At the same time, however, such social behavior promotes inter-group prejudice and conflict. The more general point is that our biological nature makes some experiences easier to learn and harder to unlearn than others.

Some bad experiences are so hard to forget that they create the condition known as post-traumatic stress syndrome (PTSD). Traumas, emotional upset, grief—all can be more than we can bear. Some people have traumatic memories so violent and intense that their emotional and psychological health is compromised—sometimes permanently.

Psychiatrist Richard McNally's recent book, *Remembering Trauma*[80], reviews the various studies of memory effects of PTSD. Many people think that memories of horrific events are driven underground, repressed, only to surface at some later time, such as during psychotherapy or a later period of extreme stress. McNally asserts that most such claims of repressed memory are little more than psychiatric folklore that is not supported by empirical evidence.

PTSD effects can be long lasting and cumulative, and even lead to high anxiety, nightmares, and flashbacks. But what has this got to do with memory? You might argue, along the lines I have already used, that alertness and even anxiety can promote the focus and concentration that would actually enhance memory. The problem is that excessive stress and the cortisol it releases actually kill neurons. Worse yet, it kills neurons in the most important memory area of the brain, the hippocampus.

You don't have to be a combat soldier to develop PTSD. Any bad experience in ordinary daily living is a learning experience that can be remembered for a long time. Sensory cues, sometimes not even recognized consciously, can trigger recall of disturbing memories or even just the negative emotions that went with the bad event. Sometimes this is the basis for so-called "anxiety attacks."

As I explained earlier on memory consolidation, the original learning could have been disrupted by other, non-threatening events and distractions. This often corrupts the facts of the situation and magnifies the accompanying emotion. Unfortunately, the emotions of bad experiences typically get rehearsed extensively immediately after learning, and that enhances consolidation of the distressed emotional state at the time.

Anxiety disorders are among the most common mental health problems and are often treated with so-called extinction therapies. That is, therapy is geared toward unlearning our fears by deliberately re-living the disturbing event under safe conditions and thereby learning we can cope successfully.

As Pavlov's animal conditioning studies showed, if you repeatedly ring a bell and then stress a rat, it soon learns to become distressed the next time it hears that bell, even after you stop the stress. In the lab, this is manifested by the rat showing freeze behavior. But, if you repeat the bell enough times without the stress, the conditioned response (freeze behavior) eventually becomes extinguished.

At first, scientists thought that memory of the conditioned response (CR) is erased during extinction, but even Pavlov recognized that extinction is a new learning experience. Think of it as learning to unlearn. Extinction creates a new memory that competes with the memory of the original CR. Both memories co-exist. However, over time the extinction memory may be lost, and the CR can return. Presumably, the rules for effective consolidation apply to extinction learning as well as to CR learning. The implication is that, just as ordinary learning needs rehearsal, so does extinction learning.

---

**Memory Myth Buster**

*When you extinguish a memory, it goes away.* WRONG. Extinction just creates a new memory of the unlearning process. It competes with the original un-extinguished memory and may be more easily forgotten.

---

Also relevant here is that memory consolidation is greatly influenced by the psychological impact of the experience, which is magnified by strong emotion and the hormones such emotions release during stressful events.

Most phobias and emotional traumas arise from a conditioned association between a neutral stimulus and the traumatic event, much like the conditioning discovered by Pavlov and his dogs. If one repeats the conditioning cue, without re-presenting the bad event, the patient may develop a new memory in which the cue becomes innocuous because it is no longer associated with the bad event. The problem here is the extinction effect can wear off over time, because the original fear memory was more firmly established and was never erased.

Modern psychotherapy for phobias and PTSD often involves re-living the original bad event under reassuring conditions by talking about it and even writing about it. But this has to be done with conscious re-assessment and realization that the original negative emotions and fear are no longer applicable because the re-living is a simulation in a safe environment. Therapeutic strategies based on rational re-living of events have been suggested by psychiatry professor G. J. Quirk.[81]

---

**Memory Myth Buster**

*PTSD is permanent and can't be treated.* WRONG. At least it doesn't have to be. Professionally-guided "talk therapy" is helpful, and there is a new treatment involving a common blood-pressure medication that interferes with consolidation of recalled memories (see below).

---

In traditional therapy for PTSD, the bad memories are recalled in a therapy session and the therapist helps the patient re-appraise the situation and deal with the emotions. Therapy for PTSD and other anxiety disorders might be more effective if it was approached as a conventional learning experience whose memory consolidation is affected in all the usual ways.

Re-learning of an extinguished response occurs much more readily than it does for an initial extinction learning. This is an example of priming. It's like re-learning a foreign language. It goes easier the second time and the memory might be even more dependable.

Since memory of an emotional conditioned response (CR) learning experience and its extinction can co-exist, these two memories compete for which one is strong enough to survive long-term. Sadly, the original CR memory is often stronger. Cues are extremely important to both forming and retrieving memory. It seems likely that in typical human situations, there are many more explicit cues for CR memories than for extinction memories. Therapy should be aimed at enriching the number and variety of cues associated with extinction learning. So far, nobody has given that much thought.

I am not a psychiatrist, but here is an example of a therapy approach this kind of research suggests to me:

If you are afraid of heights, it could be because some frightening event happened, perhaps years ago, that involved a high place. You may not even remember what caused the fear, but clearly any high place would provide plenty of cues to trigger the memory of that original conditioned learning experience. Now, if you progressively force yourself in small steps to go to high places, under clearly safe conditions, you can learn to extinguish this memory by thinking about how irrational your fear is. For instance, walking up a staircase should not evoke fear if there is no way you can fall off. These new extinction learning experiences need to be consciously attended, rehearsed, protected from interfering stimuli, and otherwise nurtured to promote consolidation. You should strive to construct all sorts of cues that can be associated with your extinction trials. These cues should strengthen the consolidation of your extinction learning and moreover, make the extinction memory stronger and more retrievable in the face of other cues that were associated with the original CR. Like any other memory, the extinction cues and environment need to be re-experienced often at periodic intervals so the extinction memory is strengthened at the expense of the original CR that created the anxiety disorder. To promote consolidation, you may need to repeat the extinction experience several times at different times.

There is another aspect to emotional learning I explained earlier: learning to learn. It may be that if you have multiple anxieties they can generalize and "spread" to facilitate learning new anxieties. The corollary would be that learning how to promote extinction could also generalize. Obviously, for one's brain to learn how to do that, one begins with one relatively easy extinction learning task and then enhances those extinction skills by applying them to other situations. This is probably a basic reason why some people have unwittingly developed good coping skills.

A more recent approach to treating PTSD and anxiety attacks has arisen from the recent discovery that when a memory is recalled, it is then re-saved. During the reconsolidation time window, the memory becomes vulnerable to new information and interference, and can become distorted, maybe even abolished. This has great potential for practical consequences. Repeated rehearsal or self-testing may reinforce the traumatic memory, but it also opens a window of opportunity for changing the memory so that it is less traumatic.

The most popular current PTSD treatments have sprung from animal studies. For example, rat studies showed that if a tranquilizer is given within 60 minutes after a reactivation of a fear memory, the fear memory tends to be wiped out.[82] The tranquilizer did not prevent original formation of the memory when given immediately after training. The rationale is the traditional one of preventing consolidation by some interference, in this case a drug.

But there is a more practical drug treatment to interfere with re-consolidation and can help us to forget overwhelmingly stressful memories and thus reduce the stress that goes with those memories. The latest treatment being investigated by some researchers is based on using a common blood pressure drug, propranolol, which has a side effect of blocking the reconsolidation of emotions associated with old memories when those memories are recalled.

The rationale for the latest PTSD treatment is based on the well-established fact that traumatic events usually release large amounts of adrenalin in the blood. Adrenalin acts on the brain to promote memory formation and fear conditioning. Adrenalin helps you to remember the bad event and hopefully you can avoid facing that threat again by being prudent.

I recently had the chance to visit with U.C. Irvine's James McGaugh, who is a pioneer in research on stress effects on memory. One of his key findings from research in rats is that some animals show great sensitivity to stress by releasing huge amounts of adrenalin and cortisol. But other rats barely react at all. Most human studies lump all the individual data together in a group average, and that can obscure the role of individual differences. This is important, because people vary a lot in the way they respond to stress, both psychologically and in the release of adrenalin and cortisol.

Dr. McGaugh and I agree that individual differences might be the reason post-traumatic stress disorder (PTSD) occurs in some people, while other people are not so affected by the same level of stress.

Adrenaline acts on a class of molecular receptors called beta-adrenergic receptors. Certain drugs, among them propranolol, block beta adrenalin receptors and thus might theoretically disrupt fear-induced memories. Obviously, propranolol given before or shortly after a PTSD event might interfere with consolidation of the associated bad memories. Several groups have confirmed that propranolol does impair fear-conditioned memory in both animals and humans.

The people who get PTSD may well be hypersensitive and prone to release large amounts of adrenalin and cortisol. If so, screening of PTSD patients might reveal which ones will be most responsive to adrenalin-blocking therapy with propranolol, as I will elaborate later. It also suggests that screening of troops before going into battle could identify which ones are likely to need preventive medication or post-traumatic therapy. Actually, the military is very much aware of these issues. Their current emphasis is to administer helpful drugs as soon after trauma as possible.

The original clinical application of adrenalin blocking came from Roger Pitman and colleagues.[83] They conducted a double-blind, placebo-controlled study in which a single 40 mg oral dose of propranolol was given as soon as possible (within 6 hours) after a traumatic event experienced by patients who had been rushed to a hospital emergency room. Patients then continued the medication four times a day for 10 days followed by a 9 days when the dose was progressively reduced to zero.

One and three months later, patients returned for psychological testing aimed at measuring PTSD. At one month post trauma, the number of patients with PTSD in the propranolol group was almost half that of placebo controls. Not tested was the possibility that a larger dose, especially if given early or prior to the unpleasant experience, might be even more effective, since there probably is a narrow window of opportunity for the drug to be beneficial in impairing the consolidation of bad memories.

Subsequently, several other groups have shown that propranolol can be an effective therapy for some PTSD patients.[84, 85] The problem is this is a prescription drug used to control blood pressure and is potentially toxic.

---

**Memory Myth Buster**

*Drugs we take for medical problems have no effect on memory, because the drugs were developed for other purposes.* WRONG. All drugs have side effects and some of these may disrupt memory formation.

---

These studies suggest the need to optimize the memory management treatment regimen in terms of drug dose and timing of administration.

Clearly a practical problem is that people don't carry the drug around every day in anticipation of experiences a PTSD-inducing event. But, in my opinion, it is time for emergency rooms and crisis centers to start including memory-control regimens. The medical and psychiatric communities need to put more emphasis on treatment for maladaptive memory.

Under the common situation where emotional trauma has already been consolidated, the obvious treatment approach for PTSD might be to have patients recall the traumatic event later while under the influence of propranolol. Indeed, this idea is being hailed in some quarters as a possible major breakthrough in treatment of PTSD. Many positive results are being reported by physicians, and the Army is considering using this approach for combat-related PTSD. The National Institute of Mental Health is now recruiting patients for a Phase IV Clinical trial.

One obvious conclusion is that propranolol might be a good PTSD preventive drug if given before an anticipated traumatic event. For example, I wonder if military psychiatrists have thought about giving propranolol to combat troops just before they engage in battle.

Another issue that nobody seems to be asking about is the possibility that people on this kind of blood pressure medication might be suffering impairments of emotional memories that they don't want to lose. Does this drug cause a general dulling of emotions? Could it aggravate the failing memories of the elderly?

These ideas also apply to curing addictions. To circumvent the need to use a drug like propranolol to help cure drug addiction to heroin, a research team of Chinese and American scientists recently developed an extinction treatment protocol that involved only manipulation of the extinction timing. Heroin addicts who experienced drug-associated memories ten minutes before extinction training sessions had reduced craving for heroin as long as 180 days later.[86]

# Key Ideas from Chapter Three

1. Get more organized. It lowers the burden on memory.

2. Develop routines and habits.

3. Use to-do lists, sticky notes, PDAs and other similar memory aids.

4. Use the "One Minute Manager" technique of deciding in one minute what to do with every new piece of mail or paperwork (act on it, file it, or chuck it).

5. Use a calendar to post appointments and activities.

6. For work, have a tote bag or briefcase that always has in it what to take home and what to bring to work.

7. Memorize only what you can't figure out.

8. Thinking about a subject, as opposed to rote memory, is the best way to learn and remember it.

9. Learning, even if forgotten, still can have a beneficial priming effect.

10. You will remember better when consciously aware of the subtle cues present in the learning environment and situation.

11. The ability to focus is a learned skill, one that can be to improved.

12. With items in a list, pay attention more and work harder to memorize items in the middle of the list.

13. Being more attentive not only gives you a richer experience in the now, but it also increases the amount of experience you will remember.

14. Attention fades when you lose interest, and you lose interest when a learning event loses its significance.

15. Items to be learned are more difficult to learn if their rehearsal are spaced to close or too separated in time.

16. When attention is divided by multitasking, information is not registered well and thus less likely to be encoded and learned.

17. Boredom results primarily from an inability to sustain attention. Work at making learning tasks interesting.

18. You can train yourself to be more attentive.

19. You remember best what grabs your attention and things that have great impact.

20. Just because you remember doesn't mean you remembered correctly.

21. Assign importance to remembering. Expect and demand of yourself success in learning.

22. Boredom is the enemy of learning.

23. Memories are formed through associations. Make associations that serve as cues for forming memory and for its recall.

24. Do not try to memorize only by rote. Rehearsal is necessary, but rehearse by including the associations as well as the object of learning.

25. Study in short segments (10-15 minutes), then rehearse as you take a short break.

26. You can train yourself to improve memory of what you read.

27. You can train yourself to improve memory of what you hear.

28. You can train yourself to improve memory of names and faces.

29.  When someone provides directions, make a drawing, rather than trying to remember the words.

30. The first six hours after learning a movement skill comprise a window of vulnerability during which the skill can be impaired or even lost by attempting to learn a second movement task.

31. Read a lot. It helps develop powers of concentration.

32. Too many interruptions disrupt focus and can impair your ability to develop powers of concentration.

33. Memorize one thing at a time. Focus, focus, focus.

34. To remember numbers, such as dates, use the number-to-word conversion system to create word images to represent the number.

35. Create mental-picture associations for things you want to remember.

36. Information presented as sound is harder to remember for most people than when presented as visual images.

37. Use the AVENUE acronym for making powerful images.

38. You can train yourself to more easily build a vocabulary.

39. Use "sound-alikes."

40. Use story chains of a sequence of mental images.

41. Use acrostics.

42. Use acronyms.

43. Use peg systems (numbered pegs, body-part pegs, room pegs, numbered space and image maps).

44. Use flashcards, but make sure some of the self-test sessions include all of the cards, even those you think you know.

45. Often, if you can't recall what you try to memorize, remembering the associated cues will help dredge up the memory.

46. Most forgetting occurs soon after learning.

47. Rehearsal and practice can change explicit memories into more automatic implicit ones.

48. Over-loading working memory will disrupt memory formation.

49. Testing promotes learning. Do it often.

50. Our ability to think depends on memory, particularly the capacity for the short-term memory we call working memory.

51. Working memory is weak and has a capacity usually limited to four or fewer independent items.

52. Working memory capacity and IQ co-vary. Learning how to increase working memory capacity will increase IQ and thinking ability.

53. The ability to pay attention decreases as working-memory load increases.

54. Protect recent memory from interferences.

55. Multitasking is very destructive of learning and memory.

56. Multitasking is likely to reduce the brain's ability to develop concentration and thinking skills.

57. Performing working-memory tasks makes you feel good.

58. Categorize learning material.

59. Study in small chunks of material and time.

60. Rehearse frequently without distractions.

61. Engage with material to be learned to make it have more impact.

62. Thinking about how you will remember something is itself a powerful form of memory rehearsal.

63. The more you think about something the more likely its memory will be consolidated. The best rehearsal is not rote repetition, but hard thinking.

64. Practice makes perfect because it actually changes pathways in the brain that mediate the memory.

65. When using flash cards for study, self-test over all the cards in the deck, not just the ones you knew the answers to when first going through the deck.

66. Over-training can be counterproductive and interfere with recall. Don't memorize things you already know or can figure out.

67. Emotions have a profound effect on memory.

68. Long-term memories have to be rehearsed occasionally or they run the risk of being forgotten.

69. Many things interfere with recall: insufficient associations, degree of confidence, stress, other people, lack of sleep, emotional stress.

70. Tip-of-the tongue (TOT) problems are reduced by thinking of as many associational cues as you can. This includes using the alphabet and phonologically related words.

71. To overcome TOT problems, you must block out wrong information and irrelevant memories.

72. Even well-established memories need refreshing from time to time.

73. Memories can change during recall. Be careful what you do during a recall episode.

74. Post-traumatic stress syndrome can be treated by manipulating memory.

75. When you extinguish a memory, it does not go away. Extinguished memory competes with the original un-extinguished memory. Extinction memory is easily forgotten and needs rehearsal, just like ordinary learning.

# IV. LIFESTYLE EFFECTS

The theme of this chapter is that what affects the brain affects the memory. Many, if not most, of our memory limitations and problems come from behaviors that have little direct connection with memory but nonetheless have profound indirect influences. We explain in this chapter, for example, how memory is affected by thinking in general, by attitude, emotions, general health, exercise, sex, music, stress, and sleep. The chapter summaries recent research that confirms that memory is affected for better or worse by lifestyle.

## Think

Thinking is great brain exercise. Exercising the brain strengthens it. There are lots of complicated explanations, but neuroscientists have clearly established that mental activity causes neurons to grow more terminals, make more synaptic connections with other neurons, and "soups up" the neurotransmitter systems of the synapses. The opposite occurs when you reduce mental activity.

The more you exercise your brain, the more capable it becomes for all sorts of mental tasks, including memory. I see this all the time with students. When they come off of summer vacation, their mental skills are rusty. As the semester progresses, if I push them intellectually, they get sharper and more proficient at learning.

As mentioned, the hippocampus is the brain structure that promotes formation of certain short-term memories into long-term memories. The hippocampus is also the one structure in the brain that clearly generates numerous newborn nerve cells, even in adults. New cells can enhance the ability of the hippocampus to create lasting memories.

To be of lasting benefit, new neurons must survive beyond just being born. Insight into the requirements for neuron survival has come in a recent study in which rats were injected with a chemical DNA marker that allowed scientists to differentiate new cells from old ones.[87] Researchers concluded that neurons only survive if they make contact with targets. Without that stimulus, they die. The stimulus of learning provides a biochemical stimulus for forming new contacts (synapses) with other neurons, thus enabling new neurons to survive.

A reasonable practical take-home message for all of us is that we need to be learning constantly, every day, so no matter what the critical period is, we will be helping our new neurons to survive. Survival of new neurons means a greater biological capacity for learning.

## Adjust Your Attitude

Unfortunately, too many people learn the wrong things from their failures. They learn that they are the failure. Psychologist Martin Seligman wrote a magnificent book, *Learned Optimism*[88], which points out that both optimism and pessimism are learned attitudes. All humans develop an explanatory style, which they use to evaluate the causes of their successes and failures.

Seligman even has a test that measures one's explanatory style, on a scale that ranges from an optimist style (with negative events considered temporary, specific, and external) to a pessimist style (where negative events are perceived as permanent, pervasive, and personalized). Optimists learn from their weaknesses and failures because they believe them to be only temporary (i.e., can be overcome), not pervasive, but limited in scope and not inherent personal deficiencies. Optimists know they can fix what is wrong. Pessimists quit trying, because they have concluded that their shortcomings are permanent, pervasive, and characteristic of themselves. The effects of these contrasting styles clearly affect one's attitude about learning and ability to improve thinking and remembering.

The good news is that with counseling one can learn an explanatory style that is more adaptive and beneficial. The point is this: if you are motivated to develop a better memory and believe you can, you are much more likely to do what it takes to have a better memory.

## Motivate Yourself to Improve Memory

Attitudes and belief affect our memory because they affect our motivation to do the things that affect memory. The drive to work at improving memory ability can come when we experience the reward sensation that comes from fulfilling motivational drive.

Rewarding sensations make us happy. Happy experiences can generate the motivation to become a more effective learner. This can happen in a life-changing way. What you learn in association with happy occasions can become so deeply ingrained that it becomes a core part of your very being. It may even affect your sense of identity and self-esteem.

Where does motivation come from? At the brain level, motivation comes from basic drive states of seeking pleasure and avoiding pain or distress. There is a system in the brain that controls pleasure seeking, a "reward system" discovered by James Olds. I remember talking with the famous Dr. Olds when he visited my lab. I asked him how he got the original idea that caused him to test for the existence of a "pleasure center" in the brain. The answer is not to be found in his published papers, because it seems so unscientific.

He confided that he was stimulating rats through electrodes implanted in the brain to study another phenomenon that had nothing to do with emotions. One day he had a rat that seemed to like it when its brain was stimulated. The rat would stop whatever he was doing and look around as if trying to figure out where the stimulation came from. Then Olds would stimulate some more and soon saw that the rat started going to the area of the open field where it remembered getting the stimulation. The rat had learned an association between the stimulation and the place where it felt it. Because the rat kept seeking out that place, Olds correctly inferred that the rat desired the stimulation and was motivated to seek it out. Because other rats had not shown this behavior, Olds reasoned that the electrode was accidentally placed in an unintended brain area. Placing electrodes in a rat's brain is done under anesthesia, when the rat's head is held in a metal frame, and micromanipulators guide the placement of the electrode. Electrode location error can be as much as one millimeter or more in any direction. In a brain as small as a rat's, electrodes sometimes end up in the wrong place and cause a major unexpected behavioral effect. Olds was anxious to know where this misplaced electrode was because it must have been in a previously undiscovered "pleasure center" of the brain. He examined the brain microscopically, revealing that the electrode was in the lateral part of the hypothalamus.

A more formal test for a possible pleasure center was soon pursued. Olds now rigged rats with electrodes deliberately placed in the lateral hypothalamus and trained them to press levers. But instead of pressing levers to get a food reward, each lever press brought the rats a mild electrical stimulation in the brain's hypothesized "pleasure center". The rats learned this new association quickly and worked the levers feverishly to stimulate their brains. Some rats worked themselves to exhaustion. As a control test, Olds did not see this effect when repeating these experiments in other rats with electrodes in other locations.

So, how do we relate this to memory? The experiments tell us that there are brain systems that cause us to seek pleasure and avoid discomfort. These seeking and avoiding drives create motivation. Reward is also important for memory in a way that is more direct than merely making us more motivated. Animal studies show that rewarding the desired memory recall actually strengthens the relationship between stimulus and learned response. Recall the earlier explanation of operant conditioning of work and show animals. Thus, I assume human learning can be enhanced by rewarding correct recall. This may be one reason, for example, why good students tend to remain good students. They have learned to provide themselves with intrinsic rewards for good performance. Poor students often do not find learning rewarding in and of itself. Maybe poor students would do better if they used rewards to shape improved school performance, much like we use operant conditioning to shape the behavior of trained animals.

## If You Want to, You Will

Attitude about memorizing largely determines memory ability. Most of us, for example, have trouble remembering names—not so with salespeople. They remember names well because they NEED to. It is part of their job, their bread and butter. Effective salesmen build rapport with potential customers; they know that, to most of us, our own name is the most pleasing sound in the English language. We appreciate and react positively to near strangers who remember our name.

The point is: if you are motivated to learn, you are much more likely to succeed, whether that learning involves people's names, foreign languages, mathematic equations, or whatever.

---

### Memory Myth Buster

*You are stuck with the learning ability you have. You are born with a talent for it or not.* WRONG. This entire book provides the evidence that you can improve your ability to learn and remember. If you don't believe it at this point, I am sure your belief will change by the time you finish reading.

---

## Belief about Learning Ability Becomes a Self-fulfilling Prophecy

If you think you are not a good learner, you probably aren't. But it is not just a matter of self-awareness. If you have convinced yourself that you'll never be able to learn better, you won't take the necessary steps to improve your cognitive skills.

Loss of faith in learning ability is a common problem in seniors, for they have been told to expect mental decline, and of course there is an element of truth to that. But a recent study of memory in the elderly provides strong evidence that stereotypical beliefs about losing memory with age may actually cause poor memory, and changing one's beliefs can change your mental ability.

Earlier investigators noticed that older people do NOT have poor memories if they live in cultures (such as China) where the elderly are considered wise.[89] Knowing this fact prompted researchers to discover that memory of Americans could be manipulated in people age 60 and older by manipulating their beliefs about their own memory skills.

The manipulation involved creating a bias about memory ability. Researchers flashed words and phrases designed to subconsciously prime the subjects' brains to hold either a positive view of the elderly (i.e. "wise," "sees both sides of an issue," etc.) or a negative view (i.e. "forgetful," "becoming senile," etc.). Both before and after the intervention, subjects were given three different kinds of memory tests that are known to assess the kinds of memory decline that occur in old age.

Test results revealed a correlation between memory performance and the conditioned bias. Compared to the results of their preliminary memory tests, subjects primed with negative connotations saw their scores drop while subjects primed with positive connotations saw their scores rise.

In any case, it was clear that implicit priming with positive ideas of old age was effective, despite the fact that all the priming was done in one training session. The implications for real-world memory performance are clear: changing your attitude changes your performance! Believing makes it so. More correctly, believing motivates us to do the things that will make it so.

Memory "athletes," who not surprisingly are not elderly, also maintain that confidence is crucial to their success in memory contests. Since they can't always know what the tasks will be in a given contest, they use memory exercises and techniques that give them a greater sense of confidence in their overall cognitive ability.

---

### Memory Myth Buster

*Older people generally experience substantial memory decline as they age.* WRONG. This is not true for elderly living in cultures where age is venerated, or for most elderly who have a positive attitude about their memory ability.

---

## Control Your Emotions

Sigmund Freud made a living and became famous by showing that repressed memories, buried deep within the subconscious, can cause emotional disorders. Freud showed that the most defining period of human development is early childhood, our memories of which—conscious or repressed or distorted—stir our emotions even into old age. These memories influence belief systems and ways of thinking.

A close association between emotions and memories should not be surprising. Both are regulated by the same parts of the brain, collectively called the limbic system, which includes the hippocampus. The brain areas comprising this system are intimately interconnected. One part of this system, the amygdala, is especially involved in the emotions of fear and aggression. Another part, the hypothalamus, controls our viscera and is involved whenever emotions are "read out" into the viscera in such forms as sweaty palms, dilated pupils, ulcers, and high blood pressure. All of these functions, from behavior to physiological functions, have learned components.

## Sex and Memory

One of the most fundamental aspects of emotional effects on memory involves sex. It is hard to speak of Freud without speaking of sex. Freud had a lot to say about sex, but not much about sex and memory, other than the repression of memories involving sex. What I want to stress here is that sexual hormones do influence memory.

Over forty years ago I published several studies on memory in rats which showed that both female and male sex hormones enhanced memory while sex hormone deficits impaired it.[90]

A little reflection should reveal to us the influence of sex hormones on memory. For example, during menopause—

when the production of sex hormones decreases markedly—some women experience forgetfulness or confusion. The sudden drop in estrogen is the cause. Gradually the brain adjusts to this new hormonal environment and things stabilize; some women use hormone replacement therapy to remedy a perceived deficit.

Lack of estrogen also has an indirect effect on memories by causing depression. Some of this research is reviewed in the book, *Committed to Memory*.[91] One study of post-menopausal women showed an impaired recall thirty minutes after short prose selections. When these women were put on estrogen replacement therapy, they did markedly better. Another study showed that subjects taking estrogen performed slightly better on memorizing names and word lists. The estrogen effect is probably related to the fact that it stimulates the growth of neuronal junctions by promoting the release of a protein called nerve growth factor. But estrogen also has a more direct neurochemical effect. Many neurons in the brain have estrogen receptors. When bound with estrogen, these receptors cause the neurons to behave differently.

Similar hormone-related memory problems also occur in older men. In a study of healthy older men, twenty-five men were given 100 mg injections of testosterone for six weeks.[92] The men showed improvements in spatial memory and in verbal memory. Maybe the hairy knuckles and male pattern baldness promoted by excess testosterone also signal men who have above-average memories.

Unfortunately, both estrogen and testosterone have serious side effects (including promoting cancer). People with normal sex hormone levels should not take sex hormone medication.

## Nervous Nellie Often Forgets

We all know people who claim they are not good test takers because they get so anxious that they can't remember things which they actually know. There may be an element of face-saving here, but it is true that anxiety can interfere with memory.

Worse yet, this is a learned behavior that gets reinforced every time it occurs. In other words, our emotions can be conditioned, much like Pavlov's dogs. Such conditioning can be created for a variety of emotions: anxiety, stress, depression. The good news is that repeated association of rewarding events helps us to learn positive emotions, such as self-confidence or happiness.

Anxiety is a form of fear. Our distant ancestors could not have survived the rigors of a dangerous world without a healthy daily dose of fear—and they had to learn from and remember these fearful experiences. It is therefore no accident that animal and human brains link the functions of fear and memory in the same neural structures, in particular the hippocampus, the amygdala, and the structures with which they most directly connect.

The amygdala is particularly relevant to fear memories. The amygdala is a pair of grape-sized clusters of neurons buried deep under the cortex that lies underneath our temples. The amygdala's most important role is to subconsciously process fear and to make fearful things more memorable. Because the processing is subconscious, the amygdala also unfortunately perpetuates irrational fears and phobias.

Fear can be profound and debilitating. All sensory inputs pass through the amygdala. For instance, odor inputs go directly to the amygdala and nowhere else. No doubt that is why odors are so inextricably linked with emotional reactions.

Although anxiety is reduced by tranquilizers, sedatives, and many other drugs, such drugs promote amnesia, whether the drugs are taken just before or just after the learning event.

One research group conducted a formal test of the hypothesis that at least low-level anxiety might be good for memory.[93] They performed their experiments on rats that they had pre-selected into three test groups based on the anxiety levels they showed in an anxiety test. Anxiety level was tested by putting rats on an elevated maze, part of which had no walls. The most anxious rats avoided the open arms of the maze, where they probably feared falling off. Some rats were just the opposite and apparently loved the adventure of exploring out on the more dangerous maze arms that had no walls.

There were also two learning tasks. One was a passive avoidance task where the rats had to remember not to leave a brightly lit chamber to enter a dark chamber. Normally, rats prefer darkness, but not when it is associated with punishment in the form of mild electrical shock to their feet. The other learning task was a two-way avoidance task in which the rat had to leave whatever side of the chamber it was in whenever a warning sounded. Failure to leave right away would result in punishment. When the experimenters re-tested the rats after the learning experience for their ability to remember, they observed that a little anxiety actually improved memory.

Time (in seconds) that rats stayed in the safe side of the chamber in a passive avoidance memory task. Note that the best memory was seen in rats that had been pre-selected for their anxiousness.

# Mild Anxiety Helps Memory

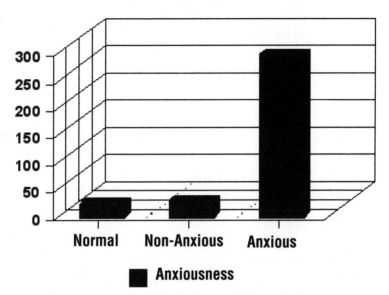

**Anxiousness**

Anxiety promotes release of adrenalin, and as was mentioned in the previous chapter, makes rats (and people) more attentive, which would magnify the registration of the learning cues. Many experiments have shown that post-training injection of adrenalin enhances memory in a variety of learning tasks. Indeed, as discussed for Post-traumatic Stress Syndrome, the adrenalin release during emotionally stressful situations is a main reason that the emotional memories are so hard to extinguish. Likewise, single post-training injections of other stress-related hormones, such as ACTH, vasopressin, and cortisone, can improve memory. But don't get excited about the idea of new memory-improving pills: ACTH or vasopressin don't survive the digestive tract and blood-brain barrier, and cortisone and adrenalin have too many bad side effects. Know also that in the study only one level of anxiety and stress condition was involved.

Clearly, memory performance could be made worse by too much anxiety and stress. Anecdotally, humans do seem to perform better under manageable stress levels, but their performance deteriorates under too much stress.

Chronic stress is especially bad for memory. Continual release of adrenal cortex hormones can kill neurons, particularly neurons in the key memory center of the hippocampus. These hormones include commonly used drugs such as cortisone and hydrocortisone. They are taken orally or by injection for severe allergies and a variety of other conditions. Physicians are supposed to prescribe these cautiously because of their undesirable side effects.

In one study, the researchers compared the effects of a single dose of cortisone versus repeated doses in adult humans.[94] Memory testing consisted of a paragraph recall task. While the single dose in the steroid-treatment group had no memory effect, recall became clearly impaired by the seventh post-treatment day. In the placebo group, recall progressively improved due to the practice effect.

Stress early in life is well known to cause multiple changes in intellectual capability and in responsiveness to stress that last into adulthood. One recent experiment on neonatal rats is particularly interesting because it relates to some things we have said about habituation (learning to unlearn) and about false memory. In this experiment[95] two groups of young rats were tested for social learning; one group had been regularly introduced to stimulating new environments as newborns, while the other group had not. When tested as adults, the rats that were used to strange new situations learned to recognize and remember an unfamiliar rat much more efficiently than the rats who had stayed in their cages—their recognition lasted over twenty-four hours, compared to two hours for the control group.

We see the effects of social learning in our pets. For example, dog trainers are well aware of the need to socialize young puppies lest they develop behavioral disorders as adults. You can see how all this could apply to young children. Lifetime coping strategies for complex social situations can be promoted by non-threatening social experience.

Why is it a good thing for the young to receive frequent stimulation? For one thing, learning to unlearn has benefits such as increased willingness to explore new experiences and learn new things. For early-socialized humans, it might mean that they are less likely to limit new learning. Babies should be socialized early, because this will reduce the learning of inflexible habits, biases, prejudices, and a small view of the world. Babies should receive lots of stimuli (mobiles, etc. over their cribs), but also they should be taken out of the crib often to get outside stimuli. Stimuli should provide hands-on engagement, not just passively seeing things. Newborn babies should receive novel stimuli under non-threatening conditions. The effects may last a lifetime.

## Music Stirs the Emotions. Emotions Stir the Memories

Another key aspect of emotion effects on memory is the influence of music. Remember what I said earlier about the problematic practice of students listening to music while they studied. But, numerous anecdotal reports suggest that stroke or dementia patients benefit from listening to music.[96] For example, Everett Dixon, a 28-year-old stroke victim, apparently learned after the stroke to walk and use his hands again from daily listening to the kind of music he had learned to like. Ann Povodator, an 85-year-old Alzheimer's patient, perks up when she listens to her beloved opera and Yiddish songs. Her daughter says, "It seems to touch something deep within her."

Caregivers commonly report that stroke or dementia patients can recall and sing songs from long ago, even when most other memories are lost. Moreover, the music can help retrieve memories that were associated with the music, not just the music itself.

Formal music therapy programs are sprouting up. Best known is the non-profit Institute for Music and Neurologic Function, directed by Concetta M. Tomaino, who lives in Garrison, New York. The Institute claims music can help premature infants gain weight, autistic children communicate, stroke patients regain speech and mobility, surgical patients alleviate pain, and psychiatric patients relieve anxiety and depression. The most effective music for adults seems to be that which the patients experienced and liked in their youth. Few of these observations come from controlled studies that rule out the possibility the improvement was going to occur anyway without the music. Nonetheless, there are apparently 5,000 certified music therapists in the U.S.

As for recall of already formed memories, listening to your favorite music will at a minimum improve emotional state, particularly in relieving stress. This alone can facilitate memory. Depression, anxiety, and stress are well known inhibitors of both memory formation and memory retrieval. Being happy not only feels good, it is also good for memory. For a good book on how to be happy, read Dr. Lyubomirsky's book, *The How of Happiness*.[97]

## How to Cope with Stress

I mentioned earlier that stress causes release of adrenalin, which helps cement bad experiences into memory. But stress also releases the hormone cortisol, and too much cortisol can impair memory by destroying synaptic connections among neurons.[98] Thus, it was no particular surprise when researchers found that stressed people performed worse than controls on delayed-recall memory tests of line-drawings and a spatial memory maze test.

Under some conditions, even mild social stress can impair memory. Maybe you have noticed that memory seems to fail you under situations where you would be embarrassed if you forgot—as in introducing a friend at a party. One study of young adult humans, for example, showed the stress hormone cortisol impaired immediate recall of stimuli that induced positive or neutral emotions (recall of induced negative emotions was not impaired by the hormone).

In another study, memory of stimuli that evoked emotions was impaired by cortisol.[99] Young healthy men were tested for their ability to recall lists of 10 positive, 10 neutral, and 10 negative words. The men were given two minutes to learn the lists and were then tested immediately. Thirty minutes later they were given a psychosocial stress which included a fictitious job interview in front of live interviewers and counting backwards in steps of 17 in front of judges. Control groups did a five-minute speech and did the same counting, but not in the presence of judges. The next day, subjects were tested again (delayed recall) 10 minutes after cortisol injection. Researchers also measured cortisol in the saliva at several key points in time.

The stressed group had elevated cortisol levels even though the stress was mild. Recall of both negative and positive emotionally arousing words was impaired, but there was no effect with neutral words. These effects could not be attributed to decreased attention or working memory span, which memory tests showed were not affected by the stress. Providing cues for recall eliminated signs of the stress effect on emotionally charged words.

Imagine how great the deleterious effect of stress could be in situations where there is real stress, as in witnessing car accidents, crimes, or dangerous situations in which recalling what happened could be very important. Studies like this are consistent with many real-life observations with eye-witness accounts, where what is remembered may well be false.

A recent brain-scan study of aged humans with a history of chronic stress showed they had a shrunken hippocampus. In older people, the amount of cortisol in their blood correlates with the brain-scan evidence of shrinkage of the hippocampus.[100] Cortisol levels in these people were monitored once each year for 5-6 years. Subjects varied considerably in the extent of their stress, as indicated by cortisol levels and also by psychological test measures of stress. People with high cortisol levels that increased each year had nearly half the memory performance capability of the people with moderate levels of cortisol that decreased each year.

Stress consequences are especially notable in older people, because they have accumulated a lifetime of stresses. The learning ranges from negative (developing hypersensitivity to stressors) to positive (mastering coping skills). Recall the study above, where some older people became more stressed with each passing year, while others became less so each year. How much memory deficit will occur as one ages could depend on how much life stress has been endured and how one has learned to react to stress. Reducing stress should not only make for better living but also better memory.

As a senior citizen myself, I am increasingly aware that aging has its own set of stressors. I know too that stress of earlier years can linger and magnify as the years go by. Have I learned to cope or to become hyper-reactive? Learning how to reduce stress can help sustain good memory capability in old age, not to mention making life more enjoyable.

## Stress-coping Strategies

It is easy to say "relax, don't worry." But doing it is no trivial matter. Coping strategies include:

- Take charge and manage your life.
- Simplify. Get organized (see Chapter III).
- Within one minute, dispense with every piece of mail or paperwork (i.e. file it, throw it away, or act on it).
- Do first things first. Don't procrastinate.
- Manage your calendar. Learn to say "no."
- Plan to avoid stressful situations.
- Students: spread learning out, don't cram.
- Businesspeople and professionals: make realistic risk assessments, diversify, master your craft; network, have a "Plan B."

- Elderly: automate the really important things (taking medicines, immutable locations for keys, purse, etc.).
- Control self-talk, self-attitudes.
- Be aware of and reject irrational or negative thoughts.
- Challenge your emotions with facts and reason.
- Be a glass-half-full person, not a glass-half-empty person.
- Consider alternative ways to view stressful situations. Look on the bright side!
- Focus on things that are not stressful.
- Relax.
- Exercise vigorously.
- Do yoga or meditation.
- Visualize soothing scenes (beach, mountains, etc.).
- Stop and smell the roses.
- Laugh—watch your favorite comedy movies or TV shows, find a funny website, or talk with a friend who makes you smile

## Teenage Angst Is Bad for the Brain

It is not just seniors who have to worry about the memory consequences of stress. Remember being a teenager?—All the stresses of dating, parents, bullies, frustrated attempts to be popular, and your grades? It seems that adolescence is an especially vulnerable time. The human brain undergoes great anatomical and biochemical change during the highly stressful adolescent and teen years. Brain scans show that the human cerebral cortex loses grey matter during adolescence, maybe because of stress-induced cortisol.[101] The effect is more pronounced in males than females. Until now, the reason for brain tissue loss has not been clear, but now we may be able to explain it by looking at the stresses that afflict teenagers.

## Lighten up! Feeling bad makes your memory bad, too

It is easy, almost natural, to get depressed in this modern world of increasing concerns, confusion and conflict. And bad memory seems to go with the territory. For example, in the aftermath of the 9/11 attacks, many people remembered watching both planes strike the World Trade Center Towers on television. The problem is, on that morning there was no video of the first plane hitting; only the second crash was filmed. Notably, they remembered the disaster well— it is now indelibly stamped on everyone's memory. But the associated details were not remembered well. Clearly, the emotional distress of the attack corrupted memory, which leads us to consider the role of bad emotions on memory.

In Chapter II, I explained "state-dependent learning," and here I want to remind you that recall is more effective if it is performed under the same mental states that were present during the initial learning. Our emotional states influence memory because they are full of cues that include not only physical settings (room, climate, scenery, etc.) but also the emotional and physiological symptoms of the state in which learning occurred. Gordon Bower at Stanford, for example, showed that memory retrieval is also mood dependent.[102] In one study of this matter, seventeen college students kept week-long diaries of their emotions. They were then put through hypnosis and suggestion exercises designed to promote either happy or unhappy states of mind. After mood manipulation, students were tested on their ability to recall events from their diaries. Happy students remembered more of the pleasant incidents in their diary. Unhappy students remembered more of the sad and unpleasant incidents. Observations like these also illustrate why states of depression are so persistent. Mood acts like a filter when recalling memories. Depression primes us to remember things in a worse light, thus reiterating and deepening the depressive state. The corollary point, however, is that optimism is self-reinforcing, too. This is why modern depression therapy often involves checking our emotional biases and revisiting past events in a calmer, more objective way.

Sadness and depression also seem to interfere with memory capability in general. A team of researchers at the University of Michigan School of Nursing published a study showing difficulties with short-term memory and concentration can be signs of clinical depression. The chief investigators, Reg Williams and colleagues had noticed depressed patients often complained of poor memory and inability to concentrate. One patient could even predict her own bouts of depression when she started making errors in her checkbook.[103]

The research used a series of computer-based and written tests to measure the ability to focus on a task at hand and short-term memory, in this case, the ability to recall an event that happened within two minutes. People in the depressed group performed more poorly on a task of balancing a checkbook. The depressed group was undergoing drug therapy and counseling at the time, and their scores on the checkbook balancing task reached the same level as controls at the end of therapy.

In another study, J. M. Strang and colleagues[104] compared five measures of working memory ability in 26 patients diagnosed with "Gulf War Syndrome," 55 clinically depressed patients, and 40 healthy subjects as controls. Both the GWS and depressed patients had an equal degree of impairment on digit-span ability and the ability to recite months of the year backwards. Depressed patients had even greater impairment than the other two groups in the other three measures of working memory.

Yet another study has confirmed the relationship between depression and poor memory. This study was especially useful because it also examined the role of anxiety. In their test of memory performance in 3,999 Vietnam-era veterans, those with clinical diagnoses of depression (without anxiety) had impaired immediate recall of new information. However, long-term retention and recall were not impaired. Veterans whose neuropsychological tests showed them to have high levels of anxiety were impaired on all aspects of memory tested: immediate recall, total amount of information acquired, longer term retention, and retrieval. The memory impairment of veterans with depression was magnified if those veterans were also chronically anxious.

Depression creates a vicious cycle of poor memory, as numerous studies have documented. Clinically depressed people—those with profound, sustained periods of depression—have a bias for remembering negative events, especially events that involved them. Thus, the depression is continually reinforced by remembering bad things. Nondepressed people generally have the opposite bias: they tend to remember positive events that involved themselves.

## Don't Over-eat to Compensate for Unhappiness

They don't call certain foods "comfort foods" without reason. Most of us like sweets and salty food. We also tend to eat foods that are associated with happy memories and avoid foods for which we have unpleasant memory associations. These effects are often subconscious.

Remember how you hated broccoli (or eggplant, or okra, or whatever) when your mother tried to convince you it was good for you? A marketing professor at the University of Illinois, Brian Wansink, has studied how people come to identify certain foods as "comfort foods" and develop a preference for them. Through interviews all across the country his team learned nearly 40% of the foods that people defined as comfort foods were not selected because they "taste good." This range of foods deemed as comforting, yet not particularly tasty, included things such as soup, certain main dishes, and even certain vegetables.

Such foods were commonly associated with happy childhood memories. All of us probably remember the warm comfort given by chicken soup on days when we had bad colds or when our stomachs were so upset that chicken soup was all that we could hold down. No wonder we develop a certain degree of affection for such foods. I remember as a 3-year-old falling in love with Grandma's pies, which had as much to do with Grandma as it did the pies.

In Wansink's survey,[105] the favorite comfort food was ice cream. But second and third choices differed between men and women. Women named chocolate and cookies as their second and third-favorite choices, while men selected soup and pizza or pasta. Age was also a factor. People 18 to 34 preferred ice cream and cookies, while people 34 to 54 preferred soup or pasta, and those older than 55 named soup and mashed potatoes.

These differences in food preferences were generally related to past memories and to personality identification. When asked to explain why a certain food was preferred, responses typically indicated some kind of comforting emotion: "My father loved green bean casserole" ... "My mom always gave me soup when I was not feeling well" ... "We kids always got ice cream after we won baseball games."

Sugar-containing foods can enhance memory. Paul Gold at the University of Virginia performed a study where human volunteers listened to an audio-taped prose passage and then drank a glass of lemonade sweetened with either sugar or saccharine.[106] Twenty-four hours later, participants were asked to recall the prose that they had read the day before. The sugar drinkers came up with 54% more information than the substitute sugar controls. We don't know why this effect of real sugar occurred. The blood sugar level is normally regulated so well that a spoonful of sugar should not cause a spike in blood sugar levels. Maybe the positive emotions associated with sugar helps the memory. Most people think sugar tastes better than saccharine.

So what is the take-home message here? If comfort foods reinforce happy memories, maybe you should reward yourself with comfort foods when accomplishing serious or difficult learning tasks.

## Avoid Violence, Even the Vicarious Kind

Few things are as emotional as violence. Movies and media promote violence because it grabs people's emotions. But entertainment producers are shooting themselves in the foot by putting so much violence in the programs. It turns out violence makes it more difficult for viewers to remember the commercials![107]

After conducting three experiments involving college students, psychologist Brad J. Bushman of Iowa State University found that watching violent television programs impaired a person's ability to remember what was being advertised during the commercials.[107] The first experiment tested 200 students (100 male and 100 female) for their ability to recall the brand names of items from two commercials advertising Krazy Glue and Wisk laundry detergent after watching a violent or nonviolent film clip. Those who watched the violent clips recalled fewer brand names and commercial message details than did those who watched the nonviolent clips.

A second experiment tested another 200 students (100 men and 100 women) on brand recall, commercial message details and visual recognition of the brand marketed in the commercial. These students were also given a distracting task where they had to recall other glue and detergent brands immediately after watching a violent or nonviolent video. The results match those of the first experiment. Those watching the violent videotape performed more poorly on recalling the brands, remembering the commercial messages, and visually recognizing the brands from the slides.

We can't say for certain why watching violence impairs memory. But we should not be surprised that it does, either. Even vicarious violence stirs strong emotions, such as anger and fear. Emotions are governed by the same part of the brain, the limbic system, as is the formation of declarative memories. The message to advertisers is to pay attention to the potential emotional impact of the shows they sponsor.

Operating at the same time may be an interference effect on working memory. Engaging in vicarious violence may so dominate thinking it is interfering with registration and consolidation of other information. So, I challenge somebody to demonstrate that violent entertainment helps viewers remember ads, especially in a positive way.

# Take Care of Your Body

Brain and body are not independent. What affects one affects the other. This is especially true in matters of health.

## Get Aerobic Exercise

The idea that exercise might benefit memory originally came from animal research revealing that exercise increases learning and memory capability, presumably because exercise stimulates the birth of new nerve cells in the hippocampus, the part of the brain that is crucial for forming long-term memory. Animal experiments show that exercise can even trigger new neurons in the aged.[108]

It is now clear exercise benefits memory capability in humans too, both old[109] and young.[110] In addition, the state of exercise is tied to memory; that is, state-dependent memory can be demonstrated with exercise. For example, in a study of humans exercising on a bicycle, word lists learned during the exercise were recalled best during another exercise episode, while words learned not riding on a bike were recalled best under that same condition.

Even simple walking is helpful, as University of Illinois professor Arthur Kramer and colleagues have shown.[111] In a study of 124 sedentary subjects, aged 60 to 74, he showed that their memory abilities improved when a regular program of walking was conducted for only six months. The regimen consisted of walking 30–60 minutes per day, three days per week. No such improvement was seen in control groups that performed stretching or weight lifting exercises. Apparently, it is the aerobic nature of the exercise that does the trick. So, for a better memory (and heart), get that heart pumping!

It is not clear how aerobic exercise helps within only six months. Certainly, cardiovascular function can be improved in that time (I know that from my own jogging experience), but there is no evidence that circulation in the brain is improved. One thing we know for sure: exercise relieves stress and anxiety, and that alone can help memory.

## Can Exercise Help Kids Do Better in School?

Even when I was a kid, which was long before the whole notion of aerobic exercise, people said that being physically active could help you perform better in school. It was a kind of folklore, with very little research evidence. Now there is evidence. Sadly, it may have come too late: many schools have done away with or minimized physical education.

The same University of Illinois research team just mentioned reported a study on the effects of exercise on the cognitive function of children aged nine to ten. They administered some stimulus discrimination tests and academic tests for reading, spelling, and math. On one day, students were tested following a twenty-minute resting period; on another day, students walked on a treadmill before testing. The exercise consisted of twenty minutes of treadmill exercise at 60% of estimated maximum heart rate. Mental function was then tested once the heart rate returned to within 10% of pre-exercise levels. Results indicated improved performance on the tests following aerobic exercise relative to the resting session. Tests of brain responses to stimuli suggested the difference was attributable to improved attentiveness after exercise.

Note this is just from a single aerobic exercise experience. How can that be beneficial? The most obvious explanation is that exercise may generate more blood supply to the brain, but blood supply to brain is well regulated, no matter what. Another possibility is the one given above for adults: exercise relieves anxiety and stress, which are known to disrupt attentiveness and learning.

## Control Your Addictions

Addiction to drugs, sex, gambling, and other compulsions provides another example of state-dependent learning in that learning consists of an inextricably linked constellation of cues and associations. Those readers who are cigarette smokers or former smokers are very familiar with the context of smoking: after waking up, with morning coffee, having drinks with friends, after dinner, etc. When one is trying to quit smoking, the common situations in which smoking has occurred over the years become an obstacle. The pleasure of smoking is also associated with the situation in which smoking occurs.

When addicts take drugs, they not only reinforce their memories of the pleasurable effect of the drugs but also they have an associated memory of the place and conditions associated with the drug taking. Drug addicts in rehabilitation programs are warned to stay out of their old environments, and to avoid as much as practical the people and places they associate with drug use. Going back to the same friends, same neighborhood, same shops and hangouts will greatly increase the odds that the addict will go back on drugs.

Addictions, of whatever sort, have a huge learning component. Addiction begins with learning a habit and its associated perceived rewards. At some point, the addiction may progress from learning in the brain to "learning" of biochemical systems of the body.

Many scientists agree with S. E. Hyman[112] that addiction to drugs and compulsive behaviors are notoriously persistent even in the face of great effort to change. All addictions have a strong memory component that includes not only remembering how good it feels initially and also to satisfy the craving, but also memory of the addictive behavior's numerous associated environmental cues (context, people, places, paraphernalia, etc.). Too much or too powerful a memory of these things can overwhelm efforts to abstain.

The rewarding properties of addictive substances or behavior are mediated by the release of the neurotransmitter dopamine in the brain. Dopamine release can thus be thought of as the common currency for valuing a variety of positive reinforcers. Memory of past reinforcers uses that same currency. Curing the addiction is promoted not only by finding substitute reinforcers but also by extinguishing the memories of addiction. Therapies for addiction should therefore take both ideas into account.

Dopamine seems to lie at the heart of obsessive-compulsive disorders (OCD). OCD is a human behavioral disorder characterized by intrusive thoughts and obsessions and frequent, repetitive ritualized behaviors (such as hand-washing or counting) meant to alleviate these anxious thoughts. Examples include compulsive gambling, obsession with pornography, and bulimia. You can think of such behaviors as addictions, and they share some of the same brain mechanisms. For example, the dopamine neurotransmitter system is involved in addiction, and many experiments show similar dopamine involvement with compulsive lever pressing in rats.[113]

A key way to think about addictions is that they develop because the person is getting addicted to the reinforcing properties of certain neurotransmitters such as dopamine (but also norepinephrine and serotonin). All of us are addicted in one way or another. Destructive addictions need to be treated. Part of any treatment regimen involves substitution. That is, substitute healthy reinforcements for destructive ones. This is how I helped learn how to stop smoking —the endorphin release from jogging substituted for the reinforcement properties of nicotine (not to mention the fact that it's hard to smoke and jog at the same time). This is why "Alcoholics Anonymous" programs are about as effective in curing alcoholism as are medical approaches—uplifting psychology and spirituality can provide similar pleasant feelings, which replace the need for alcohol.

Drug abuse is the most destructive addiction. The addiction often begins because the user has some kind of emotional problem or need that the drugs seem to alleviate. I once taught a seminar course in drug abuse in which I began each semester with the rhetorical question, "What is the mental illness that drug abuse is supposed to cure?" The hope was that students would become introspective enough to recognize their emotional problems and deal with them through rational analysis rather than with pills.

This is the kind of question we as a society ought to ask. Often nobody knows the answer, least of all the drug abuser. The important point is that the brain has mechanisms for dealing with defeat, sadness, despair, depression, low self-esteem, and other emotional problems. Conscious introspection can help us initiate those intrinsic therapeutic capabilities.

But by taking drugs, we not only get psychologically and perhaps physically addicted, we enable the drug to hijack our coping systems and prevent them from managing our emotions and mental health. The brain has an innate capacity to create and modify emotions as well as regulate learning and memory. Drug abuse takes this power away from us and our brain.

Memories of the good feelings from drugs help to sustain the addiction. Stanislav Vorel and colleagues at the Albert Einstein College of Medicine in New York recently reported experiments to confirm this conclusion.[114] Rats that had kicked a cocaine habit, when stimulated in a memory area of the brain (hippocampus), tried desperately to get another fix. But stimulation of the reward centers in the brain did not have this "relapse" effect.

The researchers first got rats hooked on cocaine by hitching them to intravenous catheters that delivered a drug dose every time they pressed one of two levers in their cage. Then, after rats became addicted, the researchers weaned them off the drug by substituting saline for the cocaine. Within a week, rats stopped lever pressing altogether. Then, when researchers electrically stimulated the hippocampus via implanted electrodes, the rats furiously pressed the former cocaine-producing lever for five minutes or more until it became clear that the drug was not there.

## Marijuana

The New York Times ran a story not too long ago about Dawn, a 12 year old who had started smoking marijuana, because her friends were doing it.[115] She wanted to be "cool" and accepted by her friends. But after a while, Dawn realized that she was having trouble in school. "I'd learn something one day and the next day I'd have no idea what the teacher was talking about."

Pointing out to pot smokers anything negative about marijuana usually evokes defensiveness. But potheads should not be surprised that marijuana impairs memory. The facts are irrefutable.[116]

Scientists have known for some time that marijuana impairs the ability to convert short-term or working memories into lasting form. Now they know why. The protein synthesis machinery in the hippocampus is necessary to accomplish lasting memory formation, and a study of mouse hippocampus revealed that marijuana impairs the protein synthesis pathway responsible for memory consolidation.

# Alcohol

Even more widely recognized is the impairment of memory caused by alcohol. The "blackouts" that occur in alcoholics are well known. Alcoholics can have multiple episodes in their recent past for which they have no recollection.

Some recent studies from the Duke University Medical Center have indicated that alcohol disturbances of memory are more profound in both young animals and young people.[117] In an animal study, a single dose of alcohol, which was not enough to sedate rats or affect their ability to swim, caused the rats to fail at learning how to swim to a safe-island platform in a water-filled maze. The blood level of alcohol was about .08 percent, which is now the new legal safe-driving limit for humans. So even though motor function may be adequate, memory function is impaired.

Just one drink, which typically has no noticeable effect on adults, can impair learning and memory in young humans. The researchers claim that the ban on under-age drinking, which historically is based on political or moral reasons, has a sound basis in science. Young people are damaged more than adults by alcohol. The Duke scientist, Scott Swartzwelder, and his team have published two recent studies that led them to conclude that "even occasional and moderate drinking could impair a young person's memory systems much more than an adult's." In their studies, memory loss lasted throughout the time people were under the influence of alcohol and none of the information presented during that time was ever memorized. Another thing they noticed: young subjects developed tolerance more quickly than adults, meaning they need to drink more to get the same high. This might explain the rapid rise in binge drinking among teenagers.

In a study of humans aged twenty to thirty, alcohol decreased the ability of everyone to recognize words from a list that had been read to them twenty minutes earlier, but the errors were significantly correlated with age: the younger the subject, the greater the errors. Age twenty-five seemed about the cutoff: those younger did worse, those older did better. The study's author made the following logical inference about these results: "If alcohol's effects varied that much within such a narrow age range, then there's a compelling reason to believe its effects are even stronger in adolescents and children."

Back in 1974, a graduate student named Russ Stevens and I were among the first to show that alcohol does not have the same effect on all nerve cells. Our studies in rabbits revealed that some nerve cells, especially in the cortex, cerebellum, and hippocampus are more sensitive to alcohol than cells located elsewhere. Two years later we confirmed and extended the initial observations.[118]

Even mild doses of alcohol can impair memory formation, if for no other reason than it dulls the senses and the ability to focus attention. Recall our earlier chapter on the importance of attention. With electrodes chronically implanted in the brains of rabbits we could monitor the electrical discharges from neurons in different parts of the brain. We noted that the mild intoxicating doses that we used suppressed neuronal activity in some brain areas, excited other neurons (probably just released from inhibitory neurons that were suppressed), while others were unaffected. It all depended on which parts of the brain we monitored.

Later, at an alcohol research conference in Sweden, I met a bright young Russian named Yura Alexandrov.[119]

He took up alcohol research where I left off, but based his research on an important new theme: the effect of alcohol on nerve cells should depend on the neurons' "behavioral specialization." That is, the normal function of a neuron in behavior provides the key indicator for whether the neuron is especially vulnerable for alcohol. So, in his recordings of nerve cell impulses (he also used rabbits), he also kept track of the normal behavioral function of the neurons.

Because my work had shown that many of the vulnerable neurons were in the hippocampus and limbic system structures that are involved in memory, Yura recorded activity in those same areas and noted that they generally existed into two categories: those associated with movements ("M neurons"), and those associated with new learning ("L neurons"). These L neurons changed their firing as the rabbit learned a task.

Then, when Yura's team gave a moderately intoxicating dose of alcohol to the rabbits, they saw the alcohol effect was specific to L neurons. They wondered if the same thing happened in addicted rabbits. After rabbits had become partially tolerant from drinking alcohol-spiked water for eight months, the L neurons could not be found. Where did the L neurons go? Had they died? Maybe they were still there but had lost their task association. Amazingly, the L neurons became detectable again when the rabbits were given a single intoxicating challenge dose. It is as if alcohol actually restored the normal learning function.

Perhaps this is akin to human situations where an alcoholic writer writes better when he has a few alcoholic drinks. Formal studies have confirmed this. This phenomenon is a form of "state-dependent" learning, which was explained earlier.

## Amphetamines ("Speed")

Despite arousing the brain, this drug group actually impairs memory. Worse yet, the loss in memory capability seems to be permanent. Since the drug is taken mostly by young people, the brain damage is especially devastating. Even after months of abstinence, these memory impairments have been recently documented in a study by Linda Chang and colleagues at the Brookhaven National Laboratory.[120] They used two short-term memory tasks. A group of 20 recently abstinent methamphetamine abusers, who on average had been abstinent for 8 months, formed the test group, and 20 nonusers formed the control group. Each control group member was selected to match one of the members in the abuser group in terms of gender and age. Memory performance was impaired in the abuser group by 21.5% in the sequential reaction time tests and by 30% in the single digit test.

Curiously, college students take amphetamines (Ritalin and Adderal) because they think it gives them an intellectual edge. Maybe these drugs do help in the short-term, but students need to think about likely long-term consequences.

## Train Your Gut

If you think it is hard to conquer an addiction, you might think it is even harder to consciously change the visceral and glandular responses that accompany emotions. For example, if we are excited, our heart rate and blood pressure rise. If we worry chronically, we may get an upset stomach and predispose our stomach to ulcers. These visceral and glandular responses are controlled by a subdivision of the nervous system, the so-called autonomic nervous system, which lies largely outside the brain, mostly in the chest and abdominal cavities. This system has traditionally been regarded as rather stupid, and unable to learn.

Nonetheless, the autonomic nervous system can learn readily, through conditioning. Such visceral learning effects underlie psychosomatic disease, such as high blood pressure, heart palpitations, ulcers, tension headaches, facial tics, and some forms of backache.

---

### Memory Myth Buster

*The part of the brain that controls viscera (such as heart rate, blood pressure, digestion, etc.) is too stupid to learn anything.* WRONG. This system does learn, and in fact is the cause of psychosomatic diseases. Biofeedback training can teach this system to change.

---

Commitment to this myth persists in spite of the classical studies by Pavlov, who showed that dogs can learn to salivate on cue when they have come to associate that cue with receiving food. This classical conditioning explained in Chapter II, is considered the most primitive sort of learning. Even simple flatworms can be conditioned: after many pairings of a light flash and electrical shock, they learn to contract their bodies in response to light.

Consider the possibility that psychosomatic diseases emerge as a result of implicitly learned bodily responses to stressful events, events that are emotionally distressing enough to make the bodily response persist. If stress is repeated, the persistence of bodily responses may become cumulative, with the implicit memory being sufficiently "rehearsed" to become a well-entrenched long-term memory.

Such a possibility seems especially likely if stressful episodes are repeated during childhood. Consider high blood pressure, for example. Most physicians assume that the high blood pressure seen in many older people is due to their genes or diet. But many people with high blood pressure do not have plugged arteries. No experiments I know of have tested the possibility high blood pressure in adults could arise from or be aggravated by a long-term implicit memory response to childhood stress. But this is such a real possibility that parents have yet another reason to do all they can to keep their children from being chronically stressed.

As we grow through childhood, much of our behavior is conditioned by our environment. This includes the part of our nervous system controlling our viscera. For example, consider a child who fears going to school because she is unprepared for a test that day. She may display the autonomic symptoms of a queasy stomach, skin pallor, or faintness. Her mother, out of sympathy and concern, may tell the child she is sick and should stay at home. This is tantamount to rewarding the behavior. Thus, the child—and her viscera—are learning to respond to stressful situations with symptoms of physical illness. If these responses occur often enough and are continually reinforced, the child may subconsciously learn and memorize a genuine psychosomatic illness that lasts a lifetime.

Humans have a hard time controlling their visceral responses through conscious will or learning. But humans can be conditioned subconsciously through Pavlovian techniques. Neal Miller, at the Rockefeller University, was among the first to demonstrate with rats that visceral conditioning can be done[121] and therefore ought to work as therapy in humans with psychosomatic diseases.

David Shapiro and his team showed that humans were as smart as rats.[122] They taught male student volunteers to raise or lower their blood pressure as desired to elicit a reward. Anytime the pressure started to move in the desired direction they would see a Playboy photograph of a nude female. The students had no idea what functions they were supposed to control. They were just told (obviously unnecessarily) to make the pictures appear as often as possible.

This principle can be extended to develop training programs to treat, that is, "unlearn," dysfunctional visceral memories. So-called biofeedback training is a form of conditioned learning where the body is taught to lower blood pressure, slow the heart rate, or change other visceral responses. For instance, if high blood pressure developed because of repeated stresses in childhood, it might be possible to train adults to habituate to stressors by presenting the stress to adults in ways that are no longer threats to a reasoning adult.

The most valuable lesson about visceral learning is that healthful responses can be learned. A whole psychological sub-industry of bio-feedback training has emerged. Companies that market biofeedback equipment include Future Health, Allied Products, Performance Edge, Motivational Hypnosis, Applied Biofeedback, Zaz, and many others.

Visceral learning may account for many cultural differences. For example, Herbert Barry III at the University of Pittsburg, showed that the amount of crying reported in children seems to be related to the way in which their friends and parents react to their tears. If crying is rewarded by sympathy, then crying becomes more ingrained. That is no doubt the reason boys generally do not cry as often or as easily as girls after early childhood. Girls are often comforted when they cry; boys may be reprimanded by their parents or peers for not "being a man."

We could also probably extend these ideas to consider many neuroses as learned responses. Here, I would consider the possibility that the flawed thinking of neuroses may be learned. By repeating thinking errors, we could actually be memorizing how to think in neurotic or criminal ways.

## Get Enough Sleep

Many people think that the purpose of sleep is to rest the brain. But there is clear evidence that the brain is still hard at work during sleep, even when you're not dreaming. Decades ago, researchers demonstrated that many neurons fired just as much during sleep as during wakefulness, and some neurons were actually more active during sleep.

---

### Memory Myth Buster

*The purpose of sleep is to rest the brain.* WRONG —at least not entirely correct. The brain works off-line while you sleep, working, among other things, to consolidate memories of the day's events.

---

Brain waves, which are derived from neuronal firing, change during different levels of sleep. In the early stages of sleep, the brain waves (electroencephalogram, EEG) become large and of low frequency. This is called the stage of "slow-wave sleep." As the night wears on, sleep is periodically punctuated by dream episodes, in which the brain waves become smaller and higher in frequency, looking much as they do when you are awake and mentally active.

Experiments clearly show that mental function declines with lack of sleep, and in fact the decline is proportional to the amount of time spent in continuous wakefulness.[123] This decline occurs irrespective of how much sleep one gets. It is as if staying awake produces wear and tear on thinking ability.

Recent studies indicate that one of the things the brain is doing during sleep is forming memories of the day's events. Numerous studies have shown that sleep promotes the consolidation of declarative memories (those which are consciously remembered, as opposed to implicit procedural memories). In exploring how sleep might facilitate memory, Steffan Gais and colleagues in Lübeck, Germany[124] found that extensive training of humans on a declarative learning task caused a specific kind of brain-wave change during nocturnal sleep. Recall ability during awake re-testing correlated with the degree to which EEGs had changed during sleep. Thus, it would appear that important memory-forming processes are underway during sleep.

Procedural memories are also being processed during sleep.[125] One study measured the effect of sleep on learned finger and thumb movements.[126] No matter whether sleep occurred in the daytime or nighttime, sleeping after practicing hand movements enhanced the speed of sequence performance by 33.5% and reduced error rates by 30% as compared to corresponding intervals of wakefulness after the training. The effect of sleep was stable and was still demonstrable when testing was delayed another night to assure that everybody in the control group got enough sleep. Maybe piano players should take a nap after practice. In fact, a study of napping showed that it promotes hand and finger-movement learning.[127]

What happens when you cut sleep short? Students, for example, may cut back on sleep to finish ever-mounting piles of homework. Combat soldiers are trained to function under sleep-deprived conditions. But this training could be counter-productive. At my university, our Corps of Cadets has a tradition of rousing freshmen in the middle of the night and preventing them from sleeping. The idea is to make them tough. What it does for certain is make them unable to do well in school—I have seen many of them flunk out.

Sleep loss degrades many neural functions. In one study sleep loss degraded visual vigilance and word memory, and caused time-of-day fluctuations in choice reaction time, logical reasoning, and word memory. Exercise also seemed to play a role, in that non-exercising subjects degraded sooner than did exercising subjects. So, sleep-deprived couch potatoes beware!

Researchers have found that people who stay up all night after learning and practicing a new task show little improvement in their performance. No amount of sleep on following nights can make up for the toll taken by the initial all-nighter.

---

### Memory Myth Buster

*You can always catch up on lost sleep.* WRONG. At least with respect to memory, the benefits of sleep apply only to the preceding day's events.

---

Robert Stickgold and colleagues at Harvard Medical School report that people who learned a particular task did not improve their performance when tested later the same day but did improve after a night of sleep.[128] To see whether the night of sleep actually caused the improvement, Stickgold trained 24 subjects in a visual discrimination task.

Half of the subjects went to sleep that night while the other half were kept awake until the second night of the study. Both groups were allowed to sleep on the second and third nights. When both groups were later tested for recall of the visual discrimination task, those who slept the first night performed the task much faster than they had the first day. The other group showed no improvement, despite two nights of catch-up sleep.

Another compelling study for the role of sleep on memory consolidation was reported by Sean Drummond and his colleagues at San Diego State University. and the University of California, San Diego.[129] They combined memory performance with brain scanning. After a sleepless night, free recall performance fell by about half, and the brain imaging analysis showed that some parts of the cerebral cortex became very active (unlike the case when a normal sleep was allowed). This suggests that a sleep-deprived brain has to work harder than normal to form memories. It seems obvious that a rested brain has more thinking resources to draw upon.

These observations led the researchers of the study to suggest that cortical regions not normally involved in some cognitive tasks like verbal learning can be recruited to help out the regions already involved in these tasks. The researchers also emphasized that the cortical areas that work the hardest during wakefulness might have a greater need for sleep. In other words, only sleep seems to provide real rest to these cortical areas.

What about a small degree of sleep loss? A University of Pennsylvania study[130] showed even a little sleep loss can harm memory. People were assigned to sleep regimens of four, six, or eight hours of sleep each night for two weeks and tested periodically during the daytime for mental performance. Subjects who got four or even six hours of sleep performed as poorly on brain function tests as they did when kept from sleeping at all for three consecutive days. So, short-changing your sleep each night by an hour or so builds up a sleep debt that affects attention and working memory. In the study, performance decline was cumulative. An interesting aside from the study was that none of the 48 people in the study realized that their mental performance had deteriorated from the mild sleep loss. Sleep helps memory formation the most if you know you will need the information later.[131] That is, it seems that the brain prioritizes its consolidation operations during sleep to favor consolidation of information that is most important.

The study tested 193 volunteers for recall of a variety of memory tasks. Some subjects were exposed to the learning material early in the day, when there would be no sleep involved. The others were exposed to the same material late, just before the night's sleep. When subjects were told they would be tested later, they were more likely to remember if they had slept immediately after the learning. This was true for both procedural tasks (like finger-tapping sequences) and declarative tasks such as word matching or stating card-pair locations.

A similar result was obtained by a French group[132] that showed sleep's effect on memory depended on whether subjects were told to remember or forget items in a learning task. In the learning task, volunteers were shown 100 French words, one at a time. Fifty of these had accompanying instruction "to be remembered" and the other 50 "to be forgotten," presented in a pseudorandom sequence that prevented more than three words of the same type being presented consecutively. After the training session, subjects were divided into two groups, one which was sent home to continue their normal activities and to sleep on their usual schedule for the next three nights. The other group was denied the first night's sleep after training, where they stayed up all that night watching movies or playing games. Otherwise, this group was treated the same. On the fourth day, both groups were tested for ability to identify which of 100 of the original words and 100 new ones were in the original list.

Upon testing, both groups had about the same degree of correct recall for "to be remembered" words. But the sleep-deprived groups remembered more of the words they were not supposed to remember. Thus, it would seem that during sleep, the brain preserved its ability to remember words that were expected to be remembered and discriminated against remembering words that were unimportant.

## How Sleep Helps

I assume that by now the reader accepts the conclusion that sleep helps memory formation. But I have not yet explained how that works. One advantage that sleep provides for memory consolidation is that the brain does not have all the distractions that occur during daytime wakefulness. As I have stressed earlier, multiple conflicting stimuli are very disruptive to memory consolidation. Moreover, the brain is less responsive to stimuli during sleep.[133]

A good illustration of the benefit of reducing interference comes from a study of napping at the University of Lübeck in Germany.[134] They asked 24 volunteers to memorize the two-dimensional location of 15 pairs of cards with pictures of animals and everyday objects. During the study time, subjects were also exposed continuously to a slightly unpleasant odor, which was intended to be an associational cue.

Forty minutes later, the volunteers were asked to learn a second, slightly different set of card pairs. This second task was to act as an interfering disruptor of the initial learning. After the first memorization session, half of the group stayed awake and the other half took a nap. For 20 minutes during the break after the first study session, the odor cue was presented with the intent of helping to reactivate the memory of the first session. The non-sleeping group got the odor cue for 20 minutes just before starting the second learning session, while the sleep group got the odor cue during the last 20 minutes of the nap.

When both groups were tested for recall of the first set of cards, the sleep group remembered much better (85% correct versus 60% for the non-sleeping group). The explanation begins with the knowledge that when temporary memories (as for the first card set) are recalled, they are vulnerable to being destroyed by new mental activity (as with the second card set). In this study, memory was reactivated in both wakefulness and sleep by the odor cue. Yet, the memorization processes that apparently persisted during sleep made the original memories more resistant to disruption. By the time of the second interfering task some

40 minutes later, much of the initial learning had gelled during sleep, but less so during wakefulness.

## Avoid Sleep Loss Before Learning Too

So far, I have given the impression that sleep is needed soon after memorizing. But sleep is needed beforehand too. There are studies revealing lack of sleep BEFORE learning interferes with memory. The cause could be that a sleepy brain has trouble sustaining attentiveness and doesn't think too effectively.

A study by Matthew Walker and colleagues,[135] showed how sleep loss impairs memory proactively in healthy young adults. On the first day, one group was kept awake for 35 straight hours. Participants in the other group spent a normal sleep night at home. At 6 PM the next day, all subjects watched a slide show of 150 slides of landscapes, objects, and people who weren't celebrities. All subjects also got MRI brain scans. The scans showed brain areas involved in memory, such as the hippocampus, were more active in the subjects who got a normal night's sleep. It is as if these areas in sleep-deprived subjects were too tired to work well. All subjects then were sent home to have a normal night's sleep.

The next evening all subjects took a pop quiz on the slides, which were randomly mixed with 75 new slides. The test was for subjects to recognize whether they had seen each slide before. Those subjects who had been sleep deprived on the first night scored the lowest, even though they later had a night to catch up on lost sleep.

The upshot of it all is that lack of sleep is bad for remembering, whether the sleep loss occurs before or after learning events.

# Don't Skimp on the Dreaming Either

Sometimes really busy people want to cram more hours into the day by waking up early. The problem with that is that all of us do most of our dreaming early in the morning, and dreaming is very important for consolidating memories of the previous day's experiences. Dreaming is integral to human life history. In both the Bible and the Koran dreaming is considered a primary source of divine inspiration. Shakespeare treated dreams as omens. Julius Caesar's wife foresaw his assassination in a dream. Sigmund Freud called dreams the "royal road" to the subconscious. Today's experimental psychologists tell us dreams are a royal road to memory.

We know from many studies that dreaming is important for memory formation. Just how dreams promote memory consolidation remains to be discovered. It may benefit us in a completely different way than non-dream sleep does; brain activity is very high while dreaming, not suppressed.

Unlike many of my scientist colleagues, I don't think we sleep in order to consolidate memories. I think we consolidate memories as a by-product of sleeping, both dream and non-dreaming stages of sleep. My explanation is that though sleep promotes consolidation, the reason we want to sleep is for some yet undiscovered biochemical purpose and the reason we dream is because after enough sleep the brain has an auto-reset function to wake itself up.[136]

It is important to point out that dreaming is most abundant in the young. Brain signs of dreaming have even been documented in late-term fetuses.[137] Babies spend a larger amount of their sleep time with bodily signs of dreaming than adults do. But what purpose does that serve? After all, you would think babies have little to dream about. One answer is that dreaming is one of nature's ways to keep the brain stimulated. Stimulation is necessary to sculpt the circuitry in a developing brain, and dreaming helps a baby cement those memories and learn faster.

## Learn During Reverie

Does it help to study just prior to going to sleep? I remember as a young veterinary medical student how I stumbled upon what seemed to be an effective learning strategy. My learning strategy was to study hard all day, like my peers. Then on nights before an examination, a group of us would gather in one room of the fraternity house and go over old exams and discuss complicated issues. Only I was usually so tired (or lazy) that I just laid on the top of a bunk-bed and listened to everybody else talk. In my reverie I would think leisurely about everything the other fellows were saying. Then I would go off to bed, thinking about the material as I fell asleep. Everybody else was staying up several hours longer. Yet I consistently outscored these guys on the exams. They were infuriated. They worked so hard, and I loafed along and still got higher grades. Physically, I was loafing, but mentally I was focused on what was being said, integrating and using it to promote my memory consolidating processes. The good night's sleep helped me a lot more than the cramming helped my buddies.

## Learn While You Sleep

Back in the 1960s and 70s, a popular fad was "sleep learning." I tried it too. The idea was to play a tape recording of what you needed to memorize while you slept. Formal studies tended to indicate this did not work. Most early adopters found that all it did was disrupt sleep.

However, since then some new research discoveries have revealed that sleep learning might be possible. Because the brain is consolidating memories of the day's events during sleep, the sleep learning idea may not be completely without merit. Maybe the right kind of stimulus input while you sleep could promote learning, at least in terms of promoting memory consolidation of the information you already learned during the day.

So, the idea would be to see if sleep can promote memory consolidation of things you recently learned, but have not yet formed into lasting memory. How might you do that? Since memory is largely associative, maybe it would work to provide during sleep the cues that were associated with the original learning. This might have a better chance of working during the dream stage of sleep, because it is well documented that external sound stimuli (like storms, rain, etc.) are documented as capable of becoming incorporated into and changing the course of a dream. Thus, the question becomes: can audio presentation of learned association cues during dreaming promote the memory formation for the original learning items or events? The idea is that the cue might reactivate a latent memory and constitute a memory rehearsal.

---

### Memory Myth Buster

*Sleep learning is a hoax. It doesn't work.* WRONG (well it depends on how you define "sleep learning"). You do consolidate the day's learning events while sleeping, but presenting information to be learned while you sleep generally does not work. However, it might work if you presented associational cues, instead of the memorization items themselves.

Presentation of cues associated with daytime learning during a nap seems to promote "sleep learning." Testing of this idea has recently been reported: Northwestern University scientists trained human subjects to recognize the location of 50 different objects on a computer screen.[138] Each object had an associated sound. For example, the cat image was associated with a meow sound, a kettle with a whistle, etc. The subjects were then asked to nap, during which time the researchers played half of the sound cues at an unobtrusive volume and without the subjects' knowledge.

After the nap, subjects had no conscious recollection of the sound cueing. After waking, the original objects were re-presented and subjects were again tested for recall of the location of the images. Memory accuracy was greater for images that had associative cues presented during the nap than for those images for which sound cues had not been played. Simultaneous recording of brain waves (EEG) showed that the brain was responding to the sensory cues during sleep.

The principle for sleep learning seems sound. What remains is for clever entrepreneurs to develop memory-enhancing strategies that are specific for specific learning tasks. I suspect that external learning "reminders" will be more effective when presented during dream sleep, not the deep stage of sleep in which people "fall into a pit" of oblivion.

## Take Naps

I mention the possibility of learning during napping, but that awaits research on how best to do it. Some benefits of naps are well established. Daytime naps are said to rejuvenate energy and lower stress. Now there is evidence naps speed up consolidation of memories.[139] One study of learning a finger movement sequence showed that memory of the learning could be disrupted by conflicting movement training within the first two hours afterwards. But this disruption could be prevented by taking a nap right after training.[140] So, you piano students might want to take a nap right after your lessons.

Another study compared caffeine, a placebo, and naps on three distinct tasks involving verbal declarative memory, procedural motor skills, and perceptual learning. Results revealed that naps provided the best improvement on memory recall for verbal memory, and naps and caffeine were about equally effective on the other tests.[141]

## Avoid Excessive Jet Lag

One disturbance of sleep that most people have experienced is jet lag. If you have ever flown through several time zones, you know the feelings of fatigue, mental fogginess, and general discomfort that go with so-called jet lag. It should not be surprising that jet lag adversely affects memory. This is confirmed in a recent study of flight attendants, whose brain images were compared with other people that did not have repeated jet lag experiences. Kwangwook Cho, a neurologist at the University of Bristol in England, has found actual structural deterioration in these subjects in the area of the brain that is involved in spatial orientation and processing.[142]

The Cho group led another troubling study of jet lag in cabin crews which they observed that salivary cortisol levels significantly higher, indicating that their bodies were chronically stressed. Memory testing revealed no deficit in cabin crews who had been working for less than three years, but deficiencies were evident in crews with four years of service, and the degree of memory loss paralleled cortisol levels. This could indicate lasting damage to the brain's memory systems, inasmuch as persistently elevated cortisol kills neurons. This study, if it can be confirmed, means that work schedules of pilots and flight attendants need to be adjusted to make certain there is sufficient recovery time between jet lag episodes.

## Key Ideas from Chapter Four

1. Mental challenges sharpen thinking, but much of the gain goes away when the challenges go away.
2. When you are motivated to learn, you are more likely to succeed at it.
3. To better cope with stress: manage your life, plan to avoid stressful situations, control self-talk, relax.
4. Repetition of ineffective or flawed thinking can make them permanent.
5. Learning often involves subconscious conditioning that can lead to unwise behavior and to psychosomatic disease.
6. Biofeedback training can alleviate psychosomatic disease.
7. Belief about memory ability becomes a self-fulfilling prophecy.
8. Motivation comes from basic drive states for seeking reward and avoiding punishment. These drives affect learning and memory.

9. Emotions affect our ability to memorize new experiences.

10. Memory ability is enhanced by positive emotions.

11. Memory ability is impaired by too much stress, anxiety, fear, or depression.

12. Sex hormones promote memory. Deficiencies, as in menopausal women, can impair memory capability.

13. Sustained stress is bad for memory and chronic exposure to its hormones may actually kill neurons.

14. Music stirs the emotions. Emotions stir the memories. Instrumental music, without lyrics, may help memorizing.

15. Babies should be socialized early, because this will limit the learning of inflexible habits, biases, prejudices, and a small view of the world

16. Babies should receive lots of stimuli (mobiles, etc. over their cribs) but also they should be taken out of the crib often to get outside stimuli involving hands-on engagement.

17. Teenage angst is bad for the brain. Adolescence is an especially vulnerable time. Not only is the adolescent brain still being built, the brain is being re-built during teenage years.

18. Violence, even if just observed on TV or movies, is harmful to memory capability.

19. Sadness and depression are harmful to memory capability. Depressed people have learned a bias for remembering depressing things.

20. Memory decline in the elderly may be promoted by some of the blood pressure medicines they take.

21. The brain has the innate capability to create and modify emotions, and secondarily our ability to learn

and apply what we remember. Drug abuse takes this power away.

22. Tranquilizers and sedatives interfere with memory. Most drugs that have any effect on memory have a negative effect.

23. Addictions of all sorts are largely influenced by learning and memory.

24. To break bad habits and addictions, substitute positive reinforcers.

25. Exercise improves memory capability, in both young and old.

26. Memories of the day's events are consolidated during sleep. Get plenty of sleep and don't cut dream sleep short by getting up too soon.

27. Learners should not cram-study for exams. Learning should be optimized by rehearsing the same learning material on separate days where normal sleep occurred each night.

28. As far as memory is concerned, you can't catch up on sleep. Its benefits apply only to the previous day.

29. Sleep learning, though generally discredited, might work if instead of listening to items to memorize, you listened to associational cues that had you previously heard or seen in conjunction with the items you are trying to memorize.

30. The sleepy brain tries to compensate by using more brain resources than is otherwise necessary. Thus sleepy brains have fewer resources available to form new memories.

31. Lack of sleep BEFORE learning interferes with forming memory of that learning. Get plenty of sleep.

32. Naps facilitate learning of preceding information.

33. Jet lag adversely affects memory. Try to avoid demanding tasks during jet lag.

34. Sleep learning doesn't work, except that it might if cues and reminders (rather than the actual objects of memory) were presented during light and dream stages of sleep.

# V. MASTERING SPECIFIC LEARNING AND MEMORY TASKS

Many people want a memory book because they feel they have a specific memory problem, like not making good-enough grades, difficulty in remembering names, learning a foreign language, and the like. This chapter is devoted to ideas for improving memory for a host of specific tasks. The recommendations also serve to illustrate how the ideas in the previous chapters can be adapted for specific learning and memory challenges.

## Reading Skills

Despite the prevalence of television, cell phones, and web "twitter," traditional reading is still an important skill. Whether it is school, tech manuals in the workplace, or regular books, people still read, though not as much as they used to. One reason that many people don't read much is that they don't read well. For them, it is slow, hard work and they don't remember as much as they should. Students, for example, may have to read something several times before they understand and remember what they read. People with good reading skills learn most efficiently through reading. For poor readers, reading may actually be an obstacle to learning if the information is accessed in another way.

For those who know how to read well, reading is the most effective and efficient way to learn. You would think that schools teach kids how to read well. I work with middle-school teachers and they tell me that many of their students are 2–3 years behind grade level in reading proficiency. No doubt, television and the web are major contributors to this problem. Also, text messaging on cell phones is creating a whole new corrupted language. But the main culprit is probably the teaching of reading in elementary school.

Some of the blame can be placed on fads in reading teaching, such as exclusive emphasis on "phonics" or on "whole language," which may be inappropriately promoted by zealots who don't respect the need for both approaches.

Phonics is without doubt a foundational approach to language in general and to effective reading in particular. The challenge is to find ways to optimize teaching of the links between sounds and their visual symbols. Learners need to improve their awareness of sounds by focusing on the melody, dissimilarities, and intentional encoding of the sounds.

For all those who missed out on good reading skills, it is not too late. I summarize below what I think it takes to read with good speed and comprehension.

## Know Your Purpose

Read with a purpose. Know what you are looking for. Slow down and think hard about the parts that have information you are looking for. Skim everything else.

Everyone should have a purpose for their reading and think about how that purpose is being fulfilled during the actual reading. The advantage for remembering is that checking continuously for how the purpose is being fulfilled helps the reader to stay on task, to focus on the more relevant parts of the text, and to rehearse continuously as one reads. This also saves time and effort because relevant items are most attended.

Identifying the purpose should be easy if you freely choose what to read. Just ask yourself, "Why am I reading this?" If it is to be entertained or pass the time, then there is not much problem, except that sloppy reading could be forming bad reading habits.

Many of us have readings assigned to us, as in a school environment. Or the boss may hand us a manual and say, "We need you to implement these instructions." Whether the order comes from a teacher or a boss, we need to ask, "What do you want me to learn from this?" In the absence of such guidance, you should still formulate your best guess about what you should learn and remember from the reading.

## Skim First

Some reading tasks require no more than skimming. Proper skimming includes putting an emphasis on the headings, pictures, graphs, tables, and key paragraphs (which are usually at the beginning and the end). Depending on the purpose, you should slow down and read carefully only the parts that contribute to fulfilling the reading purpose.

Even material that has to be studied carefully should be skimmed first. The benefits of skimming first are that the skimming: 1) primes the memory, making it easier to remember when you read it the second time, 2) orients the thinking, helping you to know where the important content is in the document, 3) creates an overall sense and gestalt for the document, which in turn makes it easier to remember certain particulars.

Browsing on the Internet encourages people to skim read. The way content is handled on the Web is even causing writers to make wider use of Web devices, such as numbered or bulleted lists, sidebars, graphics, and text boxes. But the bad news is that the Web style makes it even harder to learn how to read in-depth; that is, the Web teaches us to skim, creating bad reading habits for in-depth reading. A related problem for learning created by the Web is that it makes us lazy about memorizing. Studies of this matter reveal that people have lower rates of recall for use in thinking or answering questions if they know they can "Google it."[143]

## Get the Mechanics Right

For in-depth reading, eyes need to move in a disciplined way. Skimming actually trains eyes to move without discipline. When you need to read carefully and remember the essence of large blocks of text, the eyes must snap from one fixation point to the next in left- to right-sequence. Moreover, the fixations should not be on individual letters or even single words, but rather on several words per fixation. Perceiving several words at once not only increases the amount of information the brain receives per fixation, but also improves comprehension.

Poor readers who stumble along from word to word actually tend to have lower comprehension because their mind is preoccupied with recognizing the letters and their arrangement in each word. That is a main reason they can't remember what they read. Countless times I have heard college students say, "I read that chapter three times, and I still can't answer your questions." When I ask thought-provoking questions about the material, they often can't answer the questions because they can't remember the meaning of what they read. Even with straightforward simple memorization questions, they often can't remember, because their focus on the words themselves kept them from associating what their eyes saw with their own pre-existing knowledge and thus facilitating remembering. In short, to remember what you read, you have to think about what the words mean.

I am not arguing against phonics, which in my view is vital for the initial learning of how to read. But phonics is just the first step in good reading practice. At some point, the reader needs to recognize whole words as complete units and then expand that capability to clusters of several words.

Among the key tactics for good mechanics of reading:

- Scan all the text not being deliberately skimmed.
- See multiple words in each eye fixation.
- Strive to expand the width of each eye fixation (on an 8.5" width, strive for three fixations or eventually two per line). This skill has to be developed in stages. First, learn how to read at five or six fixations per line. Then work on four per line. Then three.
- Snap eyes from one fixation point to another (horizontal snaps on long lines, vertical snap if whole line in a column can be seen with one fixation).

There are reading-improvement machines at reading centers that train the eyes to fixate properly, but few schools use them. I know from personal experience with such machines that they can increase reading speed markedly without a cost in lower comprehension. There are also websites that train eye movements for reading (Google "eye movement training + reading" or "speed reading software").

## Be Judicious in Highlighting and Note Taking

Use a highlighter to mark a FEW key points to act as the basis for mental pictures and reminder cues. Add key words in the margins if you don't find useful clues to highlight.

Almost all students use highlighters to identify key parts of a text. But many students either highlight too much or highlight the wrong things. They become so preoccupied in marking up the book that they don't pay enough attention to what they are reading. If many pages don't require highlights, sticky tabs on pages with highlights can greatly speed a study process for whole books.

You should only highlight key things, such as items you don't understand and items you know you should memorize for a test. As you finish a few paragraphs, ask yourself what were the important things to know and then go back and highlight key words. Use one color for things you do not fully understand (e.g. red), another color for things you know you need to memorize (e.g. yellow), and perhaps headings in a third color.

Other markup options include writing or drawing in the margins if there is enough space. You can also put yellow stickies on key pages and information can be put on the stickies. Finally, you can take notes of the text either in linear or matrix format.

It is crucial to think about the meaning of text. Think about the content in each segment in terms of what you already know and don't know. Ask yourself questions about the content. "Why did the author say that? Do I understand what is meant? What is the evidence? Do I agree with the ideas or conclusions? Why or why not? What is the practical application?" I have found that a most useful question is, "What was left out?"—to answer this question you have to make yourself remember what was stated. Apply the ideas to other situations and contexts. Generate ideas about the content.

Text needs to be rehearsed in the context of how it meets your reading purpose, why it needs to be remembered, and how it fits with important material that preceded it. Every few paragraphs or pages, depending on the information density, the reader should stop and self-quiz to make sure the important material is being memorized. Making outline notes or concept maps of such material after it is first read can be an important rehearsal aid for forming immediate memory and for later study. Thinking about reading content not only helps memory, but also increases the opportunity to gain creative insights about the subject. In short, thinking not only promotes memory formation but also understanding.

## Think in Pictures

Pictures are much easier to memorize than words. Those memory wizards who put on stage shows owe their success (as do card counters in casinos) to use of gimmicks based on mental pictures. Ordinary readers can make good use of the practice of making mental images of the meaning of text. The high-lighted key words in text, for example, if used as a starting point for mental pictures, then become very useful for memorization. One only has to spot the key words and think of the associated mental images. Sometimes it helps to make mental images of headings and sub-heads. Pictures also become easier to remember when they are clustered into similar groups or when they are chained together to tell a story (see more on this tip below).

Thinking in mental pictures requires imagination, and we are not all equal in creative imagining. But I have found that making mental-picture associations gets easier with practice. You may even develop picture imagining as a habit. Since images are vastly easier to remember than words, developing imagination skills will pay off big-time.

Mental pictures are not the only way to facilitate memory for what you read. I understand that actors use another approach for memorizing their lines for a play, movie, or TV show.[144] Actors "get into the part" and study the meaning of the script in depth, which seems to produce memory automatically for them. When the same script is memorized with mental images, it appears that the text is being looked at from the outside, as something to be memorized. Actors, on the other hand, appear to be looking at the same text from the inside, as something to be experienced. The actors probe the deep meaning of the text, which inevitably involves attending to the exact words. For example, they seem to explore why their character would use a given set of words to express a particular thought. This is still a process of association, except that actors are associating words with real meaning and context as opposed to contrived visual image meaning and context.

Both approaches require engagement. The reader has to think hard about what is being read, and that is what helps you to remember what is read.

## Rehearse As You Go Along

Read in short segments (a few paragraphs to a few pages, depending on content density), all the while thinking about and paraphrasing the meaning of what is written.

To rehearse what you are memorizing, see how many of the mental pictures you can reconstruct. Use headings and highlighted words if needed to help you reinforce the mental pictures. Rehearse the mental pictures every day or so for the first few days after reading.

Think about the content in each segment in terms of how it satisfies the purpose for reading. Ask yourself questions about the content. "How does this information fit what I already know and don't know? Why did the author say that? Do I understand what this means? What is the evidence? Do I agree with ideas or conclusions? Why or why not? What is the practical application?" How much of this do I need to memorize?" Apply the ideas to other situations and contexts. Generate ideas about the content.

## Operate Within Your Attention Span

Paying attention is central to memorization. Trying to read when you can't concentrate is wasting time. Since most people have short attention spans, they should not try to read dense material for more than 10 or 15 minutes at a time. After such a session, they should take a break and quiz themselves on what they just read. Ultimately, readers should discipline their attention so they can concentrate for longer periods.

## Rehearse Soon After Reading Is Finished

At the reading session's end, rehearse what you learned—right away. Avoid distractions and multitasking because they interfere with the consolidation processes that enable longer-term memory.

Think about and rehearse what you read at least twice later that day. Rehearse again at least once for the next few days. To rehearse what you are memorizing, see how many of the mental pictures you can reconstruct.

# Listening

Seminars and workshops are often given in a format where lecturing is the basic means of transmitting information. Many teachers, especially college professors, teach by lecturing. In my view, this is not a good way for most students to learn, but since that is the environment in which they are thrust, they must learn how to learn under those conditions. Corporate and government training typically entails PowerPoint presentations. While the images in a slide show can reinforce remembering, they are often counterproductive by being distracting from being too cluttered, monotonous, or irrelevant.

The first bit of advice is to prepare for lecture. Read about the topic ahead of time and you will get more out of the lecture. The second thing is to bring your "A-game" to the presentation. When I was a student, I always had the goal of remembering as much as I could about each lecture right then and there (so I wouldn't have to use so much of my fun time studying). As long as I was surrendering my time to be in class, why waste it by being an inefficient listener?

The third thing is to take notes properly. In my experience students get little good advice on how to take notes. Note taking is the standard process whereby information is transferred from the teacher's notes to the student's notes (sometimes without passing through the mind of either). The problem is that students are too busy writing notes and not busy enough thinking about what the teacher says and means. Good teachers hand out their notes before class so that students can pay attention to the lecture and get engaged with the content rather than with pencil and paper.

One great tactic some teachers use is to hand out "skeleton notes" that give the student freedom to couch ideas in familiar terms and to leave out things they already know or can figure out. Skeleton notes contain just major headings of an outline and perhaps key data, leaving it up to the listener to fill in whatever detail they need in their own words and diagrams. This approach really pays off when it comes time to study for exams.

Note taking should follow the principles given for "Reading Skills." If the teacher permits, use a tape recorder and use variable speed, so you can slow down for difficult parts and speed up through parts that are not particularly useful. The idea is to think about what is being said, asking yourself or the teacher questions, expressing the ideas in your own terms, making mental images, and so on. Review and edit your notes as soon after class as possible. Discuss the lecture and compare notes with others in the class.

What do you do in case you miss some key information while doing all this thinking? Tape record the lecture and play it back later to update and refine your notes and to refine and rehearse your mental pictures.

# School

Obviously, a positive attitude, motivation, and belief in one's ability to learn are central to school success. But in addition, the way students approach reading and listening make a big difference, as I have just explained.

Perhaps the biggest problem students have, especially in this age of high-tech toys such as cell phones, video games, instant messaging, and the Internet, is that students too easily succumb to distraction. Multitasking is a way of life for this generation. I explained in Chapter III how crucial it is to protect memory consolidation processes from distractions and interference.

Students typically try to memorize by rote, which is the least effective and reliable way. Students also don't self-test enough, and when they do, they tend to be lax in the way they test themselves. They over estimate what they know, and undervalue extra study.

I think that education policy is part of the problem. Little-to-no emphasis is given to effective learning strategies. Also, many educational policies are counter-productive. Here are a couple of examples:

1. The summer break is too long and disruptive.
2. Classrooms, especially in elementary schools, are filled with excessive stimuli like hanging mobiles, posters on the walls, art projects, lists, charts, and homework assignments, and all sorts of other distractions. No wonder so many kids are too jazzed up to pay attention; they are over-stimulated.
3. Curricula are not integrated. We teach subjects as if they exist in isolation, severely limiting opportunities for

students to understand relevance, make associations and apply new learning.

4. Finally, it is hardly necessary to point out that many students, especially college students, do not get enough sleep. They also tend to cram for exams, instead of spreading the learning out over time.

## Names and Faces

Don't feel bad if you have trouble remembering names and faces. Everybody does. But it is important to remember. Dale Carnegie said, "Remember that a man's name is to him the sweetest and most important sound in the English language."

Ever notice how some salespeople repeat your name frequently? They are trained to do that, because it makes such a favorable impact on customers. It makes you feel more accepting of the salesperson and perhaps even what they're selling.

The obvious first thing to do when meeting new people is to focus your attention on them and their name. Notice what they look like and how they speak and act. If their name can be spelled in more than one way, ask how they spell it: for example, "is that Kathy with a K or a C?" If they give you a business card, read it right then and there. If they or their name remind you of someone, mentioning it gives you some small talk and at the same time is a memory rehearsal. Use their name as soon and as frequently as you reasonably can. Both the mechanics of speaking the name and the hearing of the sound are powerful elements of a rehearsal strategy for remembering the name.

One popular way of remembering names and faces it to identify some special facial feature (like big nose, moles in certain places, hairline, etc.) and use that to make an association with the name. It usually helps to exaggerate the feature in your mind's eye and then find a way to associate the name (or its sound-a-like) to that facial feature. Remembering the names of some people is easy. If Mr. Bell, for example, has a large nose, you can imagine his face with a huge bell hanging down from between his eyes. Names such as Carpenter, Miller, Gable, Hammer, Badger, or Wolfe have built-in images. For other names, you can take some liberties with your imagination. Mrs. Hubbard, for example, might be envisioned as "Old Mother" Hubbard. Mr. Rosenberg might be imagined as an iceberg with a rose in it. The more ridiculous your image association, the better the memory will stick.

Research, however, suggests that this approach may be counter-productive.[145] Experiments show that using verbal descriptions of facial details can actually impair subsequent recognition of the face. It seems that the brain registers images best when it can process them as a whole, rather than as a sum of its parts.

So how do we deal with that for the practical purposes of remembering names and faces? Let me suggest this: when you meet a new person think first of the whole face. Ignore facial details that might dominate your attention. See the forest, not the trees. Rehearse in your mind's eye what the whole face looks like.

Now, how do you pin the name to that image? This gets even trickier, for now you have to try to make an association of the name with a whole face. Maybe the conventional approach would still work, if you first have cemented in your mind the whole-face image. In some cases, you can make an association with the whole face.

Anytime you meet a group of new people, set a goal for remembering three people well. Then, as this skill is acquired, raise the goal to five, then seven, then ten or more people. You will discover that you become progressively better at this fundamental social skill.

Maybe shortcuts can work. In some social environments, you don't need to remember the face; it's the name that is important. In that case, write it down on a notepad and quiz yourself on what you wrote down. I have seen seminar presenters use this tactic with great effect. They jot down the names of a few people they meet before the presentation, and then call on them at various times. "I met John a minute ago. Where is John?" John holds up his hand, and the presenter asks him for his thoughts on the matter. If the people are in fixed locations—say, seated around a conference table—draw yourself a little map, showing names (and any special characteristics) in the proper place. As explained earlier, spatial location of information is a useful memory cue. A common problem I have experienced with unfamiliar people around a conference table is that they mumble their name when asked to introduce themselves. You don't want to do that with your name.

In other situations, you need only the first name, or the last name. In a few situations, it is only the face that has to be remembered. The point is, limit the memory work load whenever you can.

# Numbers

Sometimes people have a need to remember certain numbers, such as birthdates, historical dates, credit card numbers, phone numbers, addresses, TV channels, etc.

Ordinarily, numbers are hard to remember, but there is a simple, powerful system to help.

First assign a different consonant sound to each number between zero and nine. Then, when given a number to remember, make a word out of it—string the consonant sounds together for each digit, filling in vowel sounds as needed to make complete words.

A set of rules determines how to construct number-associated images. You have to memorize these rules, and that is a hassle—but worth it. The rules dictate what letters and sounds go with numbers 1 through 0, as follows:

| Number | Letter Sound | Mnemonic Aid |
| --- | --- | --- |
| 1 | t or d | Each has one down stroke |
| 2 | n or kn/gn | Two down strokes; kn and gn have the same n sound |
| 3 | m | Three down strokes |
| 4 | r | Last letter of word four |
| 5 | L | L is Roman numeral for 5 |
| 6 | j, ch, sh, soft g | Reverse J looks like 6; other letters have a g sound, as in judge |
| 7 | k, ck, hard g or c | K is made from a backward leaning 7 |
| 8 | t, ph, v | Join an F with another F turned upside down and it looks like 8 |
| 9 | p or b | Backwards p or a rotated b look like 9 |
| 0 | z, s, soft c | Z as in zero, soft c as in cent |

It may seem like a lot of trouble to memorize these sounds, but once you have it's a cinch to memorize numbers. You can construct all sorts of word-derived images based on these rules, which was illustrated also under "Peg Systems."

The words you make up from these consonants can be a single word that includes all the consonants, or several words that are sequentially linked. See the table for some examples of how this system can be applied to phone numbers. Area codes don't have to be memorized if it's the same as your local one. But if not, you can use a separate word for the area code.

| bank | 696-2180 | n, t, f, y | notify (imagine handing a note to teller to ask for withdrawal) |
| daughter | 822-6753 | j, k, l, m | joke + lame (you tell a joke to your daughter and she laughs so hard she falls down and breaks her leg [becomes lame]) |
| congressman | 512-9281 | b, n, f, t | Benefit (you host a fund-raising benefit for your congressman) |
| tennis partner | 844-4719 | r, k, t, p | racket + pee (you make a bad shot in your doubles game and you get so mad that you throw down the racket and urinate on it) |

This method can be useful for linking dates and events. For example if you wanted to remember that the Declaration of Independence was signed on July 4, 1776, you could build a memorable picture as follows: a number code for 1776 could be dog (17) and cage (76). Couple this with whatever image comes to mind for the Declaration, such as the liberty bell. Now picture your dog sleeping in its cage crate, being awakened by the ringing bell. For the link to July 4, you might want to add a firecracker image that goes off after the bell rings, like a Pavlov experiment where the bell rings, unconditioned firecracker stimulus goes off, and dog responds with jumping around in his cage. To practice this system, you might develop images for remembering family birthdays and anniversaries. I did this with my nine grandchildren, one at a time about a month or so before their next birthday.

## Dates

We all have key dates to remember: birthdays, anniversaries, deadlines, and the like. My approach is to have a stock mental image for each month and couple that image with the number code image for the day in the month. Monthly images should be whatever comes naturally to you. For example, living in my part of Texas, I conjure images of a hard freeze (icicles) for January, rain for February, tornados for March, bluebonnets for April, and so on. So, if my wedding anniversary is April 11, my mental picture is of my wife holding a baby (tot) in a field of bluebonnets and I am taking a picture of the scene. Now I also need to have an image to remember my anniversary. What comes to mind? A wedding ring! So now, I construct this image of a wedding ring totally surrounding like a frame around this picture of my wife, our tot, and the field of bluebonnets. Any time during the year that I ask myself, "When is my anniversary?"

I immediately think of wedding ring and that brings up the picture of bluebonnets and our tot.

To remember a birthday of a specific person, I have to have a mental picture that always comes to mind. In the case of my son, for example, he likes to hunt, and conjuring an imaging of him hunting is easy. He was born in August. My Texas image of August is hot, hot, hot, so I visualize him hunting without any clothes on because it is so hot. The target of his hunting is the number-code image for his day of birth. All of this is easy to integrate into one image.

# Alphabet Letters

Sometimes we have to remember letters, for example, the letters on car license plates or locations in a huge parking lot or stock-market symbols. A good way to do that is to have a mental library of images for each letter of the alphabet. Though some memory books give example lists, it saves you the time of memorizing their list if you just use whatever comes to mind for each letter. Having animal images is a good approach, and you should use animals that are sure to come to mind. For example, I live in Texas and wrote a book on armadillos, so for me the choice for the letter A is armadillos. Then I use a picture of an armadillo any time I have to remember the letter A. So if I parked my car at a stadium parking lot on row A7, I picture the car parked next to an armadillo hole in the lot, and to get it to come out I have to insert a key (code number for 7) into the hole.

Other images might be B = bear, C = cat, D = dog, E = elephant— whatever works best for you. You can do a similar thing for any letter and/or letter-number combination. Just use the letter image integrated with the number code image.

# Places

Why is it men get lost so easily? Women will say it is because they won't ask for directions. Well, as a man, I have on rare occasion stopped to ask locals for guidance. One problem is that they tend to forget that you don't know the area like they do, and give convoluted, rapid-fire directions: "Go down to the third stop sign and make a right, then you're gonna turn left at the second red light, go about four to six blocks until you reach the museum, then turn right, go past the school, merge onto the right exit lane, go down the access road to Joe's Diner, pull into his parking lot..." Well, you get the idea: I got lost after the second turn.

The simple solution: make a drawing as the verbal instructions are being presented. Drawings are easier to remember than words, and in the worst case, you can always cheat by looking at your drawing. You could jot the directions down, but a drawing is easier to remember.

# Computer Passwords

You could of course, store your passwords on your computer or in a "cloud" file like Evernote. The problem is that hackers can get to them. Assign aliases to the websites you need passwords for, and if you pick aliases that only have meaning for you, you can store the aliases in a computer file or computer sticky note. An example comes from a Dagwood cartoon joke. He is depicted at his computer, all frustrated because he can't remember his password. Blondie says, "Could it be something you love?" "Oh yes," Dagwood replies, "it must be 'pastrami'!"

One trick for sites that require changing the password every few months is to insert a number or symbol somewhere in the word. So the first time I use it, the password might be xxxxxxx6, then the next time it would be xxxxxxx7, and so on. Or you could use the same number (or symbol) and move its position in the character string.

Another useful tactic is creating a password for each website using a phrase or sentence related to that website. You can then take the first letter of each word in the sentence and make that your password, or otherwise recreate the sentence using some combination of characters. For example, if you're making a password for your Amazon. com account, you might use the sentence, "My favorite book is *To Kill a Mockingbird*." Your password could then be "mfbitkam," or even "mfbi2kam." If necessary, you can write your phrase or key down somewhere without worrying about someone hacking into your account if they find it.

## Jokes

Everybody wishes they could remember jokes better. I don't know how comedians do it, memorizing a long string of new jokes for a monologue. I have read maybe a dozen biographies of comedians, and none of them revealed how they memorize long monologs. It may be like magicians' secrets. But you can be sure they all had some sort of gimmick. That capability was a job requirement before the age of the teleprompter.

One thing I know they must do is reduce a joke to its bare minimum. They can always ad lib the details. Then, I bet these elements are made into a mental image collage or sequence of linked images.

Jokes, except for one-liners, fit well into a story-chain approach for memorizing. Jokes begin with a set up, followed by a story line, and then a surprise, and hopefully funny, ending.[146] You only have to memorize three key points: 1) the cast of characters, 2) the setting, and 3) the funny action. Everything else you can ad lib. Then take the three things and make a mental picture.

Below, I will show you an old Texas joke to illustrate the general technique for memorizing jokes. Here, the only part you need to memorize is in bold.

> Two guys from Canada, Joe and Sam, were ***driving through Texas to Mexico***. They came to a town with the city limit ***sign that said "Mexia***, population 6,552." Joe said, "I wonder how you ***pronounce Mexia***. Must be "mex ... eee ... a." No, said Sam, "That is a Mexican name. It should be "ma ... hay ... uh." After some heated argument, Joe says, "We need lunch. Let's stop at this ***Dairy Queen*** here and ask the ***waitress*** how her town is pronounced." So when the waitress comes to take their order, Joe asks her, "Excuse me, can you first settle an argument we have? How do you pronounce the name of this place?" With a quizzical look and some hesitation, she slowly says ***"daaay .... reee... queen."***

The mental picture is easy to construct: car, road sign showing Mexia, and Dairy Queen restaurant.

# Vocabulary

A strong vocabulary marks you as well educated. It makes both your reading and your writing more effective. So how do you build vocabulary? I have a couple of ideas based on memory principles.

**Learn word prefixes and suffixes.** Prefixes and suffixes are great aids. "Pre" suggests before or ahead of time; "ism" suggests a state of being, "re" suggests back or again, and so on.

**Learn word families**. Many words come from the same family. Here are some word groups. If you know what one word in the group means, you can get the general idea for the others from the context in which they are used. The other words will be easier to remember because they are similar to the word you already know.

despise, despicable, despot, despotism, despoil

habit, habitat, habitation, habitual, habitué

jet, jettison, jetstream, jetty, jetset, jetlag, jetsam

line, liner, lineman, linear, line drive, line-up

parent, paternal, pater, patriarch, paternity, patrician, patricide

Create "AVENUE" images for strange new words. Examples:

Gazebo: see yourself staring (gazing) at the ugliest boy (bo) you ever saw standing in a building that only has a roof, no walls. Feel disgust.

Adumbrate (meaning incomplete understanding or explanation): see a "dumb brat" with a dunce cap, sitting in the corner partially hidden by a screen. Sense the pain he must feel at being so ostracized and tries to hide.

Daguerreotype (an early photographic process on metal plate): visualize a picture on a sheet of metal and you have stabbed it with a dagger because you hate it so much.

Perspicacious (meaning especially insightful): see yourself working up a sweat (perspire), scratching your head with question marks around it, then jumping up with a eureka moment when you realize you figured it out.

## Foreign Languages

In this globally interconnected world, many people want to learn a foreign language. In my own case, decades ago I stumbled through Russian and French because they were required for my Ph.D. Most recently, I am trying Spanish, because I live in Texas.

Some things I know that help learning foreign language is the use of flash cards for vocabulary (using images, not just the words).

Another thing is know is the value of strategic approaches and planning. For example, I first have to confront my negative attitude (remember what I said about how negative attitudes impair learning). I have a negative attitude about the irrational things in language. Take the gender business in Spanish and many other languages. Why does everything have to have a sex identification, like male and female endings for inanimate objects? That is just plain stupid! Irregular verbs are another problem. When I was in high school, I learned Latin, which wasn't so bad because it was a much more orderly language than the modern languages that "evolved" from it. Latin wasn't broken. Why did people want to change it?

My first strategic realization was that I had to get over my pique. Who was I punishing with my negative attitude? Certainly not the people who created the irrationalities in the language. No, my attitude would be a de-motivator for me to learn. So, I tell myself, "Get over it."

Next, I think about some basic principles that might expedite my learning. You don't have to be a professor of modern languages to know that certain key components in language include the following:

1. Meaning of words. Here, try to recognize cognates (words similar to English words you already know). For other words, try to think of mental images that represent the meaning.
2. Gender identification. Fortunately, you can usually predict whether a word is male or female just from the meaning of the word. Most macho-type words are male; soft, feminine type words are usually female. Unfortunately, there are exceptions, which you just have to memorize by brute force.

3. Verb conjugation. Look for patterns. All "regular" verbs have the same pattern. In Spanish, all verbs end in AR, ER, or IR. The conjugation pattern is similar. For each, you drop the infinitive ending and add endings to the stem of the word. For AR words, the ending is either o, as, a (singular) or amos, ais, or an (plural). For ER words, the endings are o, es, e (singular) or emos, eis, en (plural). For IR words, the endings are o, es, e (singular), or imos, is, en (plural). Even irregular verbs have generally predictable patterns, except for a couple of endings.

4. Counting. Here, again, look for patterns. In Spanish you have to brute-force memorize the first 19 numbers, but thereafter predictable patterns emerge.

5. Articles, like "a," and "the." In Spanish, you only have to remember "un" for "a." But, since the article has to be a gender match to the word it refers to, you have to add an "a" (una) to refer to female words. If you are referring to a definite person, you must use "el" or "la," depending on the person's gender. Plural references add an "s" (as in "los/las")

6. Pronouns, like I, you, he, etc. In Spanish, there is a definite pattern that includes gender recognition and singular vs. plural.

Well, you probably don't want to learn Spanish, so I won't expand further. My point here is that learning is greatly facilitated when you look for patterns. Memorize the patterns, and it is easier to memorize the specifics.

Even how the patterns are displayed spatially may matter, depending on what works for you. For example, which of the following pattern for the Spanish words for "this, that, these, those" would work best for you?

| this | esta | F |
|------|------|---|
| that | esa | F |
| these | estas | F |
| those | esás | F |
| this | esto or este | M |
| that | eso or ese | M |
| these | estos | M or ? |
| those | esos | M or ? |

| this | these | that | those | Gender |
|------|-------|------|-------|--------|
| esto/este | estos | eso/este | esos | M or ? |
| esta | estas | esa | esás | F |

| | M or M/? | F |
|------|----------|---|
| this | esto/este | esta |
| that | eso/ese | esa |
| these | estos | estas |
| those | esos | esás |

There are, of course, other ways a table of this information could be laid out. My bet is you would find one layout easier to memorize than another. My Spanish teacher, by the way, laid things out like the first table, only she made it harder to memorize by having M and M or ? listed separately. You don't need to do that, since M or ? can refer to the same word no matter what. Another pattern you might notice is that the letter "t" occurs in Spanish for "this" and "these," but not the other two words. Also, you only have to memorize the masculine (ending in o or e) because the feminine is the same word, only with "a" instead of "o" or "e."

The point is this: structure your learning material in ways that work best for you. Develop a strategy. Look for patterns. A strategic approach should also include developing ways to categorize things in the most useful way for memorization.

## Playing Cards

To remember playing cards, you can incorporate the number system described earlier, as follows: first you construct a code word that represents both the suit and the value of the card. You can use the number code to find the letter to designate the card value and a letter to represent the suit (for clubs, use a c or k, s for spades, d for diamonds, and r for hearts (it is easier to generate words with an r than words with an h).

This could yield, for example, the following for clubs: 1 (the ace) = tack, 2 = neck, 3 = mike, 4 = rock, 5 = lock, 6 = check, 7 = cocoa, 8 = factory, 9 = package, 10 = sack. For the face cards, use the first letter, j for jack, q for queen, and a k for king. Thus for clubs, you would have jack (the kind kids play with) for the jack, quack for queen, and cake for king.

I won't take up book space to generate code words for all 52 cards, but you can do it yourself if you are a serious card player. You would have to memorize 52 code words, but since they are created using the number system you already know, that is not as big a chore as you might imagine. As cards are played, you visualize the code word's image as being smashed or changed in some dramatic way: As the 4 of clubs is played, envision a rock breaking on the table. An ace of clubs could be seen as a tack getting stuck in the table and remaining there. Or you could string these images into a story chain.

Even more powerful imaging methods are used by "memory athletes" in contests that test how fast they can memorize the sequential ordering of cards. Since this is not a common chore for ordinary folks, I refer you to Joshua Foer's book, *Moonwalking with Einstein*.

# Music

Music is hard for most people to learn. You not only have to memorize the notes, their timing, and sequence, but you have to train the body parts like fingers, lips, and tongue to execute the notes.

"You've probably heard the old joke: "How do I get to Carnegie Hall?" "Practice, practice, practice!" Well music practice does take time, and it's probably not a satisfying answer for people looking to learn music quickly. But surely there are techniques and strategies to expedite the process. Here's one method I've created using related memory principles:

1. Skim the whole score to identify hard and easy parts and phrases that repeat. Then start at the beginning, memorizing in chunks, one or a few bars at a time, depending on the capacity of your working memory. After memorizing a bar or phrase, see if you can play it without peeking. Musicians do not learn a new piece from beginning to end all at once. They often start at the beginning of a piece and learn a small section until they get it right. Then they learn the next piece. Then they

practice stitching the pieces together. They repeat this process until they get to the end.

2. Memorize the mechanical acts needed to play the notes (keys on a piano, valves on a clarinet, etc.). Learn one hand at a time. Look at the hands and keys while playing.

3. Play what you have just memorized from memory and repeat until you feel it is mastered. Play one hand at a time, then play with both together. Don't peek at the score until after you have played the section. Check for any errors in your recall.

4. Play the chunk slowly at first, then test the tempo by playing with a metronome.

5. Move to a different chunk and repeat steps 1–3. Add one bar or phrase at a time. Mark sections of the score as they are learned.

6. Join the latest chunk with those previously learned and play from the beginning.

7. In the next practice session, rehearse what was learned in the previous session before moving on to new material.

## Skilled Movements

A most common form of procedural memory is the learning of skilled movements, which includes skills ranging from playing golf to playing the piano. While much remains to be discovered in this area of learning, some research reveals ways to improve motor learning. The applications of these discoveries have profound implications. Athletic coaches would be well advised to ponder these discoveries. So also would physical therapists and music teachers, among others.

## Learn by Watching

People have long known that they can improve their physical skills by visualizing themselves performing in perfect form. Visualizing ideal movements in the "mind's eye" is a common technique used by athletes. It works. Athletes commonly film themselves or watch themselves in a mirror. Then they rehearse perfect movements by imagining themselves performing perfectly—a beautiful golf swing, or a double-fake pump shot in basketball, or throwing a touchdown pass, or whatever.

What many do not know is that improved learning can come from watching others perform perfect movements.[147] The idea is to practice the movement one is trying to learn in the mind's eye.

Observational learning could be very helpful for rehabilitation of patients who have difficulty in generating movements or who are unable to understand verbal instructions. I would add that observational motor learning could supplement actual practice learning in normal people who want to improve a motor skill for a sport, musical instrument, or work task. Actually, this is similar to the more general "visualization technique" where one prepares for a task by seeing himself performing it in the mind's eye.

## Learn One Movement Skill at a Time

As the brain learns a bodily movement, it creates a mental model (MM) of how the movement is accomplished.[148] For example, when a person plans to pick up a brick, a mental model of the amount of force required to pick up the brick is used to plan the action. The brain does not estimate the force as if it were a feather or a sack of cement, it uses its memory of how a brick feels to create a model of how much force will be needed to pick it up.

The study based on this concept explored the finding that a recently acquired MM (MM1) can be disrupted if a second MM (MM2) was introduced too soon after MM1. That is, a MM1 has to have enough time to consolidate, just as declarative memories do.

A proactive interference can also occur. A MM1 can interfere with learning a MM2, if there is not enough time separation between learning the two motor tasks. This was demonstrated in the present study by having 60 subjects learn how to make two conflicting movements using the robotic arm. The MM for both tasks could be learned but only if the training sessions were separated by at least 5 hours. If the interval was shorter, learning of the second MM (MM2) was impaired, as was the likelihood of consolidating the first MM.

My explanation is the following: Once MM1 gets consolidated, the circuits that sustain its short-term representation now become available for learning a second motor memory (MM2). That is, MM1 has proactive interfering after-effects that dissipate with consolidation of the MM1 and thus no longer interfere with learning an MM2. The "take home message" of this research is that learning different movement tasks should be separated in time.

Interference can be reduced by spreading out a motor learning task, rather than practicing in adjacent successive blocks where a skill is practiced exhaustively before switching to some other activity. For example, training people a complicated walking motion on a split-belt treadmill with each belt running at a different speed has been suggested as therapy for stroke victims. A study of practice structure compared two practice structures, one where subjects walked on the split-belt for 15 consecutive minutes with a another group that alternated between different speeds and the same speed. The next day, the group that switched on and off the differing speeds performed much better than the one that had learned in a constant 15 minute condition.[149] The authors rightly conclude that there are many important and poorly understood issues of "learning to learn," adaptation, and interference that affect movement performance.

Motor learning is a relatively new field of learning research, and I expect there will be many more studies of practice structure that will prove of great value to physical therapists and athletic trainers.

## Practice Smart

Remember what was said earlier about "deliberate practice?" The idea applies especially to learning skilled movements. Deliberate practice is crucial for sports, especially high-precision sports such as golf or tennis.[150] Whether it is learning movements such as throwing a baseball or playing the piano, one has to consciously think about the movements and learn explicitly what to do. Then, repeated practice can eventually automate this learning and make it implicit memory. This usually takes lots of practice, done in the right way.

Even without practice, the commands for a given task became essentially hardwired into the brain after five or six hours. This makes it easier to understand why an adult who learned to ride a bicycle as a child can go through several decades of adult life without riding a bike and still be able to ride without falling.

During this five-to-six -hour "re-wiring" consolidation interval, memory of the task is vulnerable. Trying to learn something else, especially another motor task, is likely to undo the already accomplished learning.[151] This possibility could have enormous implications for the way skills training is conducted in educational, industrial, and athletic settings. Take the training of a football quarterback, for example. If the coach wants him to work on his passing, the workout should be limited to just that, and not end the passing workout with practice on running the option.

Want to learn how to touch-type? Or play the piano? Or hit a bull's-eye with football passes? Maybe you should do your learning at night. Some intriguing recent research raises the possibility such motor skills may be learned better with night-time training than with training in the morning. Some evidence exists that implicit learning can occur "off-line" (i.e., when not being practiced) during the day. Moreover, the time of day for consolidations of implicit learning is a factor. In one study, off-line consolidation was more resistant to interference when training occurred at 8 PM, compared with 8 AM.[152] In both groups, skill was demonstrably better after the off-line interval. The sleep was a likely contributor to the beneficial effect.

---

### Memory Myth Buster

*The time of day has no bearing on learning effectiveness.* WRONG. Some people are morning people and some are night owls. It does make a difference. Motor skills seem best learned in the evening.

---

# Improving the Golf Game (and other sports)

What does all this tell you about how to lower your golf score or raise your bowling score? HOW you practice should make an enormous difference. Just putting in the same total amount of practice time is not the most important thing.

I will summarize these ideas as they might apply to improve a golf swing. I suggest:

- Watch videos of golfers noted for their swings. Visualize yourself making such beautiful swings.

- Avoid hitting several buckets of golf balls on a driving range with the same club. Such stereotyped repetitive drill would quickly produce diminishing returns. Maybe interspersing driving practice with a two-iron might be o.k., because the swings are similar, but the two-iron provides a different challenge.

- Avoid back-to-back practices of driving and making chip shots to a green. The swing mechanics are quite different and likely to produce learning interference.

- Allow at least six hours between practice sessions, so that what you learn in an early session has a chance to consolidate before you practice something else.

- Take a nap after a practice session (see next section).

- Consider practicing in the evening, as opposed to the morning.

- Make certain to get a full night's sleep after practice.

# Learned Movements Promoted by Sleep

Memory of motor learning develops "off-line," without practice, after the learning session. This off-line processing even occurs during sleep. Sleeping between learning two different movement tasks is much more effective than trying to learn them back-to-back.

Another study[153] showed movement speed was improved with no loss of accuracy by 20% after a night's sleep, whereas no improvement occurred after an equivalent amount of wakefulness.

Stage of sleep seems to matter. A typical person spends only about one-fifth of a night's sleep in the dream stage, with most of that occurring in the morning hours. Yet this is the time when movement memories are preferentially consolidated. One study[154] revealed that movement skills learned during the daytime improved more during late sleep, whereas recall of word lists improved more during early night's sleep. Obviously, cutting a night's sleep short (which reduces the amount of dream-sleep time) could impair procedural memory.

Other studies of kinds of procedural memory show that dream sleep has a preferential benefit for procedural memories. Early morning is when we consolidate memories of learned movements. If you cut your night sleep short by getting up early, procedural memory can be impaired. At least, that is the finding of Dr. Robert Stickgold's research group[155] who studied memories of college student volunteers under conditions where they spotted targets on a computer screen and pressed a button as soon as they realized they had seen a target. Students who slept less than six hours showed no improvement the next day after training. But improvement did occur if students slept more than six hours, and the improvement was proportional to the length of time beyond six hours. For those who slept more than eight hours, improvement of the skill was proportional to the amount of slow wave sleep they got in the first quarter of the night's sleep and to the amount of dream sleep that occurred in the last quarter of the night's sleep. Thus, both phases of sleep have an important effect on memory formation in these tests. The enhanced performance grew over time, with the well-rested subjects performing even better when re-tested two days to a week after the initial training session.

Even naps during the daytime are helpful for motor memory. This is true whether the non-practice interval is during the day or during sleep at night. For example, one study examined how well subjects remembered a finger-to-thumb movement task after a 90-minute daytime nap.[156]

Half of the subjects were allowed to take an afternoon 90-minute nap after training, while the other group stayed awake. The group that napped showed a distinct improvement in task performance when tested that evening. After a night's sleep, both groups showed the same improvement in acquired skill. So, it would appear the nap just speeded up the consolidation process, rather than improving on the improvement a regular night's sleep can produce.

The role of napping on interference effects was also tested. In this experiment, another group of subjects learned a different thumb-to-finger movement sequence two hours after practicing the first task. Learning a second task right after the first prevented improvement in performance of the first task either that evening or the next day after a normal night's sleep. However, the experimenters created yet another group of subjects that were allowed a 90-minute nap between learning the first movement task and the second movement task. In this case, performance on the first task was improved when they were tested the next day after a normal night's sleep. This study indicates that if you need to learn a "how to" kind of task quickly, you should take a nap soon afterward.

\* \* \* \* \*

You would not have come this far in your quest for a better memory if you did not have the need or the desire to improve your learning and memory and to reap the rewards that accompany a sharper, better brain. I hope by now you better understand how the brain learns and remembers and are aware of many principles, tips, and tricks that will indeed work for you. Of course, these ideas do you no good as long as they remain trapped in the pages of this book. Once you start using these ideas you will indeed become more competent, and that, in turn, will help build your confidence, which just makes learning even easier!

*Believe in the reality that the more you know,*
*the more you can know.*

## Key Ideas from Chapter Five

1. Advice for school: have a positive attitude, don't multitask, self-test more.

2. Remembering names and faces: make sure the name registers, focus on spelling of name, use the name, write it down, make associations with facial features, rehearse the name later.

3. Remembering places: make a drawing, spot landmarks.

4. Remembering numbers: use the number-to-letter code to create words that can be imaged in the mind's eye.

5. Remembering jokes: make a mental image of the three elements of cast of characters, setting, and funny punch line. Ad lib the rest.

6. Increasing vocabulary: learn prefixes and suffixes, create word families, create mental images.

7. Foreign language: identify cognates, use logic for most gender issues, look for patterns in verb conjugations and counting.

8. Playing cards: incorporate the numbering system, make mental images.

9. Music: skim the whole score, start at the beginning, master a few bars at a time, stitch successive bars together as they are mastered.

10. Look at how skilled people perform movement tasks. Imagine yourself doing likewise.

11. Learn one movement skill at a time.

12. Practice deliberately, consciously thinking about the movements.

13. Don't do back-to-back practice with different skills.

14. Practice movements in the right way: 1) think consciously about what is required, 2) don't try to learn unrelated movements in the same sessions, 3) mix in related movements in the same sessions to prevent drill-like repetition and habituation.

15. Consider learning movement skills in the evening.

16. Get a full night's sleep to promote consolidation of movement skills. Don't cut it short.

17. Take a nap after a training session.

# SOURCES

## CHAPTER 1

1. Martin, R., Sexton, C., and Franklin, T. (2004). "Teaching Science for All Children. Inquiry Lessons for Constructing Understanding." 3rd Edition. Old Tappan, N.J.: Allyn & Bacon.
2. Klemm, W. R. (2007). "What good is learning if you don't remember it?" J. Effective Teaching. 7(1) 61–73.
3. Peters, T. and Waterman, R. H. (1982). *In Search of Excellence*. New York: Harper Business Books.
4. Lyubomirsky, Sonja (2008) *The How To of Happiness*. New York: Penguin.
5. Klemm, W. R. (2011). *Atoms of Mind. The 'Ghost in the Machine" Materializes*. New York: Springer.
6. Klemm, W. R. (2008). *Blame Game. How To Win It*. Bryan, Tx.: Benecton.
7. Büchel, C. Coull, J. T., Friston, K. J. (1999). "The predictive value of changes in effective connecting for human learning". Science. 283 1538–1541.

## CHAPTER 2

8. Renner, M. J., and Rosenzweig, M. R. (1987). *Enriched and Impoverished Environments: Effects on Brain and Behavior*. New York: Springer–Verlag.
9. Diamond, M. et al. (1985). "Plasticity in 904 day-old male rat cerebral cortex." Experimental Neurology. 87: 309–317.
10. Diamond, Adel. (2011)." Applying what we know from scientific research in developmental cognitive neuroscience to how schools can enhance executive function in development in young children." Conference on Cognitive Neuroscience of Learning: Implications for Education. September 22-24, Aspen, Colorado.
11. Desmond, Adrian. (1999). *Huxley. From Devil's Disciple to Evolution's High Priest*. Perseus Books, Penguin, London.

12    I wrote a summary of this rather long book to inspire school children. Seehttp://peer.tamu.edu/curriculum_modules/Ecosystems/module_1/storytime6.htm

13.   Schrier, A. M. (1984). "Learning how to learn: the significance and current status of learning set formation." Primates. 25 (1): 95–102.

14.   Lightle, K. (2011). "More than just the technology." Science Scope. Summer 2011. p. 6-9.

15.   Blodgett, H.C. (1929). "The effect of the introduction of reward upon the maze performance of rats." Univ. Calif. Publ. Psychol. 4: 113–134.

16.   Harlow, H. F. (1949). "The formation of learning sets." Psychological Review. 56: 51–65. *Inquiry Thoughts, Views, and Strategies for the K-5 Classroom Foundations*. (1999). Volume 2. Arlington, VA: Division of Elementary, Secondary, and Informal Education, National Science Foundation.

17.   Dr. Harlow wrote a fascinating autobiography in Klemm, W. R. (1977) *Discovery Processes in Modern Biology*. New York: Krieger.

18.   Klemm, W. R. (2008). *Blame Game. How To Win It*. Bryan, Tx.: Benecton.

19.   Russell, Peter (1991). *The Brain Book*. New York, N.Y.: Dutton.

20.   Godden D. & Baddeley A. D. (1975). "Context-dependent memory in two natural environments: On land and under water." British Journal of Psychology. 66: 325–331.

21.   Blair, Clancy. (2011). "Executive function and school readiness." Conference on Cognitive Neuroscience of Learning: Implications for Education. September 22–24, Aspen, Colorado.

22.   Bunge, Silvia. (2011)."Intensive reasoning training alters patterns of brain connectivity at rest." Conference on Cognitive Neuroscience of Learning: Implications for Education. September 22–24, Aspen, Colorado.

23.   Xue, G. et al. (2011) "Spaced learning enhances subsequent recognition memory by reducing neural repetition suppression." J. Cognitive Neuroscience. 23: 1624–1633.

24.   Peterson, Tony (2010). *Peterson Field Guides to Birds of Eastern and Central North America*, Sixth Edition. New York: Houghton-Mifflin.

25.   Tolman, E. C. (1948). "Cognitive maps in rats and men." Psychological Review, 55, 189–208.

26.   Colvin, Geoff. (2008). *Talent Is Overrated*. London: Penguin.

27.   Rossato, J. et al. (2009). "Dopamine controls persistence of long-term memory storage." Science. 325: 1017-1020.

# Chapter 3

28. Winson, S. (1991).*Getting Organized.* New York: Warner Books.
29. Kastner, S. et al. (1998). "Mechanisms of directed attention in the human extrastriate cortex as revealed by functional MRI." Science. 282: 108-111.
30. See also McMains, S. and Kastner, S. (2011). "Interactions of top-down and bottom-up mechanisms in human visual cortex." J. Neuroscience. 31 (2): 587-597.
31. Clark, R. E., and Squire, L. R. (1998). "Classical conditioning and brain systems: the role of awareness." Science. 280 (5360): 77-81.
32. Bargh, J. A.; Chen, M.; Burrows, L. (1996). "Automaticity of social behavior: Direct effects of trait construct and stereotype activation on action." Journal of Personality and Social Psychology. 71 (2): 230–244. doi:10.1037/0022-3514.71.2.230. PMID 8765481.
33. Chabris, C., and Simons, D. (2010). *The Invisible Gorilla.* New York: Crown.
34. Kastern, S. (1998). "Mechanisms of directed attention in the human extrastriate cortex as revealed by functional MRI." Science. 282: (5386): 108-111 DOI: 10.1126/science.282.5386.108.
35. Wake Forest University Baptist Medical Center (2007). "Listen up, tune out: Training and experience can affect brain." News release, Nov. 6.
36. Gallagher, Winifred. (2009). *Rapt. Attention and the Focused Life*. New York: Penguin.
37. Alleyene, R. (2010). "Internet beats books for improving the mind, say scientists." May 29. Telegraph.Co.UK.
38. Werheid, K., et al. (2002). "The adaptive digit ordering test. Clinical application, reliability, and validity of a verbal working memory test." Arch. Clin. Neuropsychol. 17: 547–565.
39. Dijksterhuis, A. et al. (2006). "On making the right choice: the deliberation-without-attention effect." Science. 311: 1005–1007.
40. Süss, H. –M. et al. (2002). "Working-memory capacity explains reasoning ability—and a little bit more." Intelligence. 30:261–288.
41. Flynn, J. R. (1987). "Massive IQ gains in 14 nations: What IQ tests really measure." Psych. Bull. 101 (2) 171–191.
42. Jaeggi, S. M. et al. (2008). "Improving fluid intelligence with training on working memory." Proc. Natl. Acad. Science. www.pnas.org/cgi/doi/10.1073/pnas.0801268105.

43. For the actual procedure, see http://www.soakyourhead.com/.

44. Ramsden, S. et al. (2011) "Verbal and non-verbal intelligence changes in the teenage brain." Nature. Doi:10.1038/nature10514.

45. Wajima, Kayo, and Sawaguchi, T. (2005). "The effect of working memory training on general intelligence in children." Society for Neuroscience Abstracts. Abstract 772.11.

46. Olesen, P. J., Westerberg, H., and Kingberg, T. (2004). "Increased prefrontal and parietal activity after training of working memory." Nature Neuroscience. 7: 75–79.

47. Jaeggi, S. M. et al. (2008). "Improving fluid intelligence with training on working memory." Proc. Natl. Acad. Science. www.pnas.org/cgi/doi/10.1073/pnas.0801268105.

48. For the actual procedure, see http://www.soakyourhead.com/.

49. Verhaeghen, P., Cerella, J., and Basak, C. (2004). "A working memory workout: how to expand the focus of serial attention from one to four items in 10 hours or less." J. Exp. Psychol., Learning, Memory and Cognition. 30 (6): 1322–1337.

50. deFockert, J. W. et al. (2001). "The role of working memory in visual selective attention." Science. 291: 1803–1806.

51. Macrae, C. N., and Lewis, H. L. (2002). "Do I know you? Processing orientation and face recognition." Psychological Science. 13 (2): 194–196.

52. Jonides, J., and Nee, D. E. (2006). "Brain mechanisms of proactive interference in working memory." Neuroscience. 139: 181–193.

53. Goldman-Rakic, P. S. (1996). "Regional and cellular fractionation of working memory." Proc. Nat. Acad. Sci. 93: 13473.

54. McNab, F. et al. (2009). "Changes in cortical dopamine D1 receptor binding associated with cognitive training." Science. 323: 800–802.

55. McGaugh, J. L. (2000). "Memory a century of consolidation." Science. 14: 248–251.

56. Foerde, K., et al. (2006). "Modulation of competing memory systems by distraction." Proc. Nat. Acad. Sci. 103: 11778–11783.

57. Ibid.

58. Ophir, E., Nass, C. and Wagner, A. D. (2009). "Cognitive control in media multitaskers." Proceedings of the National Academy of Science. Aug. 24. doi: 10.1073/pnas0903620106.

59. Clapp, W. C. et al. (2011). "Deficit in switching between functional brain networks underlies the impact of multitasking on working memory in older adults." Proc. Soc. Nat. Acad. Sci. (U.S.A.). doi:10.1073/pnas.1015297108.

60. Dux, P. E., et al. (2007). "Isolation of a central bottleneck of information processing with time-resolved fMRI." Neuron. 52 (6): 1109–1120.

61. Wilkinson, L., Scholey, A., and Wesnes, K. (2002). "Chewing gum selectively improves aspects of memory in healthy volunteers." Appetite. 38: 235–236.

62. Pyc, Mary A., and Rawson, K. A. (2010). "Why testing improves memory: mediator effectiveness hypothesis." Science. 330: 335.

63. Karpicke, Jeffrey D., and Roedinger, Henry L. III. (2008). "The critical importance of retrieval for learning." Science. 319: 966–968.

64. Mednick, Sara, et al. (2002). "The restorative effect of naps on perceptual deterioration." Nature Neuroscience. 5 (7): 677–681.

65. Schacter, D. (1995). *Memory Distortion*. Cambridge, Mass.: Harvard University Press. 59.

66. Rupp, Rebecca. (1998). *Committed to Memory*. New York: Crown Publishers.

67. Rigney, J. W., and Lutz, K. A. (1976). "Effect of graphic analogies of concepts in chemistry on learning and attitudes." J. Educ. Psychology. 68: 305–311.

68. Brady, T. F. (2009). "Visual long-term memory has a massive storage capacity for object details." Proc. Natl. Acad. Sci. USA. 106: 6008–6010.

69. Cohen, M. A. et al. (2009). "Auditory recognition memory is inferior to visual recognition memory." Proc. Natl. Acad. Sci. USA. 106 (14): 6008–6010.

70. Foer, Joshua. (2011). *Moonwalking With Einstein*, New York: Penguin.

71. Ibid

72. Vaughn, Dean. (2007). *How to Remember Anything*. N.Y.: St. Martin's Press.

73. Baker, Robert A. (1996). *Hidden Memories*. Amherst, N.Y.: Prometheus Books.

74. Bartlett, F. C. (1932). *Remembering*. Cambridge Mass.: Cambridge University Press.

75. Haskell, Robert E. (1999). *Between the Lines*. Insight Books, New York: Insight Books.

76. Polyn, Sean M. et al. (2005). "Category-specific cortical activity precedes retrieval during memory search." Science. 310: 1963–1966.

77. Rovee-Collier, Carolyn, and Boller, Kimberly. (1995). "Interference or facilitation in infant memory?" p. 61–104. In *Interference and Inhibition*

*in Cognition*. Edited by Frank N. Dempster and Charles J. Brainerd. New York.: Academic Press.

78. Baker, Robert A. (1996). *Hidden Memories*. Amherst, N.Y.: Prometheus Books.

79. Kuhl, B. A. et al. (2007). "Decreased demands on cognitive control reveal the neural processing benefits of forgetting." Nature Neuroscience. Published online: 3 June; | doi:10.1038/nn1918. http://www.nature.com/neuro/journal/vaop/ncurrent/suppinfo/nn1918_S1.html

80. Smith, D. G., Standing, L., and de Man, A. (1992). "Verbal memory elicited by ambient odor." Percept. Motor Skills. 74 (2): 339–343.

81. Tulving, Endel. (1974). "Cue-dependent forgetting." American Scientist. 62: 74–73.

82. Barad, Mark. (2006). "Is extinction of fear erasure or inhibition? Why both, of course." Learning and Memory. 13: 108–109.

83. Quirk, G. J. and Mueller, D. (2008). "Neural mechanisms of extinction learning and retrieval. Neuropsychopharmacology." 33: 56–72. Doi: 10.1038/sj.npp.1301.555.

84. Eisenberg, M., Kobilo, T., Berman, D. E., and Dudai, Y. (2003). "Stability of retrieved memory: inverse correlation with trace dominance." Science. 301: 1102–1104.

85. Olsson, A. et al. (2005). "The role of social groups in the persistence of learned fear." Science. 309: 785–787.

86. McNally, Richard J. (2003). *Remembering Trauma*. Cambridge, Mass.: Belknap Press.

87. Quirk, G. J. et al. (2006). "Prefrontal mechanisms in extinction of conditioned fear." Biological Psychiatry. 60: 337–343.

88. Bustos, S. G, H. Maldonado, and Molina, V. A. (2006). "Midazolam disrupts fear memory reconsolidation." Neuroscience. 138: 831–842.

89. Pitman, R. K. et al. (2002). "Pilot study of secondary prevention of posttraumatic stress disorder with propranalol." Biol. Psychiat. 51 (2): 189–192.

90. Kindt, M., Soeter, M., and Vervliet, B. (2009). "Beyond extinction: erasing human fear responses and preventing the return of fear." Nature Neuroscience. DOI: 10.1038/nn.2271.

91. Vaiva, G. Et al. (2003). "Immediate treatment with propranalol decreases posttraumatic stress disorder two months after trauma." Biol. Psychiat. 54 (9): 947–949.

92. Xue, Y.-X. et al (2012). "A memory retrieval-extinction procedure to prevent drug craving and relapse." Science. 336:241–245.

# Chapter 4

93. Epp, J. D., Spritzer, M. D., and Gales, L. A. M. (2007). "Hippocampus-dependent learning promotes survival of new neurons in the dentate gyrus at a specific time during cell maturation." Behavioural Neuroscience. 149: 273–285.

94. Seligman, M. E. P. (1991). *Learned Optimism*. New York: A. A. Knopf.

95. Levy B. R, and Langer, E. (1994) "Aging free from negative stereotypes: Successful memory among the American deaf and in China." Journal of Personality and Social Psychology. 66:935–943.

96. Klemm, W. R. (1969). "ECS and estrous cycle interactions in one-trial avoidance behavior of rats." Communications in Behavioral Biology. 4: 59–65.

97. Klemm, W. R. (1969). "ECS effects on one-trial avoidance behavior in intact and gonadectomized male rats." Communications in Behavioral Biology. 4: 55–58.

98. Rupp, Rebecca. (1998). *Committed to Memory*. New York: Crown Publishers.

99. Cherrier, M. M. et al. (2001). "Testosterone supplementation improves spatial and verbal memory in healthy older men." Neurology. 57: 80–88.

100. Ribeiro, R. L. et al. (1999). "The 'anxiety state' and its relation with rat models of memory and habituation." Neurobiology of Learning and Memory. 72: 78–94.

101. Newcomer, J. W., Selke, G., Melson, A.K., Hershey, T., Craft, S., Richards, K., Anderson, A. L. (1999). "Decreased memory performance in healthy humans induced by stress-level cortisol treatment." Arch. Gen. Psychiatry. 56:527–533.

102. Newcomer, J. W., et al. (1994). "Glucocorticoid-induced impairment in declarative memory performance in adult humans." J. Neuroscience. 14: 2047–2053.

103. Tang, A. C., Reeb, B. C., Romeo, R. D., and McEwen, B. S. (2003). "Modification of social memory, hypothalamic-pituitary-adrenal axis, and brain asymmetry by neonatal novelty exposure." J. Neuroscience. 23: 8254–8260.

104. Beck, Melinda. (2009). "A key for unlocking memories." Wall St. Journal, Tuesday, Nov. 17, p. D1.

105. Lyubomirsky, S. (2008). *The How of Happiness*. New York: Penguin.

106. Chen, Y. et al. (2008). "Rapid loss of dendritic spines after stress involves derangement of spine dynamics of corticotrophin-releasing hormone." J. Neuroscience. 28 (11): 2903–2911.

107. Kuhlmann, S., Piel, M., and Wolf, O. T. (2005). "Impaired memory retrieval after psychosocial stress in healthy young men." J. Neuroscience. 25 (11): 2977–2982.

108. Lupien, S. J. et al. (1998). "Cortisol levels during human aging predict hippocampal atrophy and memory deficits." Nature Neuroscience. 1 (1): 69–73.

109. DeBellis, M. D. (2011). "Sex differences in brain maturation during childhood and adolescence." Cerebral Cortex. 11 (6): 552–557.doi: 10.1093/cercor/11.6.552.

110. Bower, G. (1992). "How might emotions affect learning?" p. 3–31, in Handbook of Emotion and Memory Research and Theory, edited by S. –A. Christianson, Hillsdale, New Jersey: Lawrence A. Erlbaum. Associates.

111. Bower, Gordon. (1981). "Mood and memory." American Psychology. Feb., p. 129–148.

112. Williams, R. A., et al. (2000). "Changes in directed attention and short-term memory in depression." J. Psychiatr. Res. 34: 227–238.

113. Strang, J. M., et al. (2001). "Attention and working memory in Gulf War Syndrome and depression." Arch. Clin. Neuropsych. 16: 799.

114. Wansink, Brian, et al. (2003), "Exploring Comfort Food Preferences Across Gender and Age, "Physiology and Behavior, 79:4–5, 739–747.

115. Gold, Paul. (1987). "Sweet Memories." American Scientist. 73: 151–155.

116. Bushman, B. J., and Anderson, C. A. (2001). "Media Violence and the American Public. Scientific Facts Versus Media Misinformation." American Psychological Association. Inc. 0003–066X/OI/$5.00 56 (6/7): 477–489 DOI: 10.1037//0003–066X.56.6–7.477 22.

117. van Praag, H., et al. (2005). "Exercise enhances learning and hippocampal neurogenesis in aged mice." J. Neuroscience. 25 (38): 8680–8685.

118. Colcombe, S. J. et al. (2006). "Aerobic exercise training increases brain volume in aging humans." The Journals of Gerontology, Series A: Biological Sciences and medical Sciences. 61: 1166–1170.

119. Hillman, C. H., et al. (2009). "The effect of acute treadmill walking on cognitive control and academic achievement in preadolescent children." Neuroscience. 31;159(3):1044–54.

120. Hillman, C. H., Kirk, I. E., and Kramer. A. R. (2008). "Be smart, exercise your heart: exercise effects on brain and cognition." Nature Reviews Neuroscience. 9: 58–65. doi: 10.1038.nrn2298.

121. Voss, M.W., et al. (2010). "Plasticity of brain networks in a randomized intervention trial of exercise training in older adults." Frontiers in Aging Neuroscience. 2: 1–17.

122. Berke, J. d. and S. E. Hyman, S. E. (2000). "Addiction, Dopamine, and the Molecular Mechanisms of Memory," Neuron. 515532 (http://www.neuron.org/cgi/content/full/25/3/515/).

123. van Praag, H., et al. (2005). "Exercise enhances learning and hippocampal neurogenesis in aged mice." J. Neuroscience. 25 (38): 8680–8685.

124. Vorel, S. R., et al. (2001). "Relapse to cocaine seeking after hippocampus theta burst stimulation." Science. 292: 1175–1178.

125. Ibid.

126. Puighermanal, E. et al. (2009). "Cannabinoid modulation of hippocampal long-term memory is mediated by mTOR signaling." Nature Neuroscience. On-line edition, Aug. 2; doi:10.1038/ nn.2369.

127. Yan, H., et al. (2009). Developmental sensitivity of hippocampal interneurons to ethanol: Involvement of the hyperpolarization-activated current." Journal of Neurophysiology. 101: 67–83. http://www.sciencedaily.com/releases/2001/01/010117074808.htp.

128. Klemm, W. R. and Stevens, R. E. (1974). "Alcohol effects on EEG and multiple-unit activity in various brain regions of rats." Bran Res. 70: 361–368.

129. Klemm, W. R., et al. (1976). "Ethanol-induced regional and dose-response differences in multiple-unit activity in rabbits." Psychopharmacology. 49: 235–244.

130. Alexandrov, Y. I., et al. (2000). "Neuronal subserving of behavior before and after chronic ethanol treatment." Alcohol. 22: 97–106.

131. Chang, L. et al. (2002). "Perfusion MRI and computerized test abnormalities in abstinent methamphetamine users." Psychiatry Research Neuroimaging. 114: 65–79.

132. Miller, Neal. (1968). "Learning of visceral and glandular responses." Science. 163: 434–445.

133. Shapiro, D., et al. (1969). "Effects of feedback and reinforcement on the control of human systolic blood pressure." Science. 163: 588–589.

134. Van Dongen, H.P., et al. (2003). "The cumulative cost of additional wakefulness: dose-response effects on neurobehavioral function and sleep restriction and total sleep deprivation." Sleep. 26 (3): 247–248.

135. Gais, S. et al. (2002). "Learning-dependent increases in sleep spindle density." J. Neuroscience. 22: 6830–6834.

136. Kantak, S. S. et al. (2010). "Neural substrates of motor memory consolidation depend on practice structure." Nature Neuroscience. July. doi: 10.1038/nn.2596.

137. Fischer, S., et al. (2002). "Sleep forms memory for finger skills." Proc. National Academy of Science. 99: 11987–11001.

138. Korman, M. et al. (2009). "Daytime sleep condenses the time course of motor memory consolidation." Nature Neuroscience. 10 (9): 1206–1213.

139. Stickgold, R. et al. (2000). "Visual discrimination task improvement: a multi-step process occurring during sleep." J. Cognitive Neuroscience. 12: 246–254.

140. Drummond, S., et al. (2000). "Altered brain response to verbal learning following sleep deprivation." Nature. 403: 655–657.

141. Van Dongen, H.P., et al. (2003). "The cumulative cost of additional wakefulness: dose-response effects on neurobehavioral function and sleep restriction and total sleep deprivation." Sleep. 26 (3): 247–248.

142. Wilhelm, I. et al. (2011). "Sleep selectively enhances memory expected to be of future relevance." J. Neuroscience. 31 (5): 1563–1569.

143. Rauchs, G. et al. (2011). "Sleep contributes to the strengthening of some memories over others, depending on hippocampal activity at learning." J. Neuroscience. 31 (7): 2563–2568.

144. Czisch M. et al. (2002)." Altered processing of acoustic stimuli during sleep: Reduced auditory activation and visual deactivation detected by a combined fMRI/EEG study." Neuroimage. 16(1): 251–258.

145. Diekelmann, S. et al. (2011). "Labile or stabile: opposing consequences for memory when reactivated during waking and sleep." Nature Neuroscience. doi:10.1038.nn.2744.

146. Yoo, S. S, et al. (2007). "A defi cit in the ability to form new human memories without sleep." Nature Neuroscience. 10: 385–392.

147. Klemm, W. R. (2011). "Why does REM sleep occur? A wake-up hypothesis." Frontiers in Neuroscience. 5 (73): 1–12. Doi: 10.3389/fnsys.2011.00073.

148. Parmelee, A., et al. (1967). "Sleep states in premature infants." Devel. Med. Child Neurol. 9, 70–77.

149. Roffwarg, H. P., Muzio, N. N., and Dement, W. C. (1966). "Ontogenetic development of the human sleep-dream cycle." Science. 152, 604–619.

150. Rudoy, J. D. et al. (2009). "Strengthening individual memories by reactivating them during sleep." Science. 326: 1079.

151. Maquet, P. et al. (2002). "Be caught napping: you're doing more than resting your eyes." Nature Neuroscience. 5 (7): 618–619.

152. Korman, M. et al. (2007). "Daytime sleep condenses the time course of motor memory consolidation." Nature Neuroscience. 10 (9): 1206–1213.

153. Mednick, S. C. et al. (2008). "Comparing the benefits of caffeine, naps, and placebo on verbal, motor, and perceptual memory." Behavioural Brain Res. Doi: 10.1016/bbr.2008.04.028.

154. Cho, K. et al.(2000). "Chronic jet lag produces cognitive deficits." J. Neurosci. 20: RC66: 1–5.

# CHAPTER 5

155. Sparrow, B. et al. (2011). "Google effects on memory: cognitive consequences of having information at your fingertips." Science. 333: 776–778.

156. Noice, H., and Noice, T. (2000). "Two approaches to learning a theatrical script," p. 444–455. In Memory Observed, edited by Ulric Neisser and Ira Hyman, Jr. New York: Worth Publishers.

157. Macrae, C. N., and Lewis, H. L. (2002). "Do I know you? Processing orientation and face recognition." Psychological Science. 13 (2): 194–196.

158. Van Munching, P. (1997). How to Remember Jokes. New York: Workman

159. Stefan, K. et al. (2005). "Formation of a motor memory by action observation." J. Neuroscience. 25 (4): 9339–9346.

160. Shadmehr, R., and Brfashers-Krug, T. (1997). "Functional stages in the formation of human long-term motor memory." J. Neuroscience. 17(1): 409–419.

161. Malone, L. A. et al. (2011). "Motor adaptation training for faster relearning." J. Neuroscience. 31 (42): 15136–15143.

162. Ericsson, K. A. et al. (1993). "The role of deliberate practice in the acquisition of expert performance." Psychological review. 100: 363–406.

163. Cohen, D. A., and Robertson, E. M. (2011). "Preventing interference between different memory tasks." Nature Neuroscience. 14 (8): 953–955.

164. Robertson, E. M. et al. (2005). "Off-line learning and the primary motor cortex." J. Neuroscience. 25 (27): 6372–6378.

165. Walker, M. P. et al. (2002). "Practice with sleep makes perfect: sleep-dependent motor still learning." Neuron. 35: 205–211.

166. Plihal, W., and Born, J. (1997). "Effects of early and late nocturnal sleep on declarative and procedural memory." J. Cognitive Neuroscience. 9: 534–547.

167. Stickgold, R. (2000). "Visual discrimination task improvement: a multi-step process during sleep." Journal of Cognitive Neuroscience. 12 (2):246–254.

168. Korman, M. et al. (2009). "Daytime sleep condenses the time course of motor memory consolidation." Nature Neuroscience. 10 (9): 1206–1213.